Reuben Cox

LEWIS HYDE

COMMON AS AIR

Lewis Hyde is the author of *The Gift*, *This Error Is the Sign of Love*, and *Trickster Makes This World* (FSG, 1998). A MacArthur Fellow and former director of undergraduate creative writing at Harvard University, Hyde teaches during the fall semesters at Kenyon College, where he is the Richard L. Thomas Professor of Creative Writing. During the rest of the year he lives in Cambridge, Massachusetts, where he is a faculty associate at Harvard's Berkman Center for Internet and Society.

For more information, visit www.lewishyde.com and www.fsgbooks.com/commonasair.

ALSO BY LEWIS HYDE

The Gift

This Error Is the Sign of Love

Trickster Makes This World

COMMON AS AIR

COMMON
AS AIR

REVOLUTION,

ART,

AND OWNERSHIP

LEWIS HYDE

FARRAR, STRAUS AND GIROUX

NEW YORK

FARRAR, STRAUS AND GIROUX
18 West 18th Street, New York 10011

An excerpt from chapter 6, "Liberty to Communicate," originally appeared, in slightly different form, in *The Kenyon Review*. An excerpt from chapter 3, "The Enclosure of Culture," originally appeared, in slightly different form, in *Tin House*.

Grateful acknowledgment is made to the White House Historical Association for permission to reprint David Marlin's painting of Benjamin Franklin.

The Library of Congress has cataloged the hardcover edition as follows:
Hyde, Lewis, 1945–
    Common as air : revolution, art, and ownership / Lewis Hyde. — 1st ed.
        p.   cm.
    Includes bibliographical references and index.
    ISBN 978-0-374-22313-7 (hbk. : alk. paper)
    1. Information commons.   2. Arts.   3. Culture.   4. Intellectual property.
I. Title.

ZA3270.H93 2010
001—dc22

                                                                    2010002388

Paperback ISBN: 978-0-374-53279-6

Designed by Abby Kagan

www.fsgbooks.com

1   3   5   7   9   10   8   6   4   2

The cover image derives from an engraving illustrating Benjamin Franklin's "Suppositions and Conjectures towards forming an Hypothesis, for the Explanation of the Aurora Borealis" as found in his *Political, Miscellaneous, and Philosophical Pieces* (London: J. Johnson, 1779). Franklin proposed that the aurora borealis was a consequence of the circulation of both air and electricity around the globe. Image courtesy of the Houghton Library, Harvard University (call number *AC7 F8545 B779p).

FOR PATSY

AND

FOR MY FATHER,

W. LEWIS HYDE (1919–2003),

WHO TAUGHT ME ABOUT DOLLOND'S CASE

Every Free-Man . . . shall have . . . the Honey that is found within his Woods.

—THE GREAT CHARTER OF THE FOREST (1217)

CONTENTS

COMMON AS AIR

1

DEFENDING THE CULTURAL COMMONS

The argument: Even as market triumphalists work
to extend the range of private property,
a movement has arisen to protect
the many things best held in common.

·

Most people act as if they had a private understanding,
but in fact the Logos is common to all.

—HERACLITUS

"THEFT IS THEFT"

Some years ago in Thailand, when drug companies priced AIDS medications at an annual cost exceeding the average Thai income, the government stepped in and set more affordable rates. In response, the pharmaceutical industry called the move illegal and ill conceived, claiming it undermined the incentive to conduct the very research that produces AIDS drugs in the first place.

During the 2008 presidential campaign, Fox News insisted that YouTube remove from its site a John McCain commercial that used unauthorized video from a Fox-moderated debate. When the McCain campaign complained about suppression of political speech, YouTube replied that copyright law gave them no choice, though they "look[ed] forward to working with Senator (or President) McCain" to improve the law.

In 2000, a British scholar published a 1,300-page anthology of modern Irish writing, twenty-four pages of which were devoted to James Joyce. Asked for permission, the Joyce estate insisted on a fee of £7,000. When the editor wrote saying he couldn't afford such a steep fee, the estate raised the price to £7,500, then changed its mind and refused permission outright. Ten years later, this anthology still lists Joyce's work in the table of contents, but pages 323 through 346 are cut from the volume.

Each of these stories revolves around what we now call "intellectual property," and as modern as these cases are, the question behind them is very old: in what sense can someone own, and therefore control other people's access to, a work of fiction or a public speech or the ideas behind a drug? The literary part of this puzzle has, by itself, a long history. Three hundred years ago in England, writers and publishers engaged in a spirited, fifty-year debate over whether or not there could even exist such a thing as "literary property."

Publishers in Scotland, for example, thought it made no sense for their competitors in London to claim exclusive ownership of, say, a book on oratory by Cicero or a popular poem like James Thomson's *The Seasons*. As one aggrieved Scot tried to explain, if a writer were to "keep his Lucubrations to himself," then perhaps "he may be said to have a Property in his Noddle." But once "he prints . . . these Lucubrations," and once someone else pays for the book and reads it, "the Person who buys has just the same Property that the Author had."

"To lucubrate": surely this is a key forgotten verb of the European Enlightenment, the root ("lux") being light itself and the action indicated being the labor of studying long into the night by the flame of a lamp. Lucubrations are the mental harvest of midnight oil, and the only way to make them "property" in the usual sense ("this is mine; you keep out") would be to keep them locked inside the skull, or so this Scottish publisher believed against the protestations of his London rivals.

Centuries have passed since arguments of this sort first appeared, but the years have neither laid them to rest nor brought much clarity to the terms of engagement. "Intellectual property" is the phrase now used to denote ownership of art and ideas, but what exactly does it mean? Does it make sense, to begin with, to say that "intellect" is the source of the "properties" in question? A novel like *Ulysses*, the know-how for making antiviral drugs, Martin Luther King, Jr.'s "Dream" speech, the poems of Rimbaud, Andy Warhol screen prints, Mississippi Delta blues, the source code for electronic voting machines: who could name the range of human powers and historical conditions that attends such creations? All that we make and do is shaped by the communities and traditions that contain us, not to mention by money, power, politics, and luck. And even should the artist or scientist think she has extracted herself from the world to stand alone in the studio, a tremendous array of faculties and mind-states may well attend her creativity.

There is intellect, of course, but also imagination, intuition, sagacity, persistence, prudence, fantasy, lust, humor, sympathy, serendipity, will, prayer, grief, courage, visual acuity, ambition, guesswork, mother wit, memory, delight, vitality, venality, kindness, generosity, fortitude, fear, awe, compassion, surrender, sincerity, humility, and the ability to integrate diametrically opposed states of mind into harmonious wholes . . . We would need quite a few new categories to fully map this territory—"dream property," "courage property," "grief property"—and even if we had that list, only half the problem would have been addressed.

For what exactly is "property"? The oil in a lamp, the light it sheds, the midnight scholar's flash of insight: can each of these be "property" and, if so, by what ample definition of the term?

I will have more to say about these questions in the chapter that follows; here I'll simply acknowledge that my own position is not as extreme as that of the Scottish publisher. I believe there can be property in all sorts of lucubrations and, in a rightly limited form, usefully so. The very first copyright law (Britain's 1710 Statute of Anne) gave "the Authors and Proprietors" of books exclusive rights to their works for as long as twenty-eight years, provided that they paid a sixpenny fee and listed their works "in the Register-Book of the Company of Stationers." For most of the twentieth century, the law in the United States was much the same: rights lasted twenty-eight years (and could be renewed once, if the owner cared) provided that works were duly registered with the copyright office. Both of these seem to me to offer sensible ways to manage the "intellectual property" found in books.

I should apparently underscore this point before going on, as a number of readers missed it when the book first came out. Some faulted me for having copyrighted my own work in apparent contradiction of its defense of cultural commons ("Oh, the irony," said a post on the NPR website); others complained that I seemed not to care about copyright at all, that I was out to "deprive artists of the right to profit from their work" (that from a review in *The Nation*). Clearly I should be more emphatic: Authors and publishers deserve to profit from the work they create and bring to the public. This is not an anti-copyright book. Copyright is a useful tool of public policy; the problem, as we shall see, is to name the policy ends toward which it is directed and then design it to serve them. Because at the moment the reach of copyright is so wildly out of balance, the emphasis in this book is on access rather than ownership, that is true, but that doesn't mean I am out to impoverish authors, myself included. As for how a better balance might be achieved, there are many suggestions in the final chapter, and I have added an afterword to this edition outlining two plausible interventions, neither of which would abolish copyright.

As I was saying, it makes sense to give the "intellectual property" in books a twenty-eight-year copyright, even a renewable one. That said, part of the task of this book is to show the degree to which a phrase like "intellectual property" serves simply to obscure a long history of philosophical, legal, and ethical argument about what sort of property lies under that heading and, once that's decided, what "rightly limited" should mean and why a limit to ownership might arise in the first place. Knowing the history of that debate not just well enough to follow the argument but well enough to *engage* with it, to take an informed position in the debate, is to my mind one of the prerequisites of cultural citizenship in the twenty-first century.

But here we come to another topic that informs this book, for cultural citizenship is itself now highly contested, sufficiently so that I take it to be the site of a new culture war. For a quick overview of the terms under which that war is being waged, one could do worse than begin with a look at the public relations campaigns that the U.S. entertainment industries have been funding, especially the antipiracy curricula that they have developed and distributed to public schools.

One such campaign, produced by the Motion Picture Association of America (MPAA), has now reached hundreds of thousands of children in classrooms from New York to Los Angeles. In most schools, teachers have been free to use the offered lesson plans or not, as they see fit, though not in California, where a 2006 law mandates that all public schools must develop an "education technology" plan in which, for example, "the implications of illegal peer-to-peer network file sharing" must be taught. (The law never mentions teaching the more interesting and revolutionary implications of *legal* file sharing.) The year 2006 was also when the industry persuaded the Boy Scouts in Los Angeles to offer a "Respect Copyright" merit badge; the MPAA wrote the curriculum for that, too.

Many of the assignments in these programs depend on role-playing exercises. The merit badge curriculum suggests, for example, that each Boy Scout "write and perform a skit about why copyright protection is important." Elementary school children get to create greeting cards and posters and hold a "publication party," at the culmination of which each child writes his or her name on a sticker that says, "You're part of the © TEAM!" and then affixes this notice to the back of the work. The sticker bears a stock "All rights reserved" copyright declaration.

In an even more elaborate exercise called "Living in a Fishbowl," the teacher gives the students cards assigning each of them to one of six roles, five of which pertain directly to conventional motion picture production: actor, set carpenter, singer, director, and producer. The sixth role is a "computer user." The movie people all have jobs and a clear story to tell: they work hard to make movies; copyright law rewards and protects that work, piracy threatens and destroys it. Online file-swapping, a typical character says, "is costing me big bucks . . . [It] just isn't fair." The computer user, on the other hand—pictured with the top of his head missing and stars shooting out of it—offers an incoherent ramble that mixes rhetorical questions ("How could it possibly be illegal . . . ?") with dismissive remarks ("It's really no big deal!"). He seems to have no job.

The students break into groups to talk about how to present each of these characters to the class; then one by one each student must sit in a circle of chairs—the "fishbowl"—and try to answer in character questions posed by the teacher. A spokesman for the MPAA describes exercises like this as offering a good way for "students to reach their own conclusions about being a good digital citizen." But of course the game itself has determined the conclusion. It is part of a program called "What's the Diff?" intended to teach the young that downloading movies is the same as shoplifting from a store ("no diff"). No student, when asked by the teacher, "What's the difference . . . ?" is really expected to hold forth on, say, the classic economic distinction between corporeal and incorporeal goods.

The offered roles are narrowly selected and well scripted. There are no archivists preserving public domain films, for example, no librarians using ad clips to teach media literacy, no critics satirizing Mickey Mouse, no documentarians of the civil rights movement, no investigative journalists, no young musicians giving their music away to build an audience, no academics sharing scientific data, no remix artists laying sixties harmonies over fifties rhythms . . . Above all, there are no blank cards encouraging students to become the active authors of their own stories. In fact, there are no real "actors" at all in the civic or educational sense, only actors in the movie sense.

Moreover, the lessons meant to inform these roles teach a series of simplifications, even falsehoods, when it comes to the ownership of art and ideas. Teachers are told and children are taught:

If you haven't paid for it, you've stolen it.

Intellectual property is no different than physical property.

As the creator of your work, you should have the right to control what people can and cannot do with your work.

Never copy someone else's creative work without permission from the copyright holder.

Students who have learned to strictly respect the intellectual work of others in order to avoid plagiarism already have a solid foundation for understanding the laws of copyright.

Every one of these assertions is either false or misleading. Take the last one, for example: copyright infringement and plagiarism in fact have almost no connection with each other; infringement is a crime defined by statute, plagiarism is an ethical violation in some—but not all—creative communities. There can be plagiarism without infringement and infringement without plagiarism; to equate the two simply muddies a useful distinction. Moreover, learning to "respect" the work of others, while often a noble goal, has nothing to do with "the laws of copyright," which contain carefully designed provisions meant precisely to protect *dis*respect wherever it deserves expression.

Or take the claim that "Intellectual property is no different than physical property," this being the ungrammatical first sentence in the Boy Scout merit badge curriculum. In fact, as we shall see, the differences are striking and important, and have been a topic of philosophical and legal analysis for centuries. But these campaigns are not out to lead the young toward the pleasures of subtle thought; they are out to command a particular model of cultural citizenship, and to that end, they need a simple tale to tell.

That tale is often built around one endlessly repeated analogy: copyright infringement is the same as shoplifting. The Recording Industry Association of America produced a public service video, for example, in which the adult moderator quizzes a high school student, asking, "What really is the difference between shoplifting and illegal downloading?," to which the student dutifully replies, "Legally . . . nothing." The answer is left to stand (though it would not stand in a court of law), and is followed quickly by the voice of a music retailer who seals the logical loop: "I don't think there's a difference, because theft is theft."

The final thing to say about these campaigns is that they often present themselves as reflecting a long and well-settled tradition of American thought. *The New York Times Magazine* once published an interview with the head of the MPAA, Dan Glickman, in which he offered a typical view, saying that "we need to educate kids so they understand the value of intellectual property" and that "the founding fathers, in our Constitution, talked about copyright. They talked about the creative juices that are necessary for a free society and protecting property rights." Here, too, we have a fable for a certain kind of citizenship, not a true attempt to educate, for Glickman's version of U.S. history is an astoundingly narrow reading of what the founders actually thought, as we shall see.

The entertainment industry's campaigns are best understood not as a late flowering of eighteenth-century thought but as a modern, post-1990 response to a striking convergence of at least three historical events. The first and broadest of these has been the rise of a "knowledge economy." Since at least the Second World War, remarkable wealth and thus remarkable power have found their sources in the laboratories and studios of industrialized agriculture, medicine, computing, and entertainment. It therefore matters to companies like Monsanto, Pfizer, Microsoft, and Disney that they control the know-how behind the goods they produce, and as for the goods themselves—especially intangible ones like a digital music file or the description of a soybean gene—it matters that the law help them guard the rights that ownership is supposed to bring, especially the exclusive right to charge fees for access.

A second historical change has, however, made it much more difficult to maintain the fences needed to make exclusivity work. In the 1990s, digital copying and the global Internet appeared almost simultaneously, and all of a sudden many of the useful old fences simply disintegrated. Once upon a time, someone had to physically lift boxes of vinyl recording disks and put them on a truck; someone had to carry tins of celluloid film to every movie theater. Once, the media themselves were slow, sticky, and local, and copying was consequently fairly cumbersome, misbehavior fairly rare, and the tools for controlling access fairly modest. There were always cheaters, of course, but on the whole the commercial and moral economies had no trouble finding common ground, and no one needed to get fourth graders to put copyright stickers on their posters.

Then, in less than a decade, the heavy, slow, and local became light, swift, and global. As with the invention of movable type or the telegraph, the appearance of the digital Internet has amounted to a phase change in the media. The old boundary markers weren't just moved, they were vaporized, and tacit understandings between owners and users got replaced by a kind of amateur anarchism on the consumer side, by ramped-up threats, lawsuits, and lobbying on the producer side, and by very little in between.

And while conventional owners are surely fighting a losing war against the material changes the Internet has brought, they nonetheless still have the kind of money and political clout that has allowed them to punctuate their propaganda campaigns with actual battles joined. The recording industry has fought hard to destroy or regulate one of the more revolutionary features of the Internet—peer-to-peer file-sharing systems—lobbying Congress to force universities to filter their networks, for example, and litigating aggressively.

Agribusiness producers have demanded that farmers who buy genetically altered seed not reproduce and save it from year to year but buy anew each spring (and they have successfully sued a Canadian farmer who, when he discovered that altered canola had accidentally appeared on his land, saved the seed and planted it again). Pharmaceutical producers have developed international trade agreements such that all nations must abide by the rules governing U.S. industrial knowledge or else be sanctioned for "piracy" (and thus managed to get the Indian Parliament to outlaw the making of generic copies of patented drugs, despite the fact that by their manufacture India had been supplying half the drugs for AIDS patients in nations too poor to otherwise afford them).

Beyond all these things, from the rise of a knowledge economy to the disruptions of the digital Internet, one final surprise of history managed to add ideological momentum to all "intellectual property" initiatives. The 1991 fall of the Soviet Union, I believe, served to remove the primary oppositional force that had kept free-market capitalism on its best behavior for half a century. Absent that force, the West entered a period of unabashed market triumphalism, during which many things long assumed to be public or common—from weather forecasting to drinking water, from academic science to the "idea" of a crustless peanut butter and jelly sandwich*—were removed from the public sphere and made subject to the exclusive rights of private ownership.

"COMMON TO ALL"

Here, however, we should come back to the thinly populated space noted earlier between the amateur anarchists of the digital age and

---

*Yes, U.S. Patent 6,004,596 for a "Sealed Crustless Sandwich" actually exists.

the old-guard content owners, for even if Western free-market capitalism was in some sense triumphant, that did not mean that anyone really knew what it should look like nor, once capitalism's exterior oppositional force had fallen, what interior forces might arise to check the unbridled greed it sometimes sets in motion. In what language, native to our own traditions, shall we speak of, say, farmers who wish to save their seed from year to year, or of patent laws designed to give the poor access to medicine, or of the remarkable new models of production that peer-to-peer file-sharing has allowed?

In answering that question, this book joins with others, and with a number of social movements, that have turned to the old idea of "the commons" as a way to approach the collective side of ownership. The next chapter will offer some history and a definition of this term; for now I want simply to note how widely deployed the language of the commons has become.

Many environmental issues are usefully approached in terms of common assets, from aquifers to wetlands to the oceans and the sky. There are, for example, many groups fighting to keep drinking water as a common resource, from Michigan's Sweetwater Alliance (formed originally "as a grassroots response to an unprecedented plan by . . . a subsidiary of Nestlé to appropriate and sell millions of gallons of water belonging to the Great Lakes Basin") to the Canadian Blue Planet Project working internationally to prevent "the private water industry, international financial institutions and others from interfering with the human right to water."

Those who concern themselves with media technology find themselves more and more speaking in terms of a commons, especially in regard to software, the architecture of the Internet, and the broadcast spectrum. Since the mid-1980s, the Free Software Foundation has not only promoted the right to freely use, copy, modify, and share computer programs; it has also developed ingenious legal tools to guard the software community's common properties against private capture. In 1991, one key innovation that led to the rise of the World Wide Web consisted simply of treating the methods by which computers communicate with each other (the Internet protocols) as common assets, not the property of some person or firm. In regard to the broadcast spectrum, there are many now who favor regulating wireless transmission as a public commons ("as we . . . regulate our highway system and our computer networks") rather than through government licenses or a system of private rights.

Arguments that arise in regard to biotechnology—about seed lines, for example, or the ownership of genetic materials—also benefit from a clear model of what it means to place limits on the market and hold some things in common. Many organizations now advocate treating the great legacy of agricultural seeds as a common good, to be preserved and shared across the globe or in their native settings, as the case may be. In the United Kingdom, the Heritage Seed Library has such a mission, as does Native Seeds/ SEARCH in the American Southwest. As for genes, the biochemist and Nobel laureate John Sulston called the book he wrote about the mapping of the human genome *The Common Thread*. "I am one of those who feel that the earth is a common good," he writes, and the book combines a passionate defense of "the common ownership of the genome" with a description of "the global consequences of ignoring common goods in the quest for short term profit."

Finally and most fully, this book is not alone in conceiving of culture as a commons, especially since the digital Internet has made so many things light, swift, and global. As early as 1971, Michael Hart, then a student at the University of Illinois, launched Project Gutenberg, now an online resource offering tens of thousands of public-domain books free to anyone with a computer terminal. Hundreds of similar projects have followed. Wikipedia, the remarkable Internet encyclopedia, may be the best known, but there are many others. The Knowledge Conservancy acquires rights to "intellectual property," then makes it available to the public for free in perpetuity. The Internet Archive is essentially a library offering permanent access to historical collections preserved in digital format. The Public Library of Science publishes a series of research journals whose authors grant to all users "a free, irrevocable, worldwide, perpetual right of access" to their work.

Other projects are not themselves cultural commons so much as their breeding grounds. Best known may be Creative Commons, a nonprofit dedicated to making it easier to share and build upon other people's work, consistent with the rules of copyright. It provides free licenses and other legal tools "to mark creative work with the freedom the creator wants it to carry." In a similar spirit, Science Commons, a Creative Commons offshoot, facilitates the sharing of knowledge in scientific research. Its NeuroCommons project, for example, is meant to enhance the study of neurodegenerative diseases by combining commons-based peer editing and annotation of data with project-specific open source software communities.

All these examples are relatively recent, to be sure, but the idea of treating knowledge as a commons is not. The aphorism from Heraclitus that stands at the head of this chapter ("the Logos is common to all") was written two and a half millennia ago. "Human intelligence is like water, air, and fire—it cannot be bought and sold; these four things the Father of Heaven made to be shared on earth in common," declares Truth in William Langland's medieval allegory, *Piers Plowman*. The less mystical, more secular founding generation in the United States held similar beliefs, as in a typical remark from a letter Thomas Jefferson wrote during his presidency: "The field of knowledge is the common property of mankind."

In fact, it is the founding generation in the United States that provides the primary source material for this book. The early Republic is the land I have chosen to visit in search of alternative visions of cultural ownership, and the founders are the allies I have enlisted to help me in that quest. What exactly, I'd like to know, *did* men like Jefferson—or John Adams, James Madison, Benjamin Franklin . . . —have to say when they "talked about" what has come to be called "intellectual property"? Not that I am looking for originalist answers; I don't believe that positions held by earlier generations have any necessary force in the present. If I find much of what the founders wrote persuasive—and I do—it is not because they were there at the creation but because their ideas can be so fruitfully brought to bear on present circumstances. I find in them a usable past, especially in that they suggest a number of ways to widen the terms of engagement beyond the "theft is theft" approach whose seed is now being so widely sown.

I realize that in drawing much of my evidence from eighteenth-century American sources I run the risk of limiting my argument to one nation's case. Perhaps I have, but I think not. Industrialized nations like the United States now aggressively export their "knowledge laws" in much the same way that the British long ago spread their "land laws" to distant colonies. Late in the nineteenth century, in country after country, British colonial governments simply erased the rules of customary common land tenure and substituted their own. In New Zealand after the Native Land Act of 1865, for example, courts refused to "recognize" anyone who showed up claiming to own land in common. In India, the Forest Acts of 1865 and 1878 similarly extinguished centuries of customary rights in the rural villages.

What happened in the nineteenth century to tangible properties is happening now to intangibles. Take as a first example a recent change in Saudi Arabian law brought about by the World Trade Organization. As the historian Carla Hesse has noted, in traditional Islamic legal practice, authors did not own the ideas expressed in their books:

> A thief who stole a book was thus not subject to the punishment for theft—the amputation of his hand. Islamic law held that he had not intended to steal the book as paper and ink, but the ideas in the book—and unlike the paper and ink, these ideas were not tangible property.

Thus when Saudi Arabia wished to join the WTO, its religious judges objected to the notion that bootlegged videos and software could be classified as stolen goods. The WTO flew a group of them to Geneva and persuaded them to change their minds.

Or take the "100 Orders" that L. Paul Bremer issued during the year that the Coalition Provisional Authority governed occupied Iraq. Issued mostly in 2004, these are a set of "binding instructions . . . to the Iraqi people" laying out a series of regulations, "penal consequences," and "changes in Iraqi law." Order 83 amends Iraqi copyright law in ways that Iraqi citizens might well have found worthy of debate: it allows ownership of "collections of works which have fallen into the public domain," and of "collections of official documents, such as texts of international laws"; it protects databases (a practice much debated in the United States and Europe); it treats computer programs "as literary works" (a common formula worldwide, but worthy of discussion nonetheless). It even protects "public recitals of the Holy Koran"—oddly so, one might think, as the Koran is taken to embody the word of Allah and its principal means of transmission has always been oral recitation from teacher to student (the word "Koran" itself means "recitation").

Another of Bremer's decrees, Order 81, amends Iraqi patent laws no less boldly. For the first time in Iraq's history, it adds "the protection of new varieties of plants" to the list of patentable things and it prohibits farmers from reproducing patented plants without permission of their owners. Most striking of all, it prohibits farmers from "re-using seeds of protected varieties."

Among the many ironies of Order 81, as an essayist for *The Ecologist* pointed out, is the fact that Iraq lies in the original fertile crescent of the Tigris-Euphrates river system, where humankind first domesticated wheat ten thousand years ago. Worldwide, there are today over 200,000 varieties of wheat, most of them developed by indigenous farmers to fit local growing conditions. Hundreds of these are found in Iraq itself, and before the 2003 invasion, almost all Iraqi farmers saved their local seed, or bought it from neighbors who did. Order 81 does not necessarily wipe out the millennia-long tradition of local plant breeding, seed-saving, and exchange, of course, but it may well do so in practice, for it lays the legal groundwork through which these ancient practices can more easily be replaced by what the order calls "the international trading system."

To come back, then, to my having chosen to base much of this book on eighteenth-century American sources, the point is that even if you are a farmer in Iraq—or a doctor in Chile, a composer in Australia, an Internet activist in China, a teacher in Zimbabwe . . . —the history of the cultural commons in the United States should be of interest, especially given that (as we shall see) the early American Republic is itself a foreign land, as it were, in relation to the nation's present practice. Where citizens of other countries wish to resist or modify cultural policies being imported from elsewhere, it will help them to know that many U.S. citizens are not only engaged in a similar task, but have at their disposal a tradition of resistance that was in fact an intrinsic part of the American Revolution.

• • •

In 1983 I published *The Gift*, a book meant to defend and illuminate the noncommercial side of artistic practice. A second book, published fifteen years later, dealt again with matters of imagination, only this time from a more mischievous point of view. *Trickster Makes This World* used a group of ancient myths to argue for the kind of disruptive intelligence all cultures need if they are to remain lively, flexible, and open to change.

The present work has roots in both of these. As with *The Gift*, my focus is on the commerce of the creative spirit, though the emphasis in this case falls more on the social side of things, on how we treat art and ideas once they have entered the public sphere. I mean this book to be a defense of the cultural commons, that vast store of unowned ideas, inventions, and works of art that we have inherited from the past and continue to enrich.

In returning to themes from *The Gift*, however, I have tried not to forget some of the lessons offered by the old trickster tales. Tricksters are the mythic characters who threaten to take the myths themselves apart. Their task is to unsettle the eternals, the *propaganda* of the faith, the seemingly foundational truths. How do they do it?

In the Norse tales, the mischief-maker Loki once approached the goddess Idunn, who tends the orchard where the Apples of Immortality grow, and persuaded her to bring a sample of her fruit out of Asgard, the Norse heaven. To fool her into leaving her post, he claimed that he had found better apples elsewhere, and asked her to bring some of her own for comparison. As soon as Idunn left the orchard, disaster struck the gods: they began to grow old and gray.

It's a simple trick, really: to show that what was assumed to be unchanging and eternal can in fact be infected by time, simply leave the garden and compare what grows there to something else. Modern tactics are the same, if more mundane, when it comes to claims about cultural truths: compare them to those from some other time or place and see how they fare. Maybe it is currently true for schoolchildren in Los Angeles that "if you haven't paid for it, you've stolen it," but is that true for children in China? Was it true during the Protestant Reformation?

The bulk of this book engages in the simple mischief of comparing current claims about cultural ownership to claims made in the eighteenth century. Even that exercise, I realize, will not get us very far from the garden of the European Enlightenment, and I want to close these introductory remarks, therefore, with a short sample of the fruits to be found if we were to wander even further afield.

If we go all the way back to the ancient world, to the old bardic and prophetic traditions, what we find is that men and women are not thought to be authors so much as vessels through which other forces act and speak. Norse legend tells of a spring at the root of the World Tree whose water bubbles up from the underworld, carrying the dissolved memories of the dead. Odin drank from it once; that cost him an eye, but nonetheless empowered him to bestow on worthy poets the mead of inspiration. Homer is not the "author" of the *Odyssey*; he disappears after the first line: "Sing in me, Muse, and through me tell the story . . . " Hesiod's voice is not his own; in *The Theogony* he has it from the muses of Mount Helicon and in *Works and Days* from the muses of Pieria. Plato presents no ideas that he himself made up, only the recovered memory of things known before the great forgetting we call birth.

Creativity in ancient China was not self-expression but an act of reverence toward earlier generations and the gods. In the *Analects*, Confucius says, "I have transmitted what was taught to me without making up anything of my own. I have been faithful to and loved the Ancients." To honor the past was a consistent virtue for a thousand years in imperial China and thus to copy the work of those who came before was a matter of respect rather than theft. Said the fifteenth-century artist Shen Zhou, "If my poems and paintings . . . should prove to be of some aid to the forgers, what is there for me to grudge about?"

A modern example of the same kind of nonproprietary assumption is given by the great Hindu mathematician Srinivasa Ramanujan, who used to say that "an equation for me has no meaning, unless it represents a thought of God." He directed his prayers toward Sarasvathi, the goddess of learning, and believed that his family deity, the goddess Namagiri, visited him in dreams to write mathematical equations on his tongue.

A long tradition in Christianity also takes the fruits of human creativity to have nonhuman origins and thus assumes that they cannot be bought or sold (nor can they really be forged, plagiarized, or stolen). Such was the traditional understanding for medieval Christians:

Scientia Donum Dei Est,
Unde Vendi Non Potest.

"Knowledge is a gift of God, therefore it cannot be sold." To sell knowledge was to traffic in the sacred and thus to engage in the sin of simony.

Reformation Protestants were particularly sensitive to simony, having charged the Catholic church with the buying and selling of ecclesiastical preferments and benefices. They believed especially in an obligation to develop God-given talent and to share its fruits with others. "Such a belief was stated stridently in the prefaces of many books as a reason for their publication," according to one scholar of early German music. The composer Martin Agricola, for example, begins his study of musical instruments imagining how God might address him at the Last Judgment: "I have heaped riches on you, so that through them you would serve your neighbor and communicate these things." Martin Luther himself inserted a *Warnung*—a warning—to greedy printers at the start of his 1545 German Bible. "Freely have I received, freely have I given, and I desire nothing in return," Luther declared, echoing the moment in Matthew when Jesus tells his disciples not to trade in the powers they have received.

The motives behind such declarations are as much pastoral as theological, for they recognize that we have duties to our neighbors as well as to God. The title page of a work by Johann Sebastian Bach displays a dedication containing this double focus: "To the highest God in his honor, / To my neighbor that he may instruct himself from it." The immensely prolific composer Michael Praetorius noted that the many Lutheran chorales he had arranged were not exactly his but more precisely "the common . . . melodies that are sung at church and at home in various places and lands." Compositions, that is, can not only be conceived as having been given by God and passed along to others, but as having come from those others in the first place, worked upon, and then returned. "If I have written much," Praetorius might have said, "it is by standing on the shoulders of the common . . ."

In speaking of common melodies and of neighbors as recipients, these artists turn toward more humanist descriptions of creativity, and toward the future, that is to say, toward the destinations of art rather than its origins. No matter its sources, for whom does the creative artist or thinker make the work? The Polish-American Nobel laureate Czeslaw Milosz once offered a reflection on the Greek concept of *storge*, usually thought of as the kind of affection that a parent feels for a child or teachers toward their students. It is also possible, Milosz wrote,

> that *storge* may be applied to the relationship between a poet and generations of readers to come: underneath the ambition to perfect one's art without hope of being rewarded by contemporaries lurks a magnanimity of gift-offering to posterity.

This is really the same lesson that another laureate, the Italian Eugenio Montale, took from his study of Dante. "The greatest lesson Dante left us," Montale wrote, is "that true poetry is always in the nature of a gift, and that it therefore presupposes the dignity of its recipient."

In closing out my introduction with this brief tour of ideas about creativity from other times and other places, I have meant simply to get a bit of distance on the idea of "intellectual property." It is an idea not just new but historically strange. It belongs to our times, to be sure, but if we are to examine it with any care it helps to know how new it really is; it's newer than automobiles, newer than lightbulbs, newer than jazz. Bowing however briefly to other ways of imagining human creativity also helps us see how much any unthinking discussion of "intellectual property" will crowd out: not just the kinds of examples I have just rehearsed, but also much of what lies ahead in this book. "The field of knowledge is the common property of mankind": what precisely were Jefferson's assumptions when he made a claim like that? And what, for that matter, did he mean by "common"?

2

WHAT IS A COMMONS?

The argument: It would be wise for most creations
of human wit and imagination to lie in a cultural commons
rather than be subject to the rules of private property.
But what is a commons?

.

The rights of man are liberty, and an equal participation
of the commonage of nature.

—PERCY BYSSHE SHELLEY, "DECLARATION OF RIGHTS," 1812

A RIGHT OF ACTION

The "commons" means many things to many people. Take John
Locke's *Second Treatise of Government* (1690), in whose chapter "Of
Property" the commons is not to be found in the contemporary
English countryside but in a time and place more reminiscent of
the Book of Genesis. "God . . . *has given the earth* . . . to mankind in common," writes Locke. Nature is "the common mother
of all," albeit a "wild common," for she lacks the improving hand
of man. For Locke, that original wilderness resembles a thing
called "America," whose "wild woods and uncultivated waste" call
to mind the world before it was first peopled by "the children of
Adam, or Noah." "In the beginning all the world was *America* . . . ;
for no such thing as *money* was any where known." Call it America
or call it Eden, in this seminal document of modern liberalism the
commons bespeaks an aboriginal first condition, one that existed

before labor, before cultivation, before the cash economy, and before the constitutional state with all its apparatus for the protection of property.

Among other things, then, the commons is sometimes the name of a primordial state, or of the longing for its return. If only the original, commodious world could be recovered, perhaps we could all be quit of the dry skin of scarcity. Perhaps life could be endlessly generative, supportive. Even a fine modern theorist of the commons like Lawrence Lessig, usually an admirably pragmatic activist, can be found drawn into dreams of plenitude. "The realist in all of us refuses to believe in Eden," he once wrote, only to add: "But I'm willing to believe in the potential of essentially infinite bandwidth." Invocations of the commons can carry with them a promise that more than air can be like air, always there for the inhaling lung: infinite bandwidth, unlimited acorns and deer, all of literature instantly available on the computer screen, unfenced prairies stretching to an unowned ocean, "that great and still remaining common of mankind" (Locke again). There are psychological, spiritual, and mythic elements to "the commons" and it is worth marking them at the outset so as to be alert to how they might refract our thinking about other, more concrete commons.

As for these last, I shall here elaborate one image of actual commons using specifics from the kind of English agricultural villages that John Locke ignored. Before entering that history, however, it will help to sketch a few matters of definition. I take a commons to be a kind of property (not "the opposite of property" as some say) and I take "property" to be, by one old dictionary definition, *a right of action.*

Consider some simple object in your house, a pencil say, and imagine all the actions that you might take in regard to it. You can use it to write a letter, but you can also give it away, or sell it, or rent it, or bequeath it to your heirs, or use it to stir soup, or break it in half, or burn it, or bury it in the backyard. We don't normally separate out all possible actions in this manner because normally what we mean by "property" is the whole bundle. If the pencil is my property, I can do anything I want with it. William Blackstone, the eighteenth-century British jurist, defined "the right of ownership" as such: "that sole and despotic dominion which one man claims and exercises over the external things of the world, in total exclusion of the right of any other individual in the universe." The word "dominion" here, by the way, was the same word that John Adams chose to describe the political power that some men hold over others, and in Adams's politics the opposite of dominion is liberty. If I own a pencil in Blackstone's sense, I am its despot; it has no liberty.

Enslaved pencils aside, if we return to this atomizing idea of a right of action, it soon becomes apparent that ownership rarely consists of the entire set of possible actions. To move from the pencil to the house where the pencil lies: if I own a house in an American city, I have many rights of action, many properties, in it, but not all. In the city where I live, for example, I cannot put a herd of cows in my yard; I cannot convert my home into a soap factory; I cannot build a tower ten stories high; I cannot even rent an office to a friend, for I live in a noncommercial zone. And all these are things I cannot do even if I own the house outright, a rare case, for most homeowners have mortgage contracts that further restrict their rights of action.

We have moved from a pencil to a house to the city where the house is found, and this last widening of the focus allows me to suggest a right of action that will complicate the picture. Adult citizens in American cities have the right to vote and this, too, can be thought of as a property. It is certainly a right of action, and one of the few remaining for which there is no market. The right to vote comes with citizenship and though there are ways in which citizens can lose it, in the normal course of events we consider it inalienable. You cannot sell your vote; you cannot give it away. There is no material property, only an action that expresses the political agency of persons who have it as a right. In fact, by its inalienability it is one of the things that makes such persons who they are.

Something along these lines is what James Madison was getting at when he wrote in a 1792 essay that "as a man is said to have a right to his property, he may be equally said to have a property in his rights." Madison's prime example was freedom of speech: "A man has a property in his opinions and the free communication of them." The right of free speech, like the right to vote, we usually think of as a "civil" rather than a property right, but the distinction begs the question of where to draw the line between the material and the social worlds. Defining property in terms of actions keeps that question open so that property is never just some physical thing (pencil or house), nor a person's rights of action, nor the social regime recognizing those rights, but some combination of these joined together. And different combinations allow, or disallow, different ways of living and acting in the world. How we imagine property is how we imagine ourselves.

In this line, note that by adding Blackstone I have begun with two related points of departure for defining what we mean by property— as rights of action or of exclusion—the one stressing the agency of owners and the other stressing limits to the agency of nonowners. Most property combines both of these in varying degrees. If I own a car, not only do I have a right to drive it, but that right depends on my ability to forbid others from doing the same. Even traditional common property, as we will shortly see, combined the right to use and the right to exclude: local villagers had access to their fields and woodlands, but by the same token all others did not.

Blackstone's chapter "Of Property" begins with "exclusion";* I began at the other end of the spectrum, with action, because questions of agency, both civic and cultural, are going to matter in the chapters that follow and thus it matters that we start by noting how our imaginings of property encourage agency rather than block it.

---

*Blackstone's point of departure still holds in many quarters. In a 1999 Supreme Court decision, Justice Antonin Scalia declared: "The hallmark of a constitutionally protected property interest is the right to exclude others."

I want "common" to be available as a verb (as in this from an old book on British law: "Generally a man may common in a forest").

What might be called the active-verb part of property will be especially marked in those areas of social life where participation is essential. In a viable self-governing nation, for example, citizens can only know themselves by way of their civic agency. True citizens are not the audience of their government, nor its consumers; they are its makers. The same may be said of a viable culture. Culture is always arising, and those who participate in its ongoing creation will rightly want to question any cultural expression that comes to them wrapped in a right to exclude.

But let us leave culture and self-governance aside for now and come back to mere pencils and houses: my point is that the idea of property as a right of action suggests, as a simple first definition, that a commons is a kind of property in which more than one person has rights. You and your spouse might own a mutual fund as "tenants in common"; your account is a commons with two commoners. In Puritan New England, the family was called "the little commonwealth"; family property was the commons of all members.

Couples and families are, however, among the smallest of possible commons, the simplest compounds, the sand and gravel of the landscape I hope to chart. To describe the more complicated commons that the term usually denotes, let us now expand on this simple definition through a look at one set of historical conditions that gave rise to the term in the first place.

ESTOVERS IN COMMON

Traditional English commons were lands held collectively by the residents of a parish or village: the fields, pastures, streams, and woods that a number of people, none of them an owner in Blackstone's sense, had the right to use in ways organized and regulated by custom. Those who held a common right of *pasturage* could graze their cattle in the fields; those with a common of *piscary* might fish the streams; those with a common of *turbary* might cut turf to burn for heat; those with a common of *estovers* might take wood necessary to heat, furnish, or repair their houses. Everyone, the poor especially, had the right to glean after the harvest.*

In fact, in regard to provisioning the poor, all these rights have larger meanings, estovers especially. The word comes from the French *estovoir*, "to be necessary"; a common of estovers is actually a right of subsistence. In 1217, when the Magna Carta guaranteed that a widow "shall have . . . her reasonable estovers in the common," it meant more than a right to firewood; it meant she should never lack for food, fuel, or shelter. Rights in common assured a baseline of provision; they were the social security of the premodern world, the "patrimony of the poor," a stay against terror.

Systems of common rights were the norm in most premodern communities. The Roman historian Tacitus, detailing the customs of first-century German tribes, indicates that they had no private property in agriculture: "Lands . . . are taken for tillage by the whole body of cultivators." Alpine grazing fields in Switzerland were village commons for millennia. Early landholding practices among Native Americans offer other parallels, as with this description in regard to California Indians:

> Sometimes people owned plots of land, particular trees, or special
> fishing places outright; in other situations they owned "rights."
> One family, for example, might own salmon-fishing rights from

---

*Theorists similarly describe any modern commons as a complex bundle of possible rights. Charlotte Hess offers this list: *access rights* (the right to enter an area and enjoy nonsubtractive benefits, e.g., to hike, canoe, enjoy nature); *extraction rights* (the right to obtain resources, e.g., to catch fish, divert water); *management rights* (the right to regulate internal use patterns and to make improvements); *exclusion rights* (the right to determine who will have rights and how those rights may be transferred); *alienation rights* (the right to sell or lease management and exclusion rights).

a particular place along a river; another family might own the eel-fishing rights there; and a third family might own the rights to cross the river at the same place.

In this case, no one absolutely owns that "place along a river"; it is, rather, the object of a set of use rights, multiply owned and embodying or reflecting the fact that communities have many interrelated members with many interrelated needs. In both this and the traditional English case, the commons is not so much the land in question as the land plus the social relations and traditional institutions that organize its use.

The system of English common land tenure lasted for over a thousand years, a span of time that can roughly be broken into three periods. In the Saxon age before the Norman conquest, it is assumed that all village lands were held and worked in common, except for a few enclosed gardens and orchards. No one person or family was the ultimate owner; what belonged to people were use rights, the commons being the place those rights were expressed. During the many centuries after the Norman conquest, the lands of any village were more likely associated with a local manor, the assumption being that the soil belonged ultimately to the lord of the manor and that rights of common were granted on condition of fealty to him and attendant acts of tribute (military service especially). The third period, the age of enclosure, ran from the early eighteenth century to the end of the nineteenth. During these two hundred years, as much as one seventh of all English common land was divided up, fenced, and converted into private property in the modern sense.

It should be said that the notion that feudal commons ultimately belonged to the lord of the manor is more likely a legal fiction promulgated during the age of enclosure than an accurate description of how feudal peoples themselves understood their situation. It would be hard to find a case during all those many centuries in which any overlord acted as owners today might act (evicting tenants, say, so as to sell land to speculators). The commons were managed collectively; no overlord alone could set in motion any significant change in how they operated. To alter any long-standing use rights, for example, required consensus agreement among the commoners and that meant, for one thing, that the commons was a very stable form, unaltered for centuries. It also meant that when landlords finally moved to enclose the land they could not simply do so; they had to go to Parliament and persuade the legislators to change the rules of the game. Most enclosure in England was "parliamentary enclosure," a legally sanctioned act of appropriation often justified by the convenient notion that the landlord's ancestors had anciently bestowed use rights upon the commoners, the idea being that if someone granted the rights in the past, his descendants might recover them in the present.

Later in this story, we will come to the colonial American idea that the best kind of property to own is "lands in fee simple," as Noah Webster wrote in his 1787 "Examination" of the Constitution, and it will be useful to pause here to explain what the phrase means because it arose by contrast to true feudal ownership. In the Middle Ages, an estate in land granted by a lord to a vassal was called either a "feud" or a "fee." A fee was not a sum of money; it was an estate held on condition of the vassal's loyalty and service. A "fee simple," on the other hand, was an estate held subject to no such obligations. A fee simple is a simple estate, an unconditional or unencumbered estate, one held free of the many reciprocal duties that were the mark of medieval hierarchy. Such a fee was also called an allodium, a term that I'll return to in a few chapters because with it comes an interesting nuance in regard to the issue of civic responsibility. For Thomas Hobbes, an allodium was land which "a Man holds," not from some king or overlord, but "from the gift of God only," the implication being that although owners of allodial land are free of feudal obligation, they are not at the same time free to ignore spiritual or public duty.

In all the grain and complexity of the story of land tenure in England before enclosure, several things are worth marking if we want these older commons to inform our thinking about more modern ones. First, a point already touched on bears stating more fully. The commons are not simply the land but the land plus the rights, customs, and institutions that organize and preserve its communal uses. The physical commons—the fields and woods and so forth—are like a theater within which the life of the community is enacted and made evident. A bit more detail about the medieval case will illustrate what I mean. Under the manorial system, an overlord had obligations to the free tenants of the manor; the tenants had rights to meadowland and so-called wastes (land not cultivated), and the lord could not alter those rights, nor diminish the amount of land involved. On the other side, these tenants typically owed the lord military service and other kinds of tribute. Below the free tenants were serfs, or "villeins," who, again, had rights in the common land, but whose obligations to the lord were fuller and more burdensome.

A serf's holdings obliged him in money, labor, and kind. Of money, for example, he was obliged to give the lord a sum upon the marriage of one of his (the serf's) daughters. Of labor, he was obliged to come with his own plow and oxen to plow the lord's acres, and when the plowing was done there was harrowing, reaping, threshing, and so forth, for an allotted number of days in the year. Of kind, he might be required to provide honey, eggs, chickens, and the like. Such a commoner had use rights in the land, but certainly no fee simple. He lived under what Daniel Defoe called "the great law of subordination." Manorial commons were the land, yes, but more substantively the land was a place where an aristocratic society staged and displayed its rigorous and inescapable hierarchies.

Feudal commons are only one case, of course; different societies will have different kinds of commons, even when at some level they all involve multiple use rights in land. English commons before the Norman conquest were much more egalitarian in practice, for example, at least according to the stories the English tell about their Saxon past.

Such historical cases aside, the idea that attention must be paid as much to social life as to the land means there are some simple questions to ask of any commons, existing or proposed: What social structures do its use rights embody? What political form does it support? Given that the commons arose in premodern agrarian villages, to what degree can the form be translated into modern contexts? If there are commons in the United States today, can they be continuous with our inherited politics and ideas about property? Can they, for example, be combined with our love of individual autonomy? Can they be democratic, pluralist, egalitarian . . . ? Can there be capitalist commons, or commons inside of or adjacent to capitalism?

BEATING THE BOUNDS

These questions aside, in addition to highlighting how commons and community map each other, the medieval case can usefully inform the modern when we turn to the question of durability. English commons lasted for centuries, possibly for millennia. To what might we attribute such remarkable longevity?

All who are in the least familiar with literature on the commons know that no discussion of that question can proceed without addressing Garrett Hardin's influential 1968 essay, "The Tragedy of the Commons." Hardin was an ecologist with a special concern for the problem of controlling human population growth; in the course of a thoughtful meditation on that topic, he digressed to consider why it so often happens that human beings find themselves destroying their own resources.

Fisheries such as those off the coast of New England are one of the examples Hardin used to illustrate the diagnosis he offered.

The fish stocks in question could be treated as a common property for centuries, so long as "the commoners" were limited in number. But there came a time when unlimited fishing with unlimited means threatened fish populations with utter collapse. Most every commons has a *carrying capacity*, a limit on its use beyond which the commons itself will begin to suffer. A forest where commoners gather wood will replenish itself so long as the commoners never exceed the forest's carrying capacity. The moment they do, the forest will die out.

As many have since pointed out, Hardin's tragic model may have been well applied to modern fisheries but it had little to do with how commons were managed historically. Hardin began, for example, by asking us to "picture a pasture open to all," and then to imagine this "all" invading it beyond its carrying capacity. But no commons was ever open to all; access was always limited in some way, a point I'll come back to shortly. Beyond this, Hardin had people using the commons who seem to have no neighbors they know or care about:

> The rational herdsman concludes that the only sensible course
> for him to pursue is to add another animal to his herd. And an-
> other . . . But this is the conclusion reached by each and every
> rational herdsman sharing a commons. Therein is the tragedy.

Hardin was prompted to this individualist daydream by his reading of an 1832 lecture on population control given by an amateur mathematician, William Forster Lloyd. Offered during the height of the enclosure period in England, Lloyd's analysis included a supposed story that Hardin did not reproduce but which is worth citing for the parallel strangeness of its assumptions:

> Suppose two persons to have a common purse, to which each
> may freely resort. The ordinary source of motives for economy is
> a foresight of the diminution in the means of future enjoyment

depending on each act of present expenditure. If a man takes a guinea out of his own purse, the remainder, which he can spend afterwards, is diminished by a guinea.

But not so, if he takes it from a fund, to which he and another have an equal right of access. The loss falling upon both, he spends a guinea with as little consideration as he would use in spending half a guinea, were the fund divided . . . Consequently . . . , the motive for economy entirely vanishes.

Just as Hardin proposes a herdsman whose reason is unable to encompass the common good, so Lloyd supposes persons who have no way to speak with each other or make joint decisions. Both writers inject laissez-faire individualism into an old agrarian village and then gravely announce that the commons is dead. From the point of view of such a village, Lloyd's assumptions are as crazy as asking us to "suppose a man to have a purse to which his left and right hand may freely resort, each unaware of the other." The "prisoner's dilemma" is the label that game theorists now give to one of the conundrums that can arise when self-interest and common purpose are set at odds. The name is telling: difficulties are not hard to generate if you assume the parties cannot communicate and it is handy therefore to begin your parable in a prison, almost as handy as assuming a herdsman who acts as if reason is blind to the presence of other commoners.

Both Hardin and Lloyd posit a kind of freedom that custom never allowed to those who held use rights in the commons. The simple fact is that the commons were a form of property that served their communities for centuries because there were strict limits on the use rights. The commons were not open; they were *stinted*. If, for example, you were a seventeenth-century English common farmer, you might have the right to cut rushes on the common, but only between Christmas and Candlemas (February 2). Or you might have the right to cut the branches of trees, but only up to a certain height and only after the tenth of November. Or you might have the right to cut the thorny evergreen shrubs called furze, but only so much as could be carried on your back, and only to heat your own house.

And these are simple restraints; most stints were more fully elaborated. If you were a farmer who held what were called "rights of common, appendant," you were constrained in the following ways: you must own land within the manor; you must actively cultivate your own land, your rights to the common pasture on "the lord's waste" arising out of your need to pasture your cattle in summer when you are cultivating; you may only pasture beasts needed in agriculture (oxen and horses to plow, sheep and cows to manure); you may only pasture your beasts during the growing season, when your land is under cultivation; you must not put more animals on the lord's land in summer than your own land can feed for the winter. In short, you must own and cultivate land distinct from the commons, and your use of the commons is limited by the size of your holding, limited in the kind of animal you may pasture, and limited to certain times of year.

In sum, use rights in the common were typically stinted, rarely absolute. No common was "open to all" and no "rational herdsman" was ever free to increase his herd at will. A true commons is a stinted thing; what Hardin described is not a commons at all but what is nowadays called an unmanaged common-pool resource.

It should be noted, too, that as the commons were stinted, so was the market in goods (especially in grain). Markets could not operate without regard for the provisioning of commoners and the poor. Farmers, for example, were obliged to bring grain to market rather than sell it in the field to wholesalers, and markets themselves were fenced, as it were, so that speculators couldn't outbid the poor. A description of "the orderly regulation of Preston market" dated 1795 reads:

> The weekly markets . . . are extremely well regulated . . . None but the town's-people are permitted to buy during the first hour,

which is from eight to nine in the morning: at nine others may
purchase: but nothing unsold must be withdrawn from the market till one o'clock, fish excepted . . .

In another town, "hucksters, higlers, and retailers" were excluded
from eight in the morning until noon.

These days it would be hard to find a time or a place where
there *wasn't* an available market, and certainly it would be hard to
find a market carefully fenced to make sure the poor could provision themselves. But in premodern England a market was a limited thing, a stinted thing. In a seven-day week, only one day was
"market day," and on market day only the afternoon hours were a
free market where anyone could buy.

As with the constraints on the commons, markets were stinted
for social and moral ends. No one was left to follow his or her
own ends without regard for the group. In *Customs in Common*,
the historian E. P. Thompson cites a pamphlet from 1768 that,
he says, "exclaimed indignantly against the supposed liberty of
every farmer to do as he likes with his own. This would be a 'natural,' not a 'civil' liberty." The pamphlet itself declares that such
liberty

> cannot then be said to be the liberty of a citizen, or of one who
> lives under the protection of any community; it is rather the lib-
> erty of a savage; therefore he who avails himself thereof, deserves
> not that protection, the power of Society affords.

To these eighteenth-century eyes, a stinted market, one constrained
by moral concerns, is a social market, while a wholly free market
operating without limits is savage.

There is one last point to make about the way that the commons
operated in premodern England. Only certain persons could use
the commons, and only for limited purposes, but once established

these uses were not to be cut off. In general no one could erect barriers to customary common rights, not the lord of the manor, not even the king. In fact, if encroachments appeared, commoners had a right to throw them down. Once a year, commoners would "beat the bounds," meaning they would perambulate the public ways and common lands armed with axes, mattocks, and crowbars to demolish any hedge, fence, ditch, stile, gate, or building that had been erected without permission. If someone sowed grazing land with wheat, villagers would destroy the crop by turning their cattle out to feed. If someone installed rabbit warrens where they did not belong, villagers would arrive with spades and dogs to root them out (one such act of resistance preserved as a commons the golf links at St. Andrews in Scotland).

Such interventions and perambulations were convivial affairs. In the north of England, laborers, crowds of boys, and the local constable made up the annual procession, the village providing them with cakes and beer. They walked their rounds during Ascension Day week, which is to say that protecting the commons and celebrating Christ's entry into heaven were one and the same. Annual perambulations assured the longevity of the commons; most of their history is therefore comic rather than tragic, if by comedy we mean a story with a social basis, a festive mood, and a happy ending.

The right to throw down encroachments was mostly a matter of local custom, but written law spelled out similar protections. As early as 1217 the Great Charter of the Forest forbade anyone to fence "arable ground" if such enclosure would be "to the Annoyance of any . . . Neighbors." Five centuries later, William Blackstone's *Commentaries on the Laws of England* enumerated the remedies available when a common right "is incommoded or diminished" or when land is "so enclose[d] . . . that the commoner is precluded from enjoying the benefit to which he is by law entitled." As late as 1827, we find a court repeating the old understanding: "If the Lord doth inclose any part, and leave not sufficient commons . . . the commoners may break down the whole inclosure."

This last pronouncement contains an echo of what is known as "the Lockean proviso," a philosopher's version of these safeguards. John Locke, in developing his theory of private property, famously claimed that things lying in the aboriginal commons become our property when we mix our labor with them, notwithstanding that they were once "common to all." Our labor removes things from "the common state" and in so doing it "excludes the common right of other men." Everyone else may then be denied access, "at least"—and here is the proviso—"at least where there is enough, and as good, left in common for others." Long before Locke, both law and custom had found ways to enact just this qualification, preserving what needs be left in common against any too intrusive exclusivity.

And how might perambulation, legal remedies, or the Lockean proviso be mapped onto the problem of preserving a cultural commons? What recourse is there if, as one scholar of intellectual property puts it, "courts or legislatures violate the proviso by creating private rights that impair the public's access to the common"? I shall let such questions hang for now, except to say that if we carry this analogy forward from the age of Locke into the nineteenth century, and return to the tangible commons for our cues, the answer would have to be "very little." This was the era of "lawless law's enclosure," as the poet John Clare called it, when Parliament could afford to turn a deaf ear on the claims of the old moral economy. To catch the tone of that unresponsive ear, witness the following exchange of letters. The date is 1824, and a commoner complains to his landlord: "Should a poor man take one of your sheep from the common, his life would be forfeited by law. But should you take the common from a hundred poor men's sheep, the law gives no redress." To which the landlord replies: "As your language is studiously offensive I must decline any further communication with you."

ALIENABLE PLOTS

With the advent of parliamentary enclosure, the old harmony between law and custom broke down and village perambulations necessarily took on an extralegal air. Often they turned into riots, and regularly they had to deal not with literal encroachments but with the abstract fences and hedges of the bureaucratic state. Beating the bounds now meant tearing notices of enclosure bills from church doors, disturbing surveyor's markers, stealing field plans and land valuation books, and, in one case, the actual burial of a court injunction in a ditch along with the offending hedge it was meant to protect.

All this was to no avail, of course. By the mid-nineteenth century, common right had been extinguished throughout England, the bulk of the commons converted to private land. Many forces lay behind the change. An emerging wool market encouraged fenced, single-use pastures for sheep, for example, while a rising industrial economy introduced rural peoples to wage labor, the freedoms of which many found preferable to the obligations of village life. The claim was also made that enclosure promoted agricultural efficiency. Separated fields could be planted with single crops to improve the soil or they could be drained to improve the health of livestock, changes which were almost impossible to effect in land held by many different people for many different uses.

The early modern phase of enclosure coincided with many other changes in how persons, their work, and their public lives were imagined, and in an associative sense the meaning of "enclosure" lies in those changes as much as in the overt fencing of fields. Enclosure meant a shift away from lives guided by customs preserved in local memory toward those guided by national law preserved in writing. It meant a shift in the value of change itself, once suspect and associated with decay, now praised and linked to growth. It meant a change in the measurement and perception of time. In the mid-eighteenth century, factory time—coordinated, precise, and finely divided—arrived to judge agrarian life and find it wanting. Enclosure took the village sundial, hung it on the wall, and added a minute hand. Before too long, it would strap the wall clock to the wrist and add a second hand. We who wear those watches, skilled now in what Wordsworth called "the usury of time," are the late inheritors of enclosure.

To my mind, though, the central meaning of enclosure's erasure of the commons lies in the way it carved those thousand-year-old beings, the commoners, into their constituent parts, then reshaped them for the new world of efficiency, law, progress, and time-as-money. A commons depends on a special sort of property that can, in theory, be broken into three parts: there is the use right, there is the commoner who acts on that right, and there is the land where the right is exercised. In theory, yes, this division can be made, but not in practice, at least not if the goal is to preserve a viable world of common holdings, for in that world these three things are one thing, and if they were picked apart that thing would cease to exist.

To illustrate by an analogy to a kind of "property" I suggested some pages back, in the United States, if you have a home in the state of Florida, say, you have the right to vote in that state's elections. All such elections have some sort of residency requirement, so the home helps establish your right. Again, we have three things (a physical place, a person, a right of action), and in a viable democracy, these things cannot be separated one from the other. In theory, perhaps, we could design a system where the right to vote belongs to the house and not the householder, but then we would have created a situation in which the rich can multiply their votes by buying up houses. Or we could, perhaps, say that the right to vote is a property that the citizen can transfer at will, though again by doing so we would open the door to the kind of plutocracy where the rich can buy more votes than the poor. Residency, resident, and right are bundled together to produce a "citizen of the state of Florida." No part can be split off as a separable property, not if we wish to preserve our kind of democracy.

But exactly this kind of severing attended the enclosure of common lands in England. During the days of parliamentary enclosure, the understanding was that people holding use rights in a commons should receive something—cash or some equivalent in private land—in exchange for the loss of those rights. In the abstract, this seems fair; it is hard to imagine how enclosure could have proceeded without some such conversion. In practice it amounts to a sea change in how persons and communities are imagined and given their agency.

To flesh this out with but one example, in 1812 the eight-thousand-acre Delamere Forest in Cheshire was enclosed, half of the land going to the king. Except in regard to a few moss pits and peat bogs, all rights of common in the forest were extinguished. The chief forester and his assistants, whose uses had included a right to raise rabbits in the woods, were given cash. Local landowners had their use rights exchanged for alienable plots of land. The tenants of these landowners, who had enjoyed a centuries-old right of estovers, got nothing, though the landowners were instructed to offer cash compensation. Such a conversion severs the land, the users, and the use rights, commodifying the first and last of these and leaving the middle term—the human being who once used the forest—changed from a commoner into a modern cash-economy individual. Thus do our practices in regard to property fit us or unfit us for particular ways of being human.

I myself find that most stories of enclosure wake in me a resistant pastoralist and therefore, just to be sure that nostalgia does not fog the edge of thought, it may be worth pausing here to say a few words in favor of the modern and against these agrarian commons. I mentioned above those feudal vassals who owed their lord the service of their swords, and below them those simple commoners obliged in honey, chickens, eggs, and time at the plow. Such people have no employers; they have lords and masters, and little or no freedom to alter the terms of their work. The great stability of the old agrarian commons was a great confinement, too; those with inherited rights to common land were the fortunate heirs of a world resistant to change, but by the same token they had little power to modify that world should they so desire.

Wage labor unsettled all that. It brought its own kinds of confinement, to be sure, but it also brought a promise of mobility and choice. To illustrate with a classic American case (to which I'll turn in a later chapter), no one wants to be Benjamin Franklin apprenticed to his bullying brother the Boston printer; everyone wants to be Franklin the runaway, setting up his own shop in Philadelphia, and advertising his do-it-yourself self by wheeling a barrow of printer's paper through the streets at dawn.

Early modern political thought long linked personal mobility with the mobility of property or, more specifically, linked political liberty with the right to hold an estate in "sole and despotic dominion." After the Puritan Revolution, the distinction between the vassal and the freeholder became marked and full of meaning. A vassal's land and sword were not his own; they were his lord's, and therefore so was he. For the freeholder, both land and sword were unencumbered and consequently so was he. A right to own land in fee simple and the "free" individual appeared together, each knit to the other. Wool was not the only crop to be taken from postfeudal fields; the modern Englishman grew there as well, a new kind of citizen—at least in the rhetoric of the time—bred to be an actor in the public sphere.

It is not hard to feel attachment to the premodern commons, but the sentiment should at least be informed. Let us not elide the fact that agrarian commoners lived embedded in a set of obligations most of us would find onerous if not actually oppressive. Enclosure and all its attendant meanings loosened up Defoe's "great law of subordination" and brought modern choice and political agency. Even

E. P. Thompson, in general a defender of the commons, is willing to concede that "the older . . . culture was in many ways otiose, intellectually vacant, devoid of quickening, and plain bloody poor."

All this said, I have not offered this short sketch of one country's actual commons in order to weigh it against the modern; the point has been to flesh out a representative image of the institution so as to bring it forward and make it new, make it an available tool for thinking about the fresh forms of common property that are now arising. To summarize, then, I began with a simple assertion: a commons is a kind of property in which more than one person has a right of action. We can now expand on this by summarizing the ground just covered. A commons is a social regime for managing a collectively owned resource. Moreover, although it is not hard to split a commons into the parts that make it up—the commoners, their use rights, the "fields" where those rights are enacted—in actual practice these parts cannot easily be separated one from another because it is the parts *bundled* that constitute the commons, that bring it into being. The things (fields, fish, songs, ideas, Internet protocols) are where common use rights meet, and that means that the things are encumbered, not readily available for private appropriation or trade. Likewise, because use rights are in an important sense what make the commoners who they are, these rights are not to be commodified either, at least not if the people and the community wish to preserve their identities. The agrarian commons I've been reviewing were not alienable things, nor were use rights alienable, nor did commoners think of market alienability as an important marker of their identity. In fact, by virtue of their common rights, commoners then and now are not individuals in the free market sense but a species, rather, of public or collective being.

Another feature of all durable commons is their stints, the constraints placed on use in the name of longevity; without these there is no true commons, only things belonging to no one or pools of resources no one manages.* Moreover, primary among the stints that sustain the commons must be counted the right to tear down encroachments. The commons is never the only kind of property at large in the land; there is always some form of despotic dominion and some form of market nearby, and for the commons to endure it must be protected from these. It needs some kind of built-in border patrol or annual perambulation, a defense against the undue conversion of use rights into rents or the fencing of open fields into sheep pastures. Almost by definition, the commons needs to stint the market, for if the "free market" is free to convert everything it meets into an exchangeable good, no commons will survive.

---

*Garrett Hardin has indicated that his original essay should have been titled "The Tragedy of the Unmanaged Commons," though better still might be "The Tragedy of Unmanaged, Laissez-Faire, Common-Pool Resources with Easy Access for Noncommunicating, Self-Interested Individuals."

3

THE ENCLOSURE OF CULTURE

The argument: Enclosure now threatens the
commons of art and ideas.

"THE ENCOURAGEMENT OF LEARNING"

The idea that durable commons may need to be stinted makes a
good point of entry into what the legal scholar James Boyle has
called "the second enclosure," the modern case in which "the
commons of the mind" have been more and more converted into
private preserves where someone's right to exclude comes before
everyone else's right to common. At first glance, it ought to seem
strange that any of the issues that arise with tangible, agricultural
commons—stinting, management, enclosure—would come into
play in regard to the creations of human wit and imagination, for,
unlike sheep meadows or fishing grounds, these things are not
generally in danger of being destroyed by overuse.

"If you have an apple and I have an apple and we exchange apples then you and I will still each have one apple. But if you have an
idea and I have an idea and we exchange these ideas, then each of
us will have two ideas." That is supposedly George Bernard Shaw's
formulation of an old idea about ideas, and about works of art
(incorporeal ones, that is—poems, tunes, ancient myths . . .). The
Iliad and the *Odyssey* can be spread throughout the world without anyone being deprived of them as a consequence. As Henry

Fielding writes in *Tom Jones*, "The ancients may be considered as a rich Common, where every Person who hath the smallest tenement in Parnassus hath a free right to fatten his Muse." Nor need your muse even have a tenement, really, nor live in the village, nor graze in summer only, for our inheritance from the ancients is an unstinted beneficence. The Pythagorean theorem, *Gilgamesh*, the poems of Sappho, the *Tao Te Ching*, or—to move closer in time— Benjamin Franklin's invention of bifocals or the autobiography that he wrote: it is in the nature of all such creations not to decline and perish but to survive and flourish in proportion to their use. "The Logos is common to all." Here lie the original comedic commons; let every new shepherdess freshly fatten her Muse, and let all nations dance on the unmuddied fields; nothing will be lost.

Not only are such cultural creations undiminished by use; once they are at large in the world it is difficult—often impossible—to make them private again. If I have a bright idea and want no one to "trespass" on it, I had better keep it to myself. In this sense, if we define property only in terms of the right to exclude, then we must say that there can be no property in revealed ideas. That was in fact one widespread belief in the eighteenth century. "The Copies of ancient Authors . . . ," a pamphleteer typically remarks, "are no more susceptible of Property than the Element of Air and Water, which are for the common Benefit of Mankind." So, too, with modern authors: should they wish to possess their lucubrations they had best not release them to the world.

The art and ideas I have pointed to in these last few paragraphs are what economists call "non-rivalrous" and "non-excludable." They are by nature abundant and gateless. The apples in that remark from George Bernard Shaw, like most tangible things, are rivalrous: if I consume them, you cannot. Ideas, inventions, melodies, and ancient epics, on the other hand, are non-rivalrous: if I consume them, so can you. Nor, once they have been made public, are they easy to make "excludable," especially when there are devices like the printing press or the Internet to disseminate them. The edition of *Poor Richard's Almanack* for 1753 carried Benjamin Franklin's clear instructions as to how to construct a lightning rod. That invention has belonged to the common stock of human knowledge ever since; nobody owns it and nobody can be excluded from it.

Rivalrous or non-rivalrous, excludable or non-excludable: economists now sort goods into categories based on the presence or absence of these traits, the limiting cases being private goods (both rivalrous and excludable) and public goods (neither rivalrous nor excludable). Public goods are not limited to the obvious cases of intangible art and ideas, either; something as concrete as a lighthouse has the same characteristics. Once it is up and running, the benefit of a lighthouse to any one ship does not lessen its benefit to all others, nor would it be easy to give exclusive light rights to paying customers and leave all others in the dark.

Public goods belong to the public domain, that great and ancient storehouse of human innovation.* The public domain surrounds us, but almost invisibly so, as if it were the dark matter in the universe of property. To illuminate but one case in point, every time you drive your car to work, you unwittingly take a ride on the public domain. Exactly how many inventions of the human mind are bundled in a working automobile? There are the four wheels, of course, and all that goes into making them: vulcanized rubber, steel-belted radials, air valves, wheel bearings and the ball bearings inside them, various kinds of grease, threaded lug nuts, metals and the metallurgy to produce them, brakes both disc and drum, devices to cool the brakes, devices to adjust them . . . And we haven't even left the ground yet; from the rubber that meets the road, to the drive shaft, to the laminated windshield, to the paint

---

*In this book, I will speak of the public domain and the cultural commons more or less interchangeably, though by the end it will be useful to distinguish them, the cultural commons being (by my definition) that part of the public domain whose customary or legal stints guard it against encroachment and enclosure.

on the roof, an automobile is a congress of thousands upon thousands of human inventions.

What would it cost if each of them were covered by a perpetual patent, and a fee had to change hands each time the dealer let a car off his lot? What is each one worth?

Luckily we have a case that names the value of a single invention. In 1962 one Robert Kearns came up with the idea for an intermittent windshield wiper and demonstrated the device to the Ford Motor Company. The Ford engineers asked Kearns a lot of questions, then sent him away. In 1969 Ford began to offer the intermittent windshield wiper under its own patents. Kearns filed a suit against Ford and others who had licensed the invention. He won $10.2 million from Ford and $11.3 million from Chrysler. In the latter case, the jury ordered Chrysler to pay ninety cents for each vehicle it had sold with intermittent wipers.

One small invention, ninety cents.

If we could multiply that by all the inventions that constitute a working automobile, we might be able to put a price on one small slice of the public domain. But of course there is no price, no fee, for the ideas behind spark plugs, rearview mirrors, turn signals, crankshafts, and so on; their patents—if they ever had them—have expired and they have taken their place in the public domain, that comedic commons to which each newborn child is heir and beneficiary.

Once we have charted the nature and the value of public goods, a question will surely arise: if, by their very nature, the fruits of human wit and imagination fall into the cultural commons, what might motivate us—*contra naturam*—to introduce a right to exclude? Why allow law, custom, or power to convert public into private goods? Why offer Benjamin Franklin, for example, despotic dominion over the manufacture of bifocals or the printing of his autobiography?

There are roughly four traditional answers to these questions. One assumes that all creative men and women have a natural right to the fruits of their labor and that, where non-excludability makes it hard to claim those fruits, society should intervene. (If it takes me ten years to write my novel, it is right and proper for the law to help me earn my rewards.) Another answer assumes that creative work is a kind of extension into the world of the creator's personality and that the work therefore deserves the same respect and protection that we accord to individuals. (My novel bears the stamp of my being; others should not be allowed to insult it, mutilate it, misattribute it, or use it to earn money without my permission.) Here the concern is not simply with just reward for effort spent but more broadly with questions of honor, respect, and reputation.

Both the labor theory and the moral rights theory, as these are called, focus on the individual creator. The third argument in support of otherwise "unnatural" exclusive rights does not ignore the individual but it begins, by contrast, with the needs of the community. If the group as a whole would benefit from a constant flow of useful and wonderful creations, and if an exclusive right would motivate creators to make these things, then why not offer it? After all, if public goods are common by nature, then their very nature is an impediment to their production (so long as producers need to earn a living). The question lying behind the labor theory— shouldn't labor have its reward?—arises here as well, but in this case the just reward for labor spent is not an end in itself but a means toward a broader, utilitarian goal of providing the greatest good for the greatest number.

But how exactly shall we know this "greatest good"? Here the utilitarian or "public benefit" model divides into two versions, the commercial and the civic. The former shies away from trying to describe "the good," trusting in market forces to reveal it, while the latter begins by nominating worthy ends, then seeks to shape the offered exclusive rights so as to achieve them. There is much to say about each of these, of course, but for now the point is simply that in both the commercial and civic form, a utilitarian theory of exclusive rights allows a taking from or enclosure of the cultural commons in the near term so as to create a larger and richer commons in the long term. It does not set the private against the public but hopes, rather, to leverage the former for the benefit of the latter.

An example from the early days of patent will illustrate the logic. In the early eighteenth century, a man named Chester Moor Hall invented a cunning way to overcome a problem in the manufacture of telescope lenses. The index of refraction of glass varies with the wavelength of light and as a result even a simple converging lens will have a bothersome problem called "color flare." To eliminate color flare, Hall devised a lens made of two kinds of glass whose indices of refraction canceled each other out. He combined a positive lens of crown glass and a negative lens of flint glass to produce what is now known as the achromatic telescope doublet.

For some reason, Hall wished to keep his discovery a secret and he therefore ordered the first two lenses to be made for him by two different opticians in London. Both of these men were too busy to do the job, however, and each subcontracted the order to a third man. This man was clever enough to realize that when he was asked to make two lenses of identical diameters, and having the same curvature on one face, someone meant to put them together. He did so and found that they produced an image free of color flare.

The technique for making an achromatic lens was then common knowledge among the instrument makers of London from about 1733 onward. These technicians, however, kept the method as a trade secret and Hall himself never published his results, being "a man of independent means, and . . . careless of fame."

As a consequence, it was necessary for a second man, John Dollond, to rediscover the telescope doublet, which he did and described in papers read before the Royal Society in 1758. He manufactured achromatic lenses, offered them for sale, and obtained a patent for his discovery.

The opticians of London begrudged this patent, however, having long known how to make telescope doublets. Eventually, Dollond's son—who had inherited the patent right upon his father's death—took one of the infringing opticians to court. The optician argued that the patent should never have been granted to Dollond because the discovery had been made many years earlier.

When the case came to trial, the opticians lost and the Dollond family won. Lord Mansfield, Lord Chief Justice of England, asserted that a patent is a contract between the inventor and the public. The commercial advantage which the inventor gains is his reward, *not for having made the invention, but for having disclosed it to the public* so that when the limited period of his patent has expired, the public gains the free use of the new idea. "It was not the person who locked up his invention in his scrutoire that ought to profit for such invention," Mansfield wrote, "but he who brought it forth for the benefit of mankind."

While it may not be obvious at first glance, copyright can be described in similar terms, as a grant whose true purpose is not so much to reward creators as to enrich the cultural commons. To see how this might be so, it helps to know the historical context of the first copyright laws. In England before the eighteenth century, a group of London printers known as the Stationers' Company dominated all publishing. A royal charter of 1557 gave these guild-like artisans exclusive and perpetual rights in duly registered books. These rights had nothing to do with rewarding authors and everything to do with the Crown's control of the press, the charter making it clear that church and state were never to be subjected to heresy, scandal, or dissent.

It was in this context—publishers enjoying a state-sanctioned monopoly over what appeared in print—that the British Parliament enacted the first-ever copyright law, the Statute of Anne, in 1710. This law gave "the Author or Proprietors" of books "the sole liberty of Printing and Reprinting . . . for the term of fourteen years" (once renewable if the author was still living).* The privilege was

---

*The word "proprietor" (meaning publisher) appears as often as the word "author": even in 1710 the legislature was more concerned with how publishers operated than with how authors made their living.

not automatic; authors and publishers had to apply for it, pay a nominal fee, and register the work in question.

Taken together, these two things—a limited term and a registration requirement—amounted to a revolution in the history of the dissemination of knowledge. In regard to printed books, at least, they brought the public domain into being. Even after 1710, most work remained unregistered (and so became public as soon as it appeared) and what did get registered enjoyed only a limited run of exclusivity, after which it was automatically released to join the ancients in that unowned commonwealth where no one needs permission to fatten a muse. These changes were a challenge to the printers of London, of course, for they had long enjoyed a protected market; they were not, however, a challenge to publishing itself, for they opened up the trade. Scottish printers, especially, entered the book business and offered classic and modern work to the public at greatly reduced prices. A cultural commons is not necessarily the opposite of a lively market; it is sometimes the precondition of one (as the Scottish printers proved).

Samuel Johnson, born about the same time as the Statute of Anne, once laid out the logic behind the new rules:

> There seems to be in authors [he told his friend Boswell] . . . a right, as it were, of creation, which should from its nature be perpetual; but the consent of nations is against it, and indeed reason and the interests of learning are against it; for were it to be perpetual, no book, however useful, could be universally diffused amongst mankind, should the proprietor take it into his head to restrain its circulation.

Johnson begins with a labor theory of ownership, then pivots ("but") and ends with a utilitarian-common-good theory. Yes, by rights authors should be owners, but the public has rights as well; learning and the general diffusion of knowledge matter. An exclusive right, especially a perpetual one, would not only mean that nothing becomes common, but that authors and booksellers could manipulate both access and price. That this not be the case, that prices be low and access easy, was a familiar concern in the eighteenth century. As one contemporary jurist wrote, dismissing a claim of unlimited ownership: "It might be dangerous to determine that the author has a perpetual property in his books . . . Such property would give him not only a right to publish, but to suppress too . . . ; this would be a fatal consequence to the public." Others stressed the matter of cost. If a perpetual right became law, it would "unavoidably raise the price of books beyond the reach of ordinary readers." Indeed, "a perpetual monopoly of books would prove more destructive to learning, and even to authors, than a second irruption of Goths and Vandals."

With such issues in mind, Samuel Johnson concluded his reflections where the Statute of Anne began, with a limit on the length of ownership:

> For the general good of the world, therefore, whatever valuable work has once been created by an author, and issued out by him, should be understood as no longer in his power, but as belonging to the publick; at the same time the author is entitled to an adequate reward. This he should have by an exclusive right to his work for a considerable number of years.

And how many years ought that to be? The statute gave a possible twenty-eight-year limit; Johnson thought that the author's life plus thirty years would be reasonable. Wherever the line falls, however, the point is that only by drawing it does the public domain come into being, and the Statute of Anne drew the line for the first time in history.

As with Lord Mansfield and patent (granted for "the benefit of mankind"), so then with these eighteenth-century thinkers and copyright. "Ordinary readers" are the object of their lucubrations, as are "learning" and "the general good" and "the publick." Limits ensure "common benefit," not private property. Even the name of the Statute of Anne pointed in this direction. When it was first debated, some wanted to call it a bill "for Securing the Property of Copies of Books." By the time it became law, the reference to "property" had been erased, the final title being "An Act for the Encouragement of Learning."

It should be added that copyright law in the United States historically assumed a similar primacy of the public domain. A 1988 review by a committee of the House of Representatives concludes with a typical summary:

> Under the U.S. Constitution, the primary objective of copyright
> law is not to reward the author, but rather to secure for the public
> the benefits derived from the author's labors. By giving authors
> an incentive to create, the public benefits in two ways: when the
> original expression is created and . . . when the limited term . . .
> expires and the creation is added to the public domain.

In the United States, the seed of this tradition was planted two centuries earlier, when the Congress enacted the nation's first copyright law and, echoing the Statute of Anne exactly, described it in the opening sentence as "an Act for the Encouragement of Learning."

"FOREVER, MINUS A DAY"

Let me retrace my steps a bit so as to come back to my point of departure, the idea that we are presently witnessing a second enclosure, a capture of cultural rather than agricultural commons. I began by saying that it is in fact odd to speak of such a thing, for, unlike fields and forests, most art and ideas are common or public by nature, being non-rivalrous and non-excludable. In fact, for a long time people thought such intangibles could not be property at all, if by that we mean things like cars and houses in which we can obviously have a right to exclude. And yet property they now are; we have invented legal devices (copyright, patent) to make art and ideas rivalrous and exclusive, and often for good reason. For one thing, exclusive rights solve a problem inherent to public goods: if there is no way to exclude, then there is no way to make money, and thus (in a pure market economy) no incentive to produce. Legally bestowed exclusive rights can solve the special problem of the non-excludability of public goods and thus, in the long run, actually enrich the commons. As I've shown, both patent and copyright were understood in just this way at the time of their inception.

As for the second enclosure, then, it should first be said that, in the simplest sense, enclosures of the cultural commons have always been with us. There has long been some knowledge kept secret; there has long been some control of the press. The governors of Venice first granted privileges to favored printers in 1469 and, by so doing, excluded all others. The 1557 charter given to the Stationers' Company in London was a form of enclosure, and was so described at the time. In one court case, it seems a certain Seymour had published an almanac to which the Company thought it had exclusive rights. They took Seymour to court and won their suit, the court opinion explaining that ever since the invention of printing a certain portion "hath been kept inclosed, never was made common." Government documents and "matters of state," for example, "were never left to any man's liberty to print." So too with the almanac in question: it was the king's prerogative to give it to the Company and he had therefore removed it from the commons.

The Statute of Anne also authorizes enclosure. If, as some eighteenth-century jurists thought, "the act of publication . . . [makes] work common to everybody," then even a fourteen-year grant has to be seen as replacing a right to common with a right to exclude. In this case, however, the substitution seems laudable; it not only beat back the larger enclosure that was the charter of the

Stationers' Company, it also—by limiting the term of the grant—established a way to feed new work into the public domain.

The idea of a properly limited exclusive right is itself a cultural innovation of the first order, or so it seems to me. The problem is to figure out what "properly limited" means, and here we come to the true second enclosure, for the history of copyright since 1710 has been the story of a limit that has lost its limit. It seems to be in the nature of all property rights that they expand over time. Those who benefit from exclusive rights have an incentive to encroach upon the commons while those who benefit only from the right to common are rarely even aware of what they have, and even more rarely do they develop any customary beating of the bounds.

A brief history of copyright in the United States will illustrate the consequent ceaseless expansion. At its inception, American copyright was a tightly focused privilege. The original term was fourteen years, once renewable; the grant applied only to "copies of maps, charts, and books"; "authors and proprietors" had to apply for the privilege. This registration requirement is important, as we've seen, for many people have no real interest in owning their work. Almost all political pamphlets published in the 1790s, for example, became common property as soon as they appeared.

In 1790, moreover, "copies" meant literal, verbatim reproductions; no one needed permission to make what are now called derivative works—translations, sequels, abridgments, and so forth. As late as 1853, a U.S. circuit court found that Harriet Beecher Stowe had no right to block an unauthorized German translation of *Uncle Tom's Cabin* (printed domestically for German-American readers), under the assumption that when an author has published a book, "his conceptions have become the common property of his readers, who cannot be deprived of the use of them." Early-nineteenth-century law encouraged translation, and why not? A translation takes time and effort; it is useful to the public; it aids in the dissemination of knowledge; it is hardly a verbatim copy of the original. To reward translators themselves with a limited exclusive right surely makes as much sense as our current practice, which gives the "proprietors" of any work full control over its fate in other languages (such that, for example, for over half a century no one was allowed to make a corrected translation of Simone de Beauvoir's classic *The Second Sex*, which existed in English only in a 1953 version made by a retired zoologist, a man who knew nothing of French philosophy and who deleted 145 pages of the original book!).

The United States never offered special privileges to favored publishers, either. The British had to struggle for years to free the ancient authors from the Stationers' Company, but no such battle was needed in America, where cheap editions flourished from the start. Farmers came home from the plow to read Homer and Tacitus, or so the story always went. The typical brag appears in Franklin's memoirs: easy access to books has "made the common tradesmen and farmers as intelligent as most gentlemen from other countries." Nor did the law offer any rights to contemporary authors in foreign lands. The United States was a pirate nation for a hundred years, and proud of it. The 1790 copyright law mentioned above (the one "for the Encouragement of Learning") contains what can only be called a piracy clause:

> *Sec. 5*: . . . Nothing in this act shall be construed to extend to prohibit the importation or vending, Reprinting or publishing within the United States, of any map, chart, book or books, written, printed, or published by any person not a citizen of the United States . . .

All these things have changed, of course. Not only do we now insist that other nations refrain from piracy, the ownership we seek to protect has vastly expanded in both scope and duration. Copyright at present subsists in any work "fixed in any tangible medium of expression, now known or later developed," and these works include not only the obvious—novels, songs, motion pictures—but *any* "fixed" thing, whether formally registered with the Copyright Office or not, be it a grocery list, a ransom note, or a child's drawing of the sun. The term for individuals is now "life-time plus 70 years" and for corporations or work made for hire it is ninety-five years. A novel written by a young author who lives to be eighty would be protected for over a century. The poems of Emily Dickinson, due to anomalies in their publishing history, are owned by Harvard University Press and will be until 2050, well over 175 years after they were written.

It was a 1976 revision of copyright law that eliminated the registration requirement, meaning that since that date *no* new creations have entered the public domain; everything carries a presumptive right to exclude. In fact, there is no statutory provision whereby a work can be given to the public domain.* Authors who do not wish to be owners must invent complicated schemes such as issuing a license to the public at large (and even that may not work: the law includes a "termination of transfer" provision whereby rights revert to the creator after a certain number of years no matter what licenses or contracts have been signed).

Default copyright has changed the very ground from which all discussion and policy must proceed. Until 1976, the point of departure was the assumed common nature of creative work; everything belonged to the commons and the exception, "intellectual property," was a small set of things removed from the commons by consent, by an overt and public action, for a short term, and for a good reason. Now the point of departure is the assumption of exclusive ownership and those who think they have a right to common are greeted by FBI warnings at the start of every movie.

These ownership rights endure for a very long time, too. The film industry lobbyist Jack Valenti, when forced to admit that the

---

*There is such a provision in patent law; an inventor has the right "to confer gratuitously the benefits of his ingenuity upon the public." Not so with copyright.

term of copyright should be limited, used to joke that from his point of view the ideal term would be "forever, minus a day." His wish has essentially been granted. When the most recent extension of copyright was challenged before the Supreme Court, a group of economists—both liberal and conservative, including five Nobel Prize winners—filed a friend of the court brief that analyzed the financial benefit of various terms. One of their conclusions was that "the current copyright term already has nearly the same present value as an infinite copyright term." In regard to money to be earned, the difference between the current term of copyright and a perpetual term is statistically trivial.*

In the copyright sphere, at least, all these things taken together are what is meant by "the second enclosure": the law grants nearly perpetual private rights to nearly every creative expression appearing in any media now known or yet to be discovered! This is one reason it seems to me that the entertainment industry's antipiracy campaigns lack moral force. Yes, people should obey the law, but doing so in this case means participating in the breach of a centuries-old understanding about the public domain.

---

*The economists assumed that "copyright provides incentives for creation by solving the special problem of non-excludability of creative works," and then tried to figure out what sort of "incentive" another twenty years offered for creators of new works. To do this, they looked at the "present value" and "future value" of the possible new earnings: "For a given amount of money today, future value is the amount that money would be worth at some point in the future. For example, if the interest rate is 7%, $1 today has a future value of $1.07 a year from now. Present value is the reciprocal of future value; thus $1.07 next year has a present value of $1 today. One dollar, received a year from now, has a present value of approximately $0.93 ($1/1.07) . . . $1 in two years is equivalent to approximately $0.87 today. The further away in time it is paid, the less that payment is worth in present value." By this reckoning, adding twenty years to the term of copyright yields a 0.33 percent increase in present-value payments to an author. The difference between such an increase and that of "an infinite copyright term" they judged to be "trivial."

If we turn briefly to patent rights, that other major sphere of "intellectual property," we will find that while they have not expanded in term the way copyright has (they used to run seventeen years; now they run twenty), they have nonetheless expanded considerably in scope. It has long been the understanding that facts, and especially facts of nature, cannot be owned. You might discover, as Sir Isaac Newton did, that the planets have elliptical orbits, but you cannot own that fact; you can only claim credit for having been the first to declare it. "When [Alessandro] Volta discovered the effect of an electric current from his battery on a frog's leg he made a great discovery but no patentable invention." When Sir Alexander Fleming noticed that penicillin mold destroys most bacteria, he uncovered a natural fact, he "lifted the veil," as they say, but he made no invention and thus had nothing to patent.

In fact, as soon as Fleming discovered it, penicillin entered the public domain, a lively competition arose to manufacture it, and the cost quickly dropped—93 percent in the first five years. Almost as quickly, the old understanding regarding facts of nature began to be challenged: drug companies managed to persuade patent offices that to isolate and purify a natural organism somehow converted it from a discovery to an invention. Thus when later generations of antibiotics like streptomycin came along, decades passed before they became as cheap as penicillin.

The simple distinction between discovery and invention has been eroded in other ways as well. We now offer patents to those who first describe gene sequences, albeit these are natural facts of great antiquity. The genetic structure of the hepatitis C virus has been patented, and as much as one fifth of the human genome is now privately controlled, including DNA segments related to diabetes, human growth hormones, and certain kinds of breast cancer.

To make matters worse, it used to be that patents were granted only for useful inventions, and inventors were required to demonstrate utility up front. Now patents are issued for DNA sequences whose purposes are wholly obscure. As one wit has said, in the United States "you get utility if you can spell it."

Even where biological utility can be demonstrated, it is often nature's utility, not ours. In a *New York Times* op-ed, the novelist Michael Crichton offered a list illustrating a disturbing trend in regard to naturally occurring correlations: "Elevated uric acid is linked to gout. Elevated homocysteine is linked to heart disease. Elevated homocysteine is linked to B-12 deficiency, so doctors should test homocysteine levels to see whether the patient needs vitamins." But, Crichton concluded, "actually, I can't make that last statement. A corporation has patented that fact, and demands a royalty for its use."

Traditional knowledge and heritage have also been the target of patent enclosure. The Indian government estimated that at the turn of the twenty-first century as many as two thousand patents were being issued annually based on indigenous medicines. The therapeutic uses of turmeric, for example, long known on the Indian subcontinent, are now privately owned.

Farmers have always saved seed from one season to the next, and for a long time, no one was allowed to introduce a right to exclude into that cycle. Not until the late sixties in Europe and the United States, that is, when "utility patents" were introduced to give plant breeders ongoing rights to the varieties they had developed. Now the farmer who saves his seeds will find they bear a crop of royalties for someone else even as they bear a crop of corn and wheat for him.

I should say that, as with agricultural enclosure in the nineteenth century, some of this loss of the commons may well have net social benefit. The search for naturally occurring antibiotics takes time, skill, and effort, for example, and these should be rewarded. Still, issuing a right to exclude is not the only way to reward good work, complicated policy questions attend each of the cases I have mentioned, and—for good or for ill—all these changes amount to an enclosure of parts of nature long thought to be our common inheritance.

"THIS BOOK CANNOT BE READ ALOUD"

The enclosure of the cultural commons is easiest to describe in regard to copyright and patent, for in these cases the changing rules are a matter of record and their context has a long history. The enclosures taking place on the Internet are another matter. The technology is new and complicated, and we have as yet very little sense of what might be the most appropriate governing social contract. One thing we do know: in the 1990s, the ease of digital copying and the rise of the World Wide Web combined to throw most of the old social contract into turmoil. As early as 1994, John Perry Barlow—a lyricist for the Grateful Dead and a cofounder of the Electronic Frontier Foundation—sketched the looming confusion:

> If our property can be infinitely reproduced and instantaneously distributed all over the planet without cost, without our knowledge, without its even leaving our possession, how can we protect it? How are we going to get paid for the work we do with our minds? And, if we can't get paid, what will assure the continued creation and distribution of such work?

It will be some time yet before we have answers to these questions. Even after the Statute of Anne, it took more than fifty years for the British to sort out what it really meant to own "literary property," and the puzzles posed by the digital Web are arguably more complicated. "Since we don't have a solution . . . ," Barlow warned, "we are sailing into the future on a sinking ship."

Either that, or maybe all ships will rise on the digital tide—all ships fitted to digital seas, that is; those built for the days when intangible goods were always delivered in tangible containers are having a harder time. Before digital came along, printed books, reels of film, phonograph records, etchings, maps, compact discs, and so forth gave nice corporeal shells to the incorporeal stuff inside them. The ideas, art, knowledge, or entertainment that they contained may well have been abundant and ungated, but they themselves were, and are, neither. Books must actually be printed with ink on paper, bound, boxed, shipped to stores, sold at cash registers, and so forth, all of which makes exclusive rights fairly easy to manage and royalties easy to reckon. Should a book be pirated, copies can be seized and destroyed, and fines levied.

In this same line, in an essay for *Wired*, the musician and music producer David Byrne asks the simple question, "What do record companies do?" and replies with a list: they "fund recording sessions; manufacture product; distribute product; market product; loan and advance money [to musicians] . . . ; handle the accounting." In short they "market the product, which is to say the container—vinyl, tape, or disc—that carried the music." But the product is not *music*; music is something "heard and experienced," always in some social setting.

> Epic songs and ballads, troubadours, courtly entertainments, church music, shamanic chants, pub sing-alongs, ceremonial music, military music, dance music—it was pretty much all tied to specific social functions . . . You couldn't take it home, copy it, sell it as a commodity . . . , or even hear it again.

Record companies don't sell music; they sell the container, and thinking that the container is the music is like thinking that a shopping cart is food or that the wine bottle is the wine. Substituting the one for the other—the container for the contained—is an old trick of language; rhetoricians call it metonymy.

From a business perspective, this is a metonymy well worth preserving: the materiality of the containers, and all the steps involved in getting them from the producer to the consumer, make the whole process sticky; it slows things down and makes them accountable. When concrete objects deliver abstract objects, a skin of scarce and exclusive property settles over the abundant and nonexclusive, stands in its stead, and makes it easy to manage right-holders' privileges.

This is one reason why the business model of the recording industry, from funding the studio session to handling the accounting, worked very well for half a century. Then several things happened at once. By Byrne's account, recording costs dropped almost to zero (it used to cost $15,000 to make a studio tape; now "an album can be made on the same laptop you use to check email"), and manufacturing and distribution costs also dropped almost to zero. With LPs and CDs, there were costs at every stage—pressing the disc, printing the labels, shipping, and so on. "No more: Digital distribution is pretty much free." Gone, too, are the economies of scale that drove the star system. On the Internet, "it's no cheaper per unit to distribute a million copies than a hundred."

A similar analysis can be applied to book publishing. What do publishers do? Ideally, they sort through a sea of submitted work, selecting for quality and/or salability; they advance royalty money to authors; they edit manuscripts; they design and print books; they advertise and promote; they sell the work to readers through various channels; they sell film, translation, and other secondary rights (and send a percentage along to authors); they keep the accounts and pay royalties . . .

And what happens to both publishers and authors (or to musicians and record companies) in a digital environment where a single copy posted on the Web can, as Barlow says, "be infinitely reproduced and instantaneously distributed all over the planet"?

We really don't know. Some will undoubtedly adapt and thrive. Barlow himself offered the Grateful Dead as a model, pointing out that not all business needs to be organized around the economics of scarcity. "Most soft goods increase in value as they become more common . . . It may often be true that the best way to raise demand for your product is to give it away." For decades the Grateful Dead allowed its fans to tape their concerts and demand didn't then fall; it rose, the Dead becoming "the largest concert draw in America, a fact that is at least in part attributable to the popularity generated by those tapes."

In the book world, the science fiction writer Cory Doctorow has taken a similar path; his books are available for free on the Web and for sale in bookstores. Neither he nor his publisher seems to be suffering.

Both of these are special cases, however (each having a large fan base and a taste for public performance), and it isn't clear how to move from their examples to a general model. What about a reclusive and unhurried poet like Elizabeth Bishop? What of a publisher whose support for young writers depends on a backlist of authors now dead? The fact is that we are redesigning this ship as we sail it, and no one can yet say how it should be fitted to serve all the ends we care about, nor what it might then look like fifty years from now.

What we can say is that the new technologies have created a medium that replaces the old distribution stickiness with a fluidity that seems to rival that of thought itself. And that change, in turn, has given rise to astounding new commons and, at the same time, to almost as astounding new enclosures. We may not be in a position to describe how the moral and commercial economies of art and ideas will look fifty years from now, but we can at least interrogate particular new models as they arise.

I earlier indicated that to my mind the "properly limited exclusive right" embodied in the Statute of Anne was a cultural innovation of the first order; it was an enclosure of print's natural commonality, yes, but one that put an end to the larger enclosure of the Stationers' Company while simultaneously initiating the formal release of work to the public domain. Where enclosures of the digital commons arise, we will have to ask if they have similar benefits (are they for "the encouragement of learning"?), or if they are merely designed to maximize the wealth and control of private owners. Do they leave us with a "generative Internet," as the legal scholar Jonathan Zittrain has called it, one where surprising and useful innovations arise precisely because so much is left up for grabs, or will we be left with digital devices so skillfully locked down that we'll wish we were back with the last century's sticky old media?

One typical puzzle raised by cyberspace will illustrate the difficulty of answering such questions. This is not a book about the Internet, but the Internet is a primary site of cultural enclosure in our age, and it will be useful to offer a sample of the kinds of choices that face us.

Take the problem of what is known as the "first sale doctrine." In physical space, it has always been hard to follow a product once it has left the store; for intangible goods in tangible containers (a book of poems, say), we have therefore long had a "first sale" rule, an understanding most people know about intuitively, though they may not know that it is also spelled out in the law. "First sale" is a limitation on an owner's exclusive rights such that once you have bought a book (or CD, or video disc, or map . . .) you may do almost anything with it that you want. You may return to it multiple times, read it to your child, copy bits into a journal, give it to a friend, loan it to a student, sell it to a stranger . . . You may not print and sell more copies, that is true, but all these other things you may do. The right of first sale creates an object-specific, downstream public domain; the copyright owner's control ends at the point of purchase.

What happens to the first sale doctrine in cyberspace? It's not even clear if it exists (technically a new copy is created each time someone downloads a file, and for all things under copyright, making that copy requires permission), and if it does exist, can any publisher be assured of selling more than one copy of a book? The first buyer could simply post it for the world at large.

That being the case, perhaps we should just eliminate first sale in the digital world. Market purists on the publishing side might welcome that; after all, with digital copying "first sale" looks more like a market failure than a consumer right. Yes, they might say, it was once hard to track every use of a book after it was sold, but happily those days are over. In cyber publishing it is easy to record every reading of a book, every passage cut and pasted, every time the work passes to a new user. Why not treat each of these as a unique commercial event and extract royalties along the way?

In a sense, this is already happening. To harvest such payments and thus to abrogate the first sale doctrine, electronic publishers have been designing their products to be as sticky as they were in the old container-based world; they have been wrapping work in "digital rights management" software or selling it under click-through licenses that effectively trump all the public domain aspects of traditional copyright.

Take, for example, an electronic book publisher's recent offering of Lewis Carroll's 1865 *Alice's Adventures in Wonderland*. The copyright notice carried the following warnings:

> **Copy:** No text selections can be copied from the book to the clipboard.
> **Print:** No printing is permitted of this book.
> **Lend:** This book cannot be lent to someone else.
> **Give:** This book cannot be given to someone else.
> **Read aloud:** This book cannot be read aloud.

Similarly, an electronic version of the U.S. Constitution, fitted to be read by a Microsoft Reader and offered for sale on Amazon.com, made it impossible for readers to print copies more than twice a year (and it is illegal to hack the code enforcing this restriction). As one wag on the Internet pointed out, if these had been the restrictions on the Constitution when it was first drafted, it would have taken six years to get copies delivered to all thirteen colonies for approval.

Yes, these are silly examples. No one is going to get arrested for hacking the Constitution or for reading *Alice* aloud. They are, however, representative of the impulse to meet the ease of digital copying with new forms of control. On the one hand, they portend the loss of the first sale doctrine and thus the enclosure of an after-market commons that has been part of the moral economy of art and ideas for centuries. On the other hand, it would seem impossible to have a first sale doctrine in cyberspace and still honor the other side of the old moral economy, the one that supported creators and publishers for centuries and—as long as copyright was rightly limited—helped enrich the commons with new work.

What is to be done? I obviously lean toward preserving existing commons wherever we can, but just as obviously there are few easy choices in this or in many of the other conflicts produced by the digital Internet. Nor is it the choices themselves that initially concern me in this book, but rather the philosophy and values that will help us make them. These at least we can work to clarify. To that end, I want to close this chapter by moving away from the kind of policy questions that something like "first sale" raises and return to the wider questions of how far and to what ends we presume to extend the right to exclude.

SILENCE AS A RESOURCE

"To study the self is to forget the self," writes the Buddhist master Dogen. "To forget the self is to be enlightened by all things." If a painter, self-forgetful, picks up her brush and sketches a cicada, or if a poet hears the mourning doves in the sunrise pines and writes a short poem, from where shall we say the work has arisen? How shall we describe the incentive to create? "If my poems and paintings . . . should prove to be of some aid to the forgers, what is there for me to grudge about?" "What difference does it make who is speaking?"

We usually say that what lies outside "intellectual property" is the public domain, but even that large preserve does not contain the fullness of potential creation, especially if we mean by it all that has first passed through the domesticating apparatus of legal ownership. All that has once been owned by someone—Jane Austen's novels, Whitman's poems, the steam engine, the transistor—is domesticated ground, but out beyond the palings are lands as yet untamed. It is a very old idea that human beings and their cultures are renewed by quitting the familiar and going (in fact or in imagination) to the desert. In many traditions, the young must go into silence or wilderness before they can emerge as real persons. It is not enough to take instruction; there has to be some contact with what lies outside our knowledge, which is to say, with our collective ignorance, how large it is, and how fertile.

The more we know and control, the less surprise and revelation. How sad if Columbus had actually landed in India, or if nature threw up no sports, or if there were no misshapen fruits for the gleaners to carry home. Ungoverned spaces make for fertile breeding grounds. A year after the first Apple II computer appeared, the company was surprised by a spike in sales. It turned out that the first spreadsheet—VisiCalc—had been written to run on the new machine. That was not a use Apple had imagined, nor one that could have appeared had their device been locked down the way many Apple products now are. The emergent properties of systems are never apparent from the conditions going in. From no single goose could you predict that flocks would fly in such fine harrows.

In the 1980s, a group of cell biologists in San Diego described and patented a particular sequence of amino acids, a family of peptides, though they had in fact no idea what role these molecules might play in human physiology. A decade later, another research group theorized that these peptides served to block the growth of blood vessels in cancer tumors. When the patent holders heard of this research, they sued for licensing fees and won a $15 million judgment. Such cases breed caution. A survey of scientists at American universities has found many who are hesitant to work on particular gene targets out of fear of unexpected fees and lawsuits. Exploratory science unfolds into the unknown, but it is difficult to conduct if patent thickets prematurely hedge the empty spaces. If the "second enclosure" means the invasion of exclusive rights into old and recognized cultural commons, perhaps we need yet another category, a "third enclosure," to name this blind prospecting, this preemptive planting of claim stakes in fields not yet understood. In these cases, we cannot even name the commons that are lost; they lie in futures now foreclosed.

Roman law used to include a kind of property called *res nullius*, "things of no one." The fish in the sea, the birds of the air, a gene sequence whose purpose no one knows: *res nullius* are those things that *could* plausibly be owned, but are not yet. If we value the surprise of the new, we need to check the impulse toward too swift an appropriation of these. We need to cultivate a practice of the wild, one whose first condition is the simple freedom to wander out, unimpeded, beyond the usual understanding and utterance. "Out of unhandselled savage nature . . . come at last Alfred and Shakespeare"—or so Emerson once claimed. His young friend Thoreau went to Walden Pond to step outside the village proper, on the chance he might learn something not talked about in the town. Solitude has its lessons, and so does silence. "Silence is audible to all men . . . ," Thoreau believed. "She is when we hear inwardly, sound when we hear outwardly." There is a direct line between Thoreau's two years at the pond and his appearance in 1848 as a tax resister able to state clearly the grounds of his refusal. Fresh speech is a translation for one's neighbors of what the inner ear has heard.

The noise of our village now surrounds us so fully it often seems there is no way to escape it. There are a number of projects in the United States whose simple goal is to set a microphone in the woods, fields, or marshes and make a record of nonhuman noises—the birds, the wind, the water—but it turns out to be almost impossible to find a square foot of land in the entire nation where you cannot hear the buzz of a chain saw or a distant airplane. In an essay called "Silence Is a Commons," Ivan Illich tells of being taken as a baby to the island of Brac on the Dalmatian coast to receive his grandfather's blessing. This was a place where daily life had altered little for five hundred years: "The very same olive-wood rafters still supported the roof of my grandfather's house. Water was still gathered from the same stone slabs on the roof. The wine was pressed in the same vats, the fish caught from the same kind of boat."

All that was about to change. "On the same boat on which I arrived in 1926, the first loudspeaker was landed on the island . . . Silence now ceased to be in the commons; it became a resource for which loudspeakers compete." As an experiment sometime, see if you can escape the loudspeakers in airports. I once paid extra money to get into an airline's "private club" because my flight was delayed and I had work to do. In an almost empty room a huge television ceaselessly delivered the news. When I turned it off (no one was watching), the attendant reprimanded me: some network had also paid to be in that room, and their terms were that the machine would never go quiet.

When I was a child in rural Connecticut, our school bus used to pass through a wooded swamp under whose canopy we sometimes saw wild ducks, beavers, or once (I thought) a bobcat with its tufted ears. In that time between sleep and the schoolroom, we would ride through the shaded tunnels of land too wet to plow. Now, I read in the paper, the buses are equipped with broadcast music and advertisements. It sedates the restless child, they say. And the school day begins with Channel One, its news and ads. Once upon a time companies fought one another for market share; now they fight for "mind share" and have discovered that elementary schools offer the richest hunting grounds. Hundreds of thousands of dollars they pay to be the only sugared drink in the school vending machines—not to sell the drink so much as to inscribe their brand on the unhandselled minds of the very young.

The composer John Cage, who had a lifelong interest in silence, used to tell a story about an event that deepened his understanding of what silence meant. In 1952 he heard that acoustical engineers at Harvard had created a completely soundproof room, an an-echoic chamber, and he arranged to spend some time in it. When he emerged, he told the technicians that it didn't work: he could hear two noises, one low and one high. "Oh," they said, "everyone hears those—the low hum is your circulating blood, the high whine is your nervous system."

There is never absolute silence, Cage concluded; there is only sound we intend to make and sound we do not intend. "Silence" in Cage's work indicates the latter, the ambient noise of non-intention. If one listens to the first recording of 4'33", his famous silent work—four minutes and thirty-three seconds during which a piano player plays nothing (though he opens and closes the piano to indicate the piece's three segments)—one can hear, among other things, the sound of rain on the roof of concert hall. For Cage, such "background" sounds are of interest, and we normally do not hear them; we screen out the trivia of life so as to focus on what we take to be the important parts, but by doing so we reduce our own awareness and confine ourselves to the story our intended noise is telling.

I say all this not simply to explain Cage's practice but to intro-duce a representative tale about the third enclosure. In 2002, the British musician Mike Batt produced an album for the rock group the Planets. Called *Classical Graffiti*, the CD featured two distinct styles and Batt decided to separate these with a track called "A One Minute Silence." He then credited the track, "tongue-in-cheek," to "Batt/Cage."

A few months later, much to Batt's surprise, the mechanicals kicked in.

Mechanicals, or more properly "compulsory mechanical li-censes," are a device much used in the music industry that allows performers to record someone else's work without having to seek permission. Music publishers grant these licenses and then, if a recording is made, "mechanical royalties" are collected and paid to the owner of the copyright. In this case, after the Planets' album had been on the market for a while, Batt received a letter from Britain's Mechanical-Copyright Protection Society. "It informed me that my silence was a copyright infringement on Cage's silence," he told *The New Yorker*. It indicated, moreover, that an initial royalty payment of over four hundred pounds had been sent to John Cage's publisher, Peters Edition.

That check found its way to the desk of one Nicholas Riddle, managing director of the London office of Peters Edition. Riddle was not entirely amused by the misuse of Cage's name and he informed Mike Batt of that fact. "This is intellectual property that needs protecting," he explained, making it clear that the publishing house was willing to go to court if need be to guard its client's reputation and interests.

There followed a season of bemused banter with apparent good humor on both sides. "Mine is a much better silent piece," Batt declared at one point. "I have been able to say in one minute what Cage could only say in four minutes and 33 seconds." Asked which bit of Cage's composition he had stolen, Batt replied, "None of it. My silence is original silence." That summer Peters Edition and Batt agreed to hold a (silent) musical runoff: at Baden-Powell House in London, the Planets performed Batt's one-minute piece and then a clarinetist from the publishing house performed Cage's *4'33"*.

Such antics notwithstanding, a few months later Batt elected to resolve the potential conflict without contesting the publisher's legal claims. On the steps of the High Court in London, he handed Riddle a check for an undisclosed sum, saying simply that he was "making this gesture of a payment to the John Cage Trust in recognition of my own personal respect for John Cage and in recognition of his brave and sometimes outrageous approach to artistic experimentation in music."

The newspapers have reported that this was a case of "copyright infringement" and that "the lawsuit claimed Batt stole his silence from Cage." This is not entirely accurate. At issue, rather, were John Cage's "moral rights," one of which (under most European law) is the right to be protected from misattribution. As Riddle told me in an e-mail, "The issue was entirely that Batt identified this silence as having Cage authorship." His crime was "misappropriating Cage's name," and that "would not do."

At this point, it is worth backing off and saying a little more about Cage's philosophy. As I've indicated, his art often created situations in which to hear and see what normally passes unnoticed. It is an art of attention and awareness and not, then, an art meant to express the artist's personality. Cage was influenced by Buddhism and in Buddhism the "self" is a thing to be thinned out, not built up, forgotten, not remembered. And while the Buddhists suggest meditation as a way to get free of the self, Cage decided to use chance operations. "I used them to free myself from the ego." Flipping coins while he composed was a good way to escape his own sense of how things ought to sound, his own likes and dislikes. He had no interest in making an art that carried the marks of his personality or taste. He loved the incidental drawings that are scattered throughout Thoreau's journals: "The thing that is beautiful about the Thoreau drawings is that they're completely lacking in self-expression."

What is of interest in the Mike Batt affair, then, is the disconnect between Cage's practice and the philosophy behind moral rights, which assumes, as some European law asserts, that the work contains "the imprint of the author's personality." United States copyright law has different roots but it sometimes touches on "personality" in a related way. A key Supreme Court case from 1903, for example, concerned whether or not there could be a copyright in something as mundane as printed posters for circus acts. In affirming that indeed there could, Justice Oliver Wendell Holmes wrote that

> an artist who draws from life . . . makes a work that is the personal reaction of an individual upon nature. Personality always contains something unique. It expresses its singularity even in

handwriting, and a very modest grade of art has in it something irreducible which is one man's alone.

Fine, but if this is the assumption behind the law, then the law should have no standing where artistic practice seeks to step beyond "unique" personality. ("Personality," Cage once said, "is a flimsy thing on which to build an art!") If, on the other hand, the law claims standing here, if litigation extends even to the fruits of self-forgetfulness, if the mechanicals kick in and checks must be exchanged on the steps of the High Court, then surely the third enclosure is upon us.

. . .

I closed the previous chapter of this book with the idea that durable commons survive because they include both customary limits to use and an acknowledged right to tear down encroachments. These points led into what should really be called the *puzzle* of the second enclosure, puzzle because limits to use usually arise to solve the problem of carrying capacity and no such problem attends "the commons of the mind." These are by their very nature both abundant and ungated, and yet for apparently good reasons (to give labor its just reward, for example) we sometimes counterplot nature and introduce the social artifice of exclusive rights. But this leaves us with potential conflicts among the things we value and thus grounds for debate about where to encroach upon a cultural commons and where to resist.

Let us then conclude this chapter by opening up the question of ends or purposes. Every form of property raises political, ethical, even eschatological questions. The catechism of the old *New England Primer* used to ask, "What is the chief end of man?," the Puritan response being, "to glorify God and to enjoy Him forever." Such declarative faith may not always be available, but that does not mean that questions about ultimate purposes disappear. In service of what ideals have we adopted the ways in which we live? To what end should one or another thing be open to common usage rather than held in private hands?

We have already seen some ways in which questions like these might be answered in regard to tangible things. In the English case, it is not hard to nominate ends, both positive and negative, of the traditional agricultural commons. They were, at various times, organized to ensure the sustainability of forests and arable lands, to give village life stability over time, to lock in the hierarchies of medieval life, and so forth. The Magna Carta and the related Great Charter of the Forest guaranteed a range of common rights— not just that every widow should have "her reasonable estovers in the common," but that "every Free-Man . . . shall have . . . the Honey that is found within his Woods," and more, which is to say that the commons were understood to serve the subsistence of households. The poor were always entitled to glean (gleaned corn could provide enough flour to last until Christmas) and they always had access to the non-arable commons and other "wastes." Gleaning and access rights were especially important in times of dearth or scarcity and, along with the stinted market that kept "hucksters, higlers, and retailers" at bay, were part of a system of communal tenure that knew one of its ends to be the provisioning of the poor.

The modern ends toward which commons might exist are similar if more various. Issues of sustainability have not left us. If we wish to preserve watersheds, the oceans and their bounty, the atmosphere, aquifers, and so on, some modern form of commons is in order. Issues of social equity and distributive justice are always with us, too—in regard to access to the Internet, for example, or in discussions of broadcast spectrum or of medicines that can be brought into the public domain.

As for the ends toward which cultural properties are dedicated, the following chapters elaborate a set of historical answers, the point of departure being a question posed: what mattered to the founding generation in the United States when they addressed themselves to what we now call "intellectual property"? As we shall see, ownership in Blackstone's sense mattered to the founders, but it was the least of their concerns and it was always approached with skepticism under the assumption that exclusive control of ideas was at odds with many of the larger purposes toward which the new nation might be dedicated. When it came to the circulation of knowledge, three things mattered above all in what used to be called the Republic of Letters: laying the ground for democratic self-governance, encouraging creative community, and enabling citizens to become public actors, both civic and creative.

If today the entertainment industry is truly interested in "educat[ing] our kids" about what "the founding fathers" meant when they "talked about copyright," then these are the frames of reference that ought to be offered to children in our grade schools. The roles we ask the very young to play could then include John Adams attacking the Stamp Act as a tax on knowledge, Benjamin Franklin encouraging skilled artisans to smuggle technical expertise out of England, James Madison explaining why unlimited copyright undermines civic and religious liberty, and Thomas Jefferson trying to get a prohibition on patent monopolies written into the Bill of Rights. The details of this curriculum lie in the chapters that follow.

4

FRAMING A COMMONWEALTH

The argument: The founders believed that created works
belong largely in the commons so as to enable
democratic self-governance.

·

Wisdom and knowledge, as well as virtue, diffused generally among the
body of the people, being necessary for the preservation of their rights and
liberties . . . , it shall be the duty of legislatures . . . , in all future periods of
this commonwealth, to cherish the interests of literature and the sciences.
—THE CONSTITUTION OF THE COMMONWEALTH OF
MASSACHUSETTS, AS DRAFTED BY JOHN ADAMS (1780)

"LEACHES HAVE SUCKED THE COMMON-WEALTH"

At the end of chapter 1, I offered a brief sample of the various ways
in which other cultures and other eras have imagined the ownership of art and ideas, running from the classical Chinese ideal
of reverence toward the ancients up to Martin Luther's typical
Reformation creed: "Freely have I received, freely have I given, and
I desire nothing in return." My project in the chapters that follow
is to move forward into the eighteenth century so as to describe
how the generation of thinkers who founded the United States
imaged what we now call "intellectual property."

The first thing to note is that both the Enlightenment and the
rise of a middle-class public sphere stand between the Reformation
and the American Revolution. In the seventeenth century, the idea

of divine origins begins to be replaced or at least augmented by the humanist idea that creativity builds on a bounty inherited from the past, or gathered from the community at hand. Sir Isaac Newton famously spoke of himself as having stood "on the shoulders of Giants." The phrase comes from a letter that he wrote to Robert Hooke in 1675, the context being a debate with Hooke about who had priority in arriving at the theory of colors. Newton manages to combine humility with an assertion of his own achievement, writing: "What Des-Cartes did was a good step. You have added much several ways, & especially in taking the colors of thin plates into philosophical consideration. If I have seen further it is by standing on the shoulders of Giants." The sociologist Robert K. Merton wrote an amusing book, *On the Shoulders of Giants*, in which he shows that this famous phrase did not originate with Newton; it was coined by Bernard of Chartres in the early twelfth century, the original aphorism being, "In comparison with the ancients, we stand like dwarfs on the shoulders of giants." The image was a commonplace by the time Newton used it, his one contribution being to erase any sense that he himself might be a dwarf.

Newton's self-conception aside, Alexander Pope's praising couplet—"Nature and nature's laws lay hid in night; / God said Let Newton be! and all was light"—shows that in the popular imagination no humanist sense of debt to one's forebears ever wholly replaced the idea that divine forces were at work. At the same time, after the Reformation those forces were thought to be concentrated in certain heroic individuals, geniuses visited by a spark of celestial insight. In a 1774 speech made during parliamentary debates over literary property, Lord Camden offered an evocative description of how we should conceive of created work if we begin with the assumption that creative individuals have been touched by a "ray of divinity":

> If there be any thing in the world common to all mankind, science and learning are in their nature *publici juris* [belonging to the

public by right], and they ought to be as free and general as air or water. They forget their Creator, as well as their fellow creatures, who wish to monopolize his noblest gifts and greatest benefits . . .

Those great men, those favoured mortals, those sublime spirits, who share that ray of divinity which we call genius, are intrusted by Providence with the delegated power of imparting to their fellow-creatures that instruction which heaven meant for universal benefit; they must not be niggards to the world, or hoard up for themselves the common stock.

Combining that Providential ray with his "great men" theory allows Camden to move from individual talent to a wider, common good. Figuring talent as among God's "noblest gifts" also allows the link to air, water, and all the other commodious gifts of creation. In Roman law, those things whose size and range make them difficult if not impossible to own—all the fish in the sea, the seas themselves, the atmosphere—belong to the category *res communes*, common things. To that list Camden is adding the fruits of science and learning (once they have been made public), and thus produces a way of speaking that has descended into the present moment. In a Supreme Court opinion from 1918, Justice Louis Brandeis declared that "[t]he general rule of law is, that the noblest of human productions—knowledge, truths ascertained, conceptions, and ideas—become, after voluntary communication to others, free as the air to common use." Brandeis's final phrase reappeared in 1999 in the title to a law review article by Yochai Benkler arguing that the First Amendment should constrain the current push to extend copyright to areas that have been in the public domain for centuries. Camden's theological justification for treating ideas as if they were "air or water" may have eroded in the last two hundred years, but the useful category of *res communes* persists.

Not all early modern writers and thinkers shared Camden's free and open view of "the common stock," of course. An oppositional group of metaphors appeared early on, one that began not with scientific giants and Providential rays but with the puzzle of how to free creative talent from its dependence on patronage. From this distance in time, we would also say that what was at stake was the problem of how to create a public sphere, a realm, that is, of thought and deliberation independent of the government, the aristocracy, and the church. Whatever the reason, early in the eighteenth century we begin to hear from authors who, even as they joined with others in speaking of noble gifts and sublime spirits, felt no need to distance themselves from the commercial book trade. An author without a patron needs to earn his keep and might not trouble himself so much with rumors about God's position on selling the fruits of imaginative labor.

The German dramatist Gotthold Lessing knew the rule Martin Luther had declared; Lessing reproduced it as "Freely hast thou received, freely thou must give!" and then dismissed it: "Luther, I answer, is an exception in many things." Lessing himself was involved in early movements to free the middle class, and writers especially, from subservience to the nobility. Why, he asks, should "the writer . . . be blamed for trying to make the offspring of his imagination as profitable as he can? Just because he works with his noblest faculties he isn't supposed to enjoy the satisfaction that the roughest handyman is able to procure?"

In England probably the prime spokesman for the commercial position was the novelist Daniel Defoe. In the period just prior to England's first copyright act, the 1710 Statute of Anne, Defoe published both a pamphlet and a series of essays in defense of authors having "exclusive Right to the Property of published books." When it came to offering reasons for this position, Defoe repeatedly drew his metaphors from family life. The pirating and printing of other men's work is "every jot as unjust as lying with their Wives, and breaking-up their Homes." After all, a later essay explained, "A Book is the Author's Property, 'tis the Child of his Inventions, the Brat of his Brain; if he sells his Property, it then becomes the Right of the Purchaser; if not, 'tis as much his own, as his Wife and Children are his own."

Defoe's familial analogy never caught on, however, probably because it becomes awkward when carried to its logical end. A man might sell the brat of his brain, yes, but he isn't supposed to sell the brats of his loins, nor his wife for that matter. Partisans of individual rights to literary property, in any event, soon dropped all talk of women and children and turned instead to land, a man of genius being pictured as the owner or steward of an estate from which he harvests a marketable crop. Joseph Addison, writing at the same time as Defoe, said of another author, "His Brain, which was his Estate, had as regular and different Produce as other Men's Land." Mark Rose, whose book *Authors and Owners* contains many such examples, reproduces a wonderful extended metaphor along these lines from Arthur Murphy, a playwright but also a lawyer much involved with legal wrangling over literary property. To cite but one fragment:

> The ancient Patriarchs of Poetry are generous, as they are rich: a great part of their possessions is let on lease to the moderns. *Dryden*, beside his own hereditary estate, had taken a large scope of ground from *Virgil*. Mr. *Pope* held *by copy* near half of *Homer's* rent-roll . . . The great *Shakespeare* sat upon a cliff, looking abroad through all creation. His possessions were very near as extensive as *Homer's*, but in some places, had not received sufficient culture.

This revisits the idea that moderns stand indebted to the ancients, but rather than figuring the relationship in terms of giants and pygmies we now get landlords and tenants with a variety of leases and rental arrangements.

As Rose explains, above all "it was on the model of the landed estate that the concept of literary property was formulated." It was soon an eighteenth-century commonplace. "The mind of a man of Genius is a fertile and pleasant field, pleasant as *Elysium*, and fertile as *Tempe*," wrote Edward Young in his 1759 *Conjectures on Original Composition*. "There are some low-minded geniuses," wrote Catharine Macaulay in 1774, "who will be apt to think they may, with as little degradation to character, traffic with a bookseller for the purchase of their mental harvest, as opulent landholders may traffic with monopolizers in grain."

The estate metaphor splits nicely at one point during late-eighteenth-century parliamentary debates over laws governing literary property: Justice Joseph Yates once argued against perpetual ownership by saying that while an author could surely own his own manuscript, publication made the work a gift to the public. "When an author prints and publishes his work, he lays it entirely open to the public, as much as when an owner of a piece of land lays it open into the highway."

In this instance, created works, once they have begun to circulate, are not like private estates but like public highways (or more precisely like land made public for having been used as a highway). They are not shoes in a shoe store but rather the sidewalks and roadways that enable the store to be in business in the first place. As such they belong to yet another Roman category of property, *res publicae*, things such as roads and harbors, bridges and ports, that belong to the public and are open to them by operation of law. This phrase, *res publicae*, is also of course the root of "republic," that form of governance in which the government belongs to the people just as the roads might belong to the people.

To simplify the argument so far, early modern debates over intellectual property appear to have been framed in two ways. The frame we might call "common stock" or "free as the air" took up the old idea of a gift of God and preserved it in a form that honored individual talent. Divine power sometimes seems to be replaced by the gathered wisdom of the human community (as in Newton's bow to giants past and present), though it is just as easy to say that theism and humanism augment each other: even those who reap what others have sown may still imagine God to be the source of the original seed.

The second frame does not necessarily conflict with the religious background of the "common stock" idea, but its point of departure is decidedly of this world, more focused on the problem of freeing individual talent from patronage and also, therefore, more at ease with commerce. Here the dominant metaphor was the landed estate, an image that had the advantage, for partisans of strong intellectual property rights, of borrowing from popular assumptions about real estate. "We conceive [that] this property is the same with that of Houses and other Estates," declared London booksellers when first threatened with a limit to the term of their copyrights. They beg the question, of course, of what exactly we assume such property entails (there are many kinds of estates, as we shall see in the next section), but as with most compelling frames, the intuitive response is what matters, not complexities hidden beneath the surface. Shouldn't all property, even a bookseller's copyright, be "safe as houses"?

These two—the commons and the estate frames—were widespread in the centuries preceding the American Revolution. They do not, however, bring us to the end of our story; there was yet a third frame that regularly stood alongside these and gave more complex meaning to each. It has come up in passing in some of what I have already cited, though it probably doesn't strike the modern ear with the resonance it must have carried some centuries ago. Listeners in 1774 would have found a range of associations at hand when Lord Camden spoke of those who would "monopolize [God's] noblest gifts." The same is true of the language in which Catharine Macaulay chooses to speak of "mental harvest." Macaulay actually stands in opposition to Lord Camden; the sentence I cite from her comes from a pamphlet published to dissent from his denigration of the commercial side of publishing (he had claimed that "Newton, Milton, Locke" never would have trafficked with "a dirty bookseller"); nonetheless, she joins her adversary in worrying about the figurative "monopolizers in grain." Monopoly is the third frame in this tradition and it can, it seems, threaten any harvest, no matter if it's gathered from a commons or from a freehold.

Monopoly had a marked historical meaning for early theorists of intellectual property, seventeenth-century Puritans having begun their argument with royal power over exactly this issue. As the historian and statesman Thomas Babington Macaulay explains in his *History of England*, Puritans in the House of Commons long felt that Queen Elizabeth had encroached upon the House's authority to manage trade, having in particular taken it "upon herself to grant patents of monopoly by scores." Macaulay lists iron, coal, oil, vinegar, saltpeter, lead, starch, yarn, skins, leather, and glass, saying that these "could be bought only at exorbitant prices."

Macaulay doesn't list printing in his *History*, but it was the case that in the late sixteenth century the queen's printer, Christopher Barker, held monopoly rights to the Bible, the Book of Common Prayer, and all statutes, proclamations, and other official documents. And Macaulay *does* mention monopoly in his 1841 parliamentary speech in opposition to a proposed extension to the term of copyright. "Copyright is monopoly, and produces all the effects which the general voice of mankind attributes to monopoly," he said, asking rhetorically if the Parliament wished to reinstate "the East India Company's monopoly of tea, or . . . Lord Essex's monopoly of sweet wines?"

The understanding of copyright as monopoly was not Macaulay's invention; it was almost as old as copyright itself. In 1694 John Locke—a strong supporter of property rights in other respects— had objected to copyrights given by government license as a form of monopoly "injurious to learning." Locke was partly concerned with religious liberty, the laws in question having been written to suppress books "offensive" to the Church of England, but mostly he was distressed that works by classic authors were not readily available to the public in well-made, cheap editions (he himself had tried to publish an edition of Aesop only to be blocked by a printer holding an exclusive right). "It is very absurd and ridiculous," he wrote to a friend in Parliament, "that any one now living should pretend to have a propriety in . . . writings of authors who lived before printing was known or used in Europe." Regarding authors yet living, Locke thought they should have control of their own work, but for a limited term only. As with Macaulay, his framing issue was monopoly privilege, not property rights.

To come back, then, to Macaulay's story of the initial resistance to monopoly, in Queen Elizabeth's time the Puritan opposition had led the House of Commons to meet "in an angry and determined mood." Crowds formed in the streets exclaiming that the Crown "should not be suffered to touch the old liberties of England." In the end, the queen wisely "declined the contest" and "redressed the grievance, thank[ing] the Commons . . . for their tender care of the general weal."

The queen's diplomatic capitulation seems not to have survived her death. Within two decades, Parliament felt called upon to pass a law directly forbidding "all monopolies." The 1624 Statute of Monopolies also made one overt exception to its general prohibition: it allowed patents "of fourteen years or under" to be granted "to the first and true inventor" of "any manner of new manufacture." Such was the first British patent law and its context makes two things clear: patents, like copyrights, were understood to be a species of monopoly, and in allowing them Parliament was granting a *privilege*, not recognizing a *right*.

It is worth pausing here to note that this distinction was central to debates over intellectual property for many years. One side argued that the history of the common law showed that authors and inventors had a natural right to their work, and that like other such rights it should exist in perpetuity; the other side replied that the common law contained no such record, that copyrights and patents "were merely privileges, which excludes the idea of a right," that such privileges come from statutes rather than nature, and that they could and should be limited in term. A 1774 British law case, *Donaldson v. Becket*, supposedly settled this question in favor of the "limited privileges" camp, as did an American case from 1834, *Wheaton v. Peters*, in which the Supreme Court confirmed the statutory or limited-privilege theory of copyright and rejected the common law or unlimited-right theory. In many regards, though, the argument persists to this day.

Putting aside the question of how exactly monopolies should be described, it would seem that British monarchs found the prerogative to grant them an undying temptation, for despite regular parliamentary resistance, the problem continued throughout the seventeenth century. One final example of parliamentary resistance is worth citing simply for its rhetorical flourish. By mid-century the list of exclusive rights given by Macaulay had swollen to include monopolies on wine, salt, the dressing of meat in taverns, beavers, belts, bone lace, pens, and even the gathering of rags. In the Long Parliament of 1640, Sir John Culpeper rose to denounce the lot of them. Monopolies, he declared, are

> a Nest of Wasps or swarm of Vermin which have over-crept the Land . . . These, like the Frogs of Egypt, have gotten possession of our Dwellings, they sup in our Cup, they dip in our Dish. They sit by our Fire. We find them in the Wash-House and Powdering-Tub; they share with the Butler in his Box. They have marked and sealed us from Head to Foot; they will not abate us a Pin. These are the Leaches that have sucked the Common-Wealth so hard, that it is almost become hectical.

I have sketched this history from the Puritans onward because I take the problem of monopolies to be a primary, albeit less obvious, contributor to the conceptual frame that the founders

inherited when they began to think about the ownership of art
and ideas. Monopoly was one of the opposing poles that organized
that frame, the other being commonwealth.

Between these two lay the figure of the landed estate, a mediating term whose boundaries remained unsettled. If the wealth of
human ingenuity, past and present, is a kind of "common stock,"
as Lord Camden says, should it be turned into private estates,
enclosed as agricultural commons were then being enclosed? Or
should concern for "the general weal" leave as much of the incorporeal commons as possible open to the public? Should the law
reserve a "republic of ideas," much as it might reserve highways,
parks, and even government itself, as a "public thing"? Or if some
combination of these two were possible, how should the parts be
apportioned? Where should the boundaries fall?

Such questions were very much in play as the Constitution was
being framed and are, in a sense, still in play today. And, however
we may conceive of them today, in the late eighteenth century they
were framed by way of an assumed struggle between monopoly
and commonwealth, an opposition out of which arose the field of
discourse available to the founders.

The constituents of that field are not hard to map. In the English
tradition, the monarch's power to grant monopoly privileges always
appeared as a restraining force in the struggle for self-governance
and religious liberty. Potentially the tool of despotism, it was especially at issue when extended to the printing trades, for there
it served to suppress political and religious diversity and dissent.
(Publishing monopolies, wrote John Locke, were designed to "let
Mother Church" remain undisturbed "in her opinions.")

Put in its positive terms, in this tradition a *lack* of monopolies
is associated with representative government and, because self-
governance depends on an informed public, with a concern for
the dissemination of knowledge and the liveliness of the public
sphere. A lack of monopolies also meant, from the Puritans in

1601 forward, the kind of religious liberty that drew out of the established church the great plurality of Protestant sects we still have today. In this line, Lord Macaulay illustrates his opposition to publishing monopolies with the case of the Wesleyan Methodists, asking what might have happened to them had John Wesley's writings been subject to seventeenth-century press restrictions. In Locke's time, there were a mere twenty printers in London, and if one died, it was the Bishop of London who chose his replacement; a century later, in Lord Camden's day, there were thirty thousand printers and booksellers, and the Church had nothing to do with them.

It is hard to say exactly what parts of the tradition the founding fathers knew directly; I doubt any of them had access to Lord Camden's parliamentary speeches, or to Locke's 1694 "Memorandum." At the same time, the way that they speak about authors and inventors shows that their approach proceeded within the frames I have been describing. I'll here give just a few examples, the first from correspondence between Thomas Jefferson and James Madison.

Jefferson was in Paris in the late 1780s when the Constitution itself was being debated, but he and Madison regularly wrote to each other about the work being done in Philadelphia. Jefferson's main complaint about the draft document Madison sent him was that it contained no Bill of Rights, and when enumerating the items such a bill ought to contain he always listed "restrictions against monopolies." Furthermore, the granting of patents is the one example he gives of what "monopoly" meant to him. In June 1788, for example, he wrote Madison saying that while he was well aware that a rule against monopolies would lessen "the incitements to ingenuity, which is spurred on by the hope of a monopoly for a limited time, as of 14 years," nonetheless, "the benefit even of limited monopolies is too doubtful to be opposed to that of their general suppression."

Madison replied several months later, disagreeing with Jefferson but using the same frame to make his point:

> With regard to Monopolies they are justly classed among the greatest nuisances in Government. But is it clear that as encouragements to literary works and ingenious discoveries, they are not too valuable to be wholly renounced . . . ? Monopolies are sacrifices of the many to the few. Where the power is in the few it is natural for them to sacrifice the many to their own partialities and corruptions. Where the power, as with us, is in the many not in the few, the danger can not be very great.

Jefferson himself slowly came around to Madison's position—that limited monopoly privileges were useful incentives—but that is not the point for the moment; for the moment the point is that both men saw "intellectual property" in terms of monopoly privileges, not property rights, and both were concerned to know how "the many" were to be protected from monopoly's potentially corrupting power. In the background lay all that I have just sketched—political and religious liberty, the dissemination of knowledge, and so forth—as is clear, for example, from a memorandum on monopolies that Madison wrote many years later in which he declared that "perpetual monopolies of every sort are forbidden . . . by the genius of free Governments," and where he expressly made the link to religious liberty.

In all of this, we have the negative pole of the monopoly versus commonwealth tension. To see the positive, we need only turn to Jefferson's most famous statement on owning ideas, his 1813 letter to Isaac McPherson.

> If nature has made any one thing less susceptible than all others of exclusive property, it is the action of the thinking power called an idea, which an individual may exclusively possess as long as he keeps it to himself; but the moment it is divulged, it

forces itself into the possession of everyone, and the receiver can-not dispossess himself of it. Its peculiar character, too, is that no one possesses the less, because every other possesses the whole of it. He who receives an idea from me, receives instruction himself without lessening mine; as he who lites his taper at mine, receives light without darkening me. That ideas should freely spread from one to another over the globe, for the moral and mutual instruc-tion of man, and improvement of his condition, seems to have been peculiarly and benevolently designed by nature, when she made them, like fire, expansible over all space, without lessening their density at any point, and like the air in which we breathe, move, and have our physical being, incapable of confinement, or exclusive appropriation.

This is the pure commonwealth position. Jefferson may have sub-stituted "nature" for Lord Camden's "Creator," and light and fire have been added to air and water, but overall his language rises from the same ground.

Finally, it should be said that Jefferson's position was also his practice. To take but one example, two years after his letter to McPherson, Jefferson himself invented an improved method for "the braking and beating [of] hemp." In a letter describing his device to a friend, Jefferson wrote:

Something of this kind has been so long wanted by the cultiva-tors of hemp, that as soon as I can speak of its effect with certainty I shall probably describe it anonymously in the public papers, in order to forestall the prevention of its use by some interloping patentee.

By the time of this letter, Jefferson had, as I say, acknowledged the utility of rewarding authors and inventors for their work (a typical remark reads: "Certainly an inventor ought to be allowed a right to the benefit of his invention for some certain time. It is equally certain it ought not to be perpetual"). But the benefit in question is not one he himself ever sought. He imagined himself, instead, as a commonwealth man, releasing his invention as an unsigned contribution to the public. That being the case, we can return to the question of exactly what kind of "estate in land" a creative person might have in a republican democracy and, for that matter, what kind of "person" might be the owner of that estate.

"EASY AND CHEAP AND SAFE"

When his father died in the spring of 1761, John Adams inherited one of several family farms. That property made the younger Adams a freeholder and a taxpayer in the town of his birth, Braintree, Massachusetts, and it consequently empowered him to vote at town meetings, something he had not been allowed to do until then, even though he was twenty-five years old, a Harvard graduate, and a practicing lawyer. In colonial Braintree, only the owners of property could have political agency. Along with that agency came civic obligation: as soon as Adams could vote, he was also elected the surveyor of highways (an unpaid office) and asked to attend to a local bridge that needed to be replaced. Adams complained that he knew nothing of such work, but the town elders said that did not matter; everyone had to take a turn at the town offices. So Adams learned what he needed to know about bridges and oversaw the construction of a new one.

I read the service part of this story as an emblematic account of what has been called "civic republicanism." We have at least two republican traditions in this country, the civic and the commercial. The commercial comes later in our history and is the one most of us are familiar with. It values above all the private individual seeking his or her own self-interest. Commercial republicanism assumes that property exists to benefit its owners and that owners gain virtue or respect in one another's eyes by increasing the market value of the goods that they command. The government in such a republic leaves citizens alone to follow their own subjective sense of the good life. Liberty is negative liberty, a lack of all coercion. Where questions of social well-being or the common good arise, government is given little role in answering them, the assumption being that if answers are to be had at all they will arise automatically if paradoxically from the summed activity of private actors seeking private ends.

All these things—self-interest, property, virtue, liberty, the public good—are situated differently in civic republicanism. Here autonomous individuals and private property are also valued, but property is assumed to exist in order to free the individual for public service. Liberty in this instance is positive liberty, citizenship being directed toward acknowledged public ends, above all toward creating and maintaining the many things that must be in place before there can be true self-governance (a diverse free press, for example, literacy, situations for public deliberation, and so forth). Social well-being in this view cannot arise simply by aggregating individual choices; private interest and public good are too often at odds. Citizens acquire virtue in the civic republic, therefore, not by productivity but by willingly allowing self-interest to bow to the public good (or by recognizing that the two are one). Civic virtue is not something anyone is born with; it is acquired through civic action, and in the story just told, John Adams began to have it by getting a bridge built in the town of Braintree.

What might intellectual property look like in the context of civic republicanism? More particularly, how might American revolutionary ideals alter the old metaphor that linked created work to a landed estate?

A nicely nuanced answer to such questions is suggested by the first political essay that John Adams ever wrote. Published in 1765, "A Dissertation on the Canon and Feudal Law" was prompted by the Stamp Act of the same year. To the members of the British

Parliament who passed it, that act was a just and simple way of rais-
ing revenue to pay debts incurred defending the Colonies during
the French and Indian wars. To most colonists and to later generations, however, the Stamp Act was a pure case of "taxation without
representation." Even if the tax were just, "the rights of Englishmen"
entitled the Americans to participate in its passage and that was
something the British Parliament consistently refused to allow.

The first thing that will strike a modern reader of Adams's essay,
then, is that he has nearly nothing to say about representation. The
essay is concerned almost entirely with intellectual freedom and
the free flow of knowledge. Adams's thesis is that for centuries the
church and the aristocracy (the "canon and feudal" powers) controlled their subjects by controlling learning and that the Stamp
Act was intended to do the same thing. In Adams's reading of history, the "Romanish clergy" maintained its hold over the people
"by reducing their minds to a state of sordid ignorance and staring
timidity"; the same was true of the monarch whose grip over "the
people in the middle ages" only loosened as they "became more
intelligent." The dual struggle against "ecclesiastical and civil tyranny" came to a head with the Puritans, who succeeded simply because they were "better read" than anyone else in England; these
were the same "sensible people" who settled America, a land where
"a native . . . who cannot read and write is as rare . . . as a comet or
an earthquake."

Adams is describing the world of Protestant literacy that
was a common source of pride and boasting in the American
Colonies. As a further emblematic example, consider the passage
in Benjamin Franklin's *Autobiography* in which he writes that his
"obscure family" had been "early in the Reformation" in England,
and that they

> continued Protestants through the reign of Queen Mary, when
> they were sometimes in danger of trouble on account of their zeal
> against popery.

They had got an English Bible, and to conceal and secure it, it was fastened open with tapes under and within the cover of a joint-stool. When my great-great-grandfather read it to his family, he turned up the joint-stool upon his knees . . . One of the children stood at the door to give notice if he saw the apparitor coming, who was an officer of the spiritual court. In that case the stool was turned down again upon its feet, when the Bible remained concealed under it as before.

Queen Mary was the Catholic monarch who ruled England during the 1550s, who reestablished papal authority, and who relentlessly punished the Protestant opposition. But the focus here is not so much the sixteenth century as the eighteenth: Franklin is telling this family fable to his son in 1771. It is an origin myth for an American patriot, a man whose sense of self was largely grounded in having independent access to knowledge. The Bible is not to be read to you in church by the priest; you are to read it yourself, alone in your own home. And that is only the beginning, for there are "political Bibles" as well (as Tom Paine called the U.S. Constitution); once individual literacy is widely established, a public sphere of deliberation and debate can begin to form.

The creation and preservation of such a public sphere is exactly what's at issue in Adams's essay. The value of "knowledge diffused generally" and the need to guard "the means" of diffusing it are the overarching themes. Chief among those means for Adams were public education and the free press. The colonists "laid very early the foundations of colleges"; they passed laws assuring that every town had a grammar school; the "education of all ranks" was made a matter of public "care and expense." As for the press, that most sacred of "the means of information," those who settled America took care "that the art of printing should be encouraged, and that it should be easy and cheap and safe for any person to communicate his thoughts to the public." None of these things is an end in itself, however; all contribute to the autonomy of mind and conscience that citizens must have if they are to be self-governing.

In listing "the means of knowledge," Adams was addressing himself by implication to the *content* of the Stamp Act, not to the question of representation in its passage. The act placed a "stamp duty" of varying amounts on the papers used in a wide range of public transactions. It covered legal affairs, real estate, trade, the sale of wine and spirits, shipping, printing, education, apprenticeships, even playing cards and dice. The seventh of the act's enumerated items displayed the typical formula and speaks to Adams's concerns:

> There shall be ... paid unto his majesty ..., for every skin or piece of vellum or parchment, or sheet or piece of paper, on which shall be engrossed, written, or printed ..., any ... certificate of any degree taken in any university, academy, college, or seminary of learning within the said colonies and plantations, a stamp duty of *two pounds.*

A later paragraph places a smaller duty on fees paid for an apprentice to learn a trade.

Edmund and Helen Morgan, in their 1953 book on the Stamp Act, add an interesting note to these items dealing with education. The American duties were higher than similar charges then found in England, the report prepared by the Treasury office in support of the act having argued that

> the Duties upon Admissions to any of the professions or to the University degrees should certainly be as high as they are in England; it would indeed be better if they were raised both here and there considerably in order to keep mean persons out of those situations in life which they disgrace.

The passage of the act itself saw no change in British rates; in England the tax on a college degree remained at two shillings and sixpence while in the colonies it was set at two pounds, an expense whose rationale was precisely counter to one of Adams's stated ideals, the "education of all ranks."

Nine paragraphs in the Stamp Act concerned the press: pamphlets and newspapers were to pay half a penny to a shilling, depending on their size; advertisements, two shillings; and almanacs two to four pence, depending on size (it was Benjamin Franklin's estimate that these duties would cut both newspaper sales and advertising in half). The duty on foreign-language publications was double the rate for English publications, a provision that promised to destroy the German-language newspapers in Philadelphia.

A look at the British context will help us understand how to read this imposition of stamp duties on colonial newspapers. Paul Starr has outlined the details in his book *The Creation of the Media*. In Great Britain, the government began instituting stamp taxes as early as 1712. Newspapers at the time were printed on half sheets of paper; they sold for a penny and were taxed half a penny, essentially a 50 percent sales tax. The taxes rose for the rest of the century "until the retail price of a single copy of a newspaper hit 6*d*, nearly a day's pay for a typical wage-earner." As with the American case, these taxes were presented as sources of revenue, but they also had the effect—welcomed by many in the government—of controlling the size and reach of the press. "The stamp tax made it impossible to operate a popular press that was at once cheap and legal"; more subtly, Starr concludes, it assured that "the public" consisted of the wealthy. As with stamp duties on learning, these taxes didn't simply raise revenue; they also helped to sort the low and mean from the high and refined.

Such a sorting was in accord with what might be called the antipublic sphere of earlier times in England. There, during a parliamentary debate on stamp taxes, Lord North had once declared that "foolish curiosity" fed the demand for newspapers, and that they should thus be thought of as luxuries, well worthy of taxation. John Adams in New England hardly saw the press in those terms,

of course, and it is not only his themes that make that clear but also
the place and manner of his essay's publication. His "Dissertation"
appeared as an unsigned contribution in an independent paper,
the *Boston Gazette*, and Adams pauses in the middle of one of his
long paragraphs to address the printers of that paper:

> And you, Messieurs printers, whatever the tyrants of the earth
> may say of your paper, are so much the more to your honor; for
> the jaws of power are always opened to devour, and her arm is
> always stretched out, if possible, to destroy the freedom of think-
> ing, speaking, and writing.

One of the printers Adams here apostrophizes was Benjamin Edes,
an original member of the Boston Sons of Liberty, part of the resistance movement summoned into being by the Stamp Act.

The *Boston Gazette* is in fact a good representative of what was
to become a lively public sphere in the young Republic. Newspapers
of its kind were a departure from the norm in both England and
the early colonies. All governments seem to prefer to control the
flow of news, and one simple way of doing so is to grant monopoly
power to some select group, understanding that they are not likely
to make trouble so long as their wealth and well-being depend on
the government's good graces. Thus when the Stuarts returned to
power in England after the English Civil War, Parliament passed
a Licensing Act (1662) under which, as we saw earlier, just twenty
master printers were allowed to operate in London. For the next three
decades, England had only one newspaper, the *London Gazette*.
It displayed beneath its logo the phrase "Printed by Authority,"
nicely proclaiming itself as good an example as any of "copy right"
as monopoly privilege and of monopoly privilege as press control.

Printers in the American Colonies operated under similar constraints well into the eighteenth century. Where they displeased
the authorities, they were regularly jailed, censored, or run out of

town. In 1690 the first newspaper ever to appear in Boston was banned after a single issue on the grounds that it was operating without a license. The first newspaper to publish regularly in the Colonies—the *Boston News-Letter*—appeared in 1704; it survived by avoiding all controversy and by getting the governor's advance approval for each issue. Like the *London Gazette*, it displayed the imprimatur "Published by Authority."

In the mid-eighteenth century, then, newspapers like the *Boston Gazette*—call them the Not-by-Authority press—were both recent and unusual. These were the media by which British civic republican voices were heard in America, the *Gazette* for example having first published the radical Whig essays known as *Cato's Letters* in 1755 and then reprinting them a half dozen times in the following decades. In the *Gazette* we have as good an example as any of the then-assumed link between liberty and a *lack* of monopoly privilege, and the "Messieurs printers" like Edes who produced that paper demonstrate the positive liberty demanded by civic republicanism: they worked to create a public good, one as useful as any bridge in Braintree, one of the many that make for a lively, deliberative public sphere, that make for a self-governing people.

Adams, as I say, published his essay as an unsigned contribution to the *Gazette*. ("What difference does it make who is speaking?") Readers in both Massachusetts and England assumed that it had been written by Jeremy Gridley, a leading lawyer in the colony, and in fact when it was included in a little book published in London in 1768, *The True Sentiments of America*, it bore Gridley's name. The point is not so much the misattribution as the fact that Adams's self-effacement was of a piece with his themes. The man behind this work is not claiming his ideas as his property; he is offering his ideas up for public deliberation. If we are trying to answer the question "How did the founders imagine intellectual property?," then Exhibit A ought to be the way in which they themselves treated their ideas. In this case, ideas were released directly to the public domain, published in a manner that clearly subordinated self-interest to the commonweal.

THE FRAMERS' ESTATE

If we now return to the old land metaphor, the one that compares a creative person's mind to an estate or a farm, and ask how it might appear in this civic republican setting, we may note that it is in the context of his attack on feudal and canon law that Adams speaks of something I mentioned in passing a few chapters back, a thing called allodial land. The noun "allodium" and the adjective "allodial" distinguish a certain kind of individual landholding from feudal landholding. Feudal estates carried a set of social obligations with them, a "feud" being land held from a lord on condition of homage and service (military service, typically, but also—as we saw earlier—requirements to work the lord's land, to give gifts when his daughters married, to provision him with such things as honey and chickens, and so on). Vassals hold their feuds from the nobles above them; freemen hold their allodiums from (to cite Thomas Hobbes again) "the gift of God only."

The presence or lack of obligation is key to the distinction between feudal and allodial, but for the full flavor of these terms it helps to see how they have been deployed historically. The latter term became popular after the Puritan Revolution in England, denoting one foundation of the new age. In that context, it did not mean so much an estate held without obligation as one in which obligation had been relocated. The holder of an allodium had no service due to any overlord, but freeholders had duties nonetheless, ones that arose from the very fact of their autonomy.

Military service makes a good example of both the obligation and its shifting locus. As the historian J.G.A. Pocock has explained, after the Revolution a man's sword was no longer his lord's, it was "his own and the commonwealth's." An allodial landholder was still expected to be available for armed conflict if the need arose, but decisions about when and whom to fight now belonged to him and his neighbors, not to any superior. Moreover, the literal sword here stands for the fact that authority itself has moved from the overlord to the conscience of the autonomous citizen. To free the sword is to free the man, free him to become that paradoxical being, a public individual. Allodial holdings served, Pocock writes, "the liberation of arms, and consequently of the personality, for free public action and civic virtue."

This is not the end of the story, either, for once someone has been empowered for "free public action," the question remains, to what end? Once the personality has been liberated, what does it do? Freehold and free lance make a free man, but free for what?

There is no single answer to such questions; the ends of freedom will vary as the historical periods vary. In the case at hand, though, the period is seventeenth-century England and in those days, especially for "commonwealthmen" such as the utopian writer James Harrington, the freedoms of allodial property were directed toward at least two acknowledged ends. One we have already seen—to free the property owner to be an actor in the public sphere, a true citizen. The other was to enable families to endure over time. Allodial land is land that can be bequeathed, passed from one generation to the next, and as such it is the vehicle for family continuity over time, for stability decade after decade.

Commonwealth economics is Greek in this regard; it is *oikonomia*, home economics, the management of an *oikos*, a home. And as with the Greeks, the end of land ownership for commonwealth idealists is not to make a profit, not merely to collect rents or harvest corn and wool, certainly not to trade or speculate in the soil itself. Allodial holdings may thus be contrasted not only with the feudal but also with the commercial. Neither feudal nor allodial land is fully alienable the way commercial land is. Allodial holdings are meant to be passed to one's heirs, and freeholders are distinct then not only from vassals but from speculators and entrepreneurs.

The founders of the American Republic were well aware of the distinction between feudal and allodial estates. Adams, as I say, mentions it in his essay, a point I'll return to. Thomas Jefferson mythologized it. In *A Summary View of the Rights of British America*, his 1774 instructions to Virginia's delegates to the Continental Congress, Jefferson declared Americans to be descended from "Saxon ancestors" who, before the eighth century, "held their lands . . . in absolute dominion, disencumbered with any superior," in the manner "which the Feudalists term Allodial." The fall into feudalism unfortunately broke our link to these ancestors. After the Battle of Hastings in 1066, lands occupied by William the Conqueror were granted out on condition of vassalage and feudalism began.

By invoking "that happy system" of Saxon forebears, Jefferson made feudal holdings the exception to the rule, the rule being that land should be held "of no superior," "in absolute right." Bringing that rule to bear on British America, Jefferson first noted that "America was not conquered by William the Norman" and then asserted that American lands "are undoubtedly of the Allodial nature." If most immigrants to Americans have not known that, if they have mistakenly believed "the fictitious principle" that some king was the original owner of the continent, that is only because they have been "laborers, not lawyers."

As I said above, the ends of freedom will vary as the historical periods vary, and in that line it should be noted that by the time that British commonwealth philosophy got to Virginia, it had undergone one important alteration. The founders understood family estates, in fact all estates held in perpetuity, as among the means by which the church, the nobles, and the monarchy had perpetuated their powers in England. They therefore looked on claims for continuity over time with some skepticism. Jefferson strongly believed that one generation had no right to bind those that followed. "*The earth belongs in usufruct to the living,*" he wrote to Madison; "the dead have neither powers nor right over it." Later in the same letter—written in Paris as the Constitution was being debated in Philadelphia—he expanded on the point:

> This principle that the earth belongs to the living and not to the dead is of very extensive application . . . It enters into the resolution of the questions, whether the nation may change the descent of lands holden in tail [i.e., limited to a specified line of heirs]; whether they may change the appropriation of lands given anciently to the church . . . ; whether they may abolish the charges and privileges attached on lands including the whole catalogue, ecclesiastical and feudal; it goes . . . to perpetual monopolies in commerce, the arts or sciences, with a long train of et ceteras.

But what should replace perpetual holdings in land, or in art and science? How regularly should the grip of those who come before us be broken? For what length of time should the living be given their dominion?

To answer that question, Jefferson, ever the scientist, studied actuarial tables created by the Comte de Buffon in France and concluded that a new generation succeeds the old one every "eighteen years, eight months," a period he regularly rounded off at nineteen years. If the present government wants to assume a public debt, for example, it should be paid off within nineteen years and not settled on future generations. As for the creations of human art and intellect, if we are to grant their authors monopoly privileges, those terms should also run no more than nineteen years. All this seems to do away with inheritance, of course, and in one sense it does, though in another sense it relocates it for purposes of democratic self-rule. If inheritance once helped to preserve great families, now it helps to enrich "the public." The intangible creations of art and science, when treated as allodial estates, are bequeathed to the community at large, not to a single family or priesthood. Civic virtue is thus translated into the structure of law such that the public domain might inherit from the private.

To return to John Adams and his own use of the term "allo-dial," the first thing to note is that when Adams finally addresses himself directly to the Stamp Act, it is to denounce it not as "taxation without representation," but as a device to destroy the public sphere by injecting it with feudal hierarchy:

> It seems very manifest from the Stamp Act itself, that a design is formed to strip us in a great measure of the means of knowledge, by loading the press, the colleges, and even an almanac and a newspaper, with restraints and duties; and to introduce the inequalities and dependencies of the feudal system, by taking from the poorer sort of people all their little subsistence, and conferring it on a set of stamp officers, distributors, and their deputies.

It is in contradistinction to such feudal dependencies that Adams introduces the topic of allodial land. He begins by saying that the colonial Puritans did *not* "hold . . . their lands allodially," explaining that "for every man to have been the sovereign lord and proprietor of the ground he occupied would have constituted a government too nearly like a commonwealth." What they did, instead, was "to hold their lands of their king" in an unmediated fashion, that is to say, with no hierarchy between them, no "mense or subordinate lords" and none of "the baser services."*

In the usage Adams adopts, "commonwealth" is equivalent to "republic," and he is saying that colonial Puritans were not ready for such a government, preferring a limited monarchy. It was probably the case that Adams himself was not ready for republican

---

*There were, in fact, not two but three kinds of land in civic republican symbology: feudal, allodial, and commercial. Of the last of these, the founders had less to say, reluctant to imagine that land itself might become commodified, the stuff of speculation. A fourth form, traditional Native American common land, was excluded entirely from the civic republican model, a point I'll address three chapters hence when we come to the Dawes Severalty Act and the fate of the common self.

government in 1765 when he wrote this essay, but he was ready for it by the time the war broke out, as his letters make clear. And from this early "Dissertation" we learn that, for Adams, in a commonwealth or a republic, each man will be "sovereign lord and proprietor" of his allodium.

By its themes and by the context of its printing, we also learn what that means for a cultural creation such as Adams's essay itself. *Republican intellectual property is an allodial estate.* It mixes private sovereignty and public service. Creators are autonomous "proprietors," but they cannot know themselves as citizens nor acquire "public virtue" until they give their creations up to the public good.

I call this sequence the Republican Two-Step. First autonomy, then service; first the private thing, then the *res publica.* Note that allodial holdings as I have described them contain a built-in model of maturation. Holding land allodially allows one to become self-possessed, and self-possession allows one to become a public person, an agent, not a servant. In feudal times it was, in a sense, each vassal's *lack* of independence that made him a member of the community, and gave the community the feeling that it might exist in perpetuity. Now personhood is reimagined to contain the promise of individual agency. Those who realized that promise, taking the second step and acting so as to acquire civic virtue, become citizens in the true sense.

Article I, section 8, clause 8 of the U.S. Constitution gives Congress the power "[t]o promote the Progress of Science and useful Arts, by securing for limited Times to Authors and Inventors the exclusive Right to their respective Writings and Discoveries." This "progress clause" is modeled, I believe, on the Republican Two-Step. Authors and inventors receive a monopoly privilege, but the privilege is limited, not perpetual, and the limit provides what I earlier called a structure of law such that the public domain might inherit from the private. First something for the individual self, then something for the public good. First a contraction on behalf of the few, then a dilation on behalf of the many. Such is the dynamic of knowledge in a free republic.

To summarize this first view of how America's revolutionaries imagined intellectual property, it will help to begin by getting the terms in order. A discursive list of key words and phrases would look something like this:

- Authors and inventors may control their work, but if we are to call what they receive "property," then it is a specific species known as **monopoly**.
- This monopoly is a **privilege** created by statute, not a natural right.
- For authors and inventors, monopoly privileges are an **encouragement** to **ingenuity** (these being the two words that both Madison and Jefferson regularly use).
- Monopoly privileges must be limited, however, not perpetual. In the European experience, perpetuities were a tool of despotism. We've seen Madison's image of the American ideal: "**Perpetual monopolies . . . are forbidden** . . . by the Genius of free governments."
- Put in positive terms, limits on monopoly privileges serve the ends of **political and religious liberty**. Always at issue for John Adams, for example, was the freedom of "the means of knowledge," meaning the institutions we now think of as belonging to **the public sphere**.
- These institutions, in turn, enable **republican self-governance**. Moreover, no republic can be self-governing unless its citizens are capable of **civic virtue**, the willing subordination of self-interest to **the public good**.
- Given this ideal, intellectual property rights are best structured so as to make them allodial holdings. Monopoly privileges are granted under condition that private holdings ripen into **common wealth**. In a democracy, therefore, **intellectual**

property is ultimately a republican estate. It is the intangible equivalent of the tangible *res publicae* (roads, bridges, harbors) or of the Republic itself.

These terms were deployed in what we might as well call the "democracy" frame. Directed ultimately toward citizenship and public life (not private property, not "theft"), the democracy frame assumed that citizens can never be truly self-governing until they have a lively public sphere, a free flow of knowledge, religious liberty, and so forth. It is not that the frame ignores "encouragements" to authors and inventors—it expressly provides them—but creating private wealth and autonomy is only the near-term purpose of these rewards. Madison understood all incentives to ingenuity to be "compensation for a benefit actually gained by the community." That formulation embodies the Republican Two-Step: first a private compensation, then a public benefit. Where monopoly privileges were granted, that is, they were means toward larger ends.

They were the means by which human ingenuity might be led to engender a republic of art, invention, and ideas. And this republic of knowledge, in turn, was taken to be an essential part of the larger political estate the founders were trying to create. The "progress clause" of the Constitution is, after all, embedded in the Constitution itself, and the Constitution established a republican democracy on American soil. That is the outer boundary of this inquiry, one of the foundational frames within which our discussions of cultural creations should be held. After all, democracy is democracy.

The question remains of how this foundational frame might be applied in the present. Here there will be much to say, the uses of any conceptual tool being as various as the issues it is brought to. Nonetheless, I will close with one sample line of thought, a response to a problem posed in the first chapter, the entertainment industry's concern with piracy.

The history just told suggests how the framers might have approached the problem. In his 1694 "Memorandum," John Locke tells the story of one Mr. Samuel Smith, who "imported from Holland Tully's Works, of a very fine edition, with new corrections made by Gronovius," based on comparisons of several ancient manuscripts. The London printer who had from the Crown the exclusive right to Tully's (i.e., Marcus Tullius Cicero's) work seized these books as they entered the country. The law allowed this printer to extract from Mr. Smith a fine for having violated his copyright. It never occurs to Locke to speak of Mr. Smith's action as "theft"; he attacks instead the printer's monopoly, calling it "absurd and ridiculous" and "injurious to learning." As for the law giving printers their privileges: "by this act scholars are subjected to the power of these dull wretches, who do not so much as understand Latin."

If we suppose that Mr. Locke himself had imported Tully from Holland, perhaps a copy of that great orator's treatise *On Duty* or his dialogue on "the good," and if we then ask how the framers of our Constitution would have responded to the case, the answer is clear: they would have understood it as Locke understood it, as a matter of liberty and learning, not as a matter of property and theft.

In the present moment, of course, we have no problem with the distribution of Greek and Roman authors; they are readily available in cheap editions, thanks to the century-long struggle that ended as the American Revolution began. At issue now is the puzzle of how to be a citizen in a mass culture dominated by corporate "content providers." All of us presently live in a soup of commercially and politically motivated stories, images, and music. I may take my children to the north woods for two weeks in August, hoping that the murmuring pines and the hemlocks will school their souls, but for the remaining fifty weeks of the year, their learning takes place in the thickets and streams of electronic media. What form should the old model of personal autonomy and civic action take for those who come of age watching forty hours of TV a week? How does a young person mature into a true citizen inside that forest of signs?

The music collective calling themselves Negativland suggests how citizens who are artists might answer:

> As artists, we find this new electrified environment irresistibly worthy of comment, criticism, and manipulation.
>
> The act of appropriating from this media assault represents a kind of liberation from our status as helpless sponges which is so desired by the advertisers who pay for it all. It is a much needed form of self-defense against the one-way, corporate-consolidated media barrage.

Fair enough; enter the forest and try to make its materials your own. And yet, as with Locke's story of importing classics from Holland, it turns out that the law stands in your way. The Negativland collective has found it impossible to comply with the law and still make their work. The recordings that they create are "typically packed with found elements, brief fragments recorded from all media." One piece can have a hundred different parts, and the problem posed by the obligation to get permissions and pay clearance fees for all these makes it literally impossible for Negativland to make their work and also comply with the law.

That "absurd and ridiculous" fact is not actually the focus I want to have here, however; I'm more interested in the point being made about passive and active receivers of the mass media, for with that Negativland manages to return us to the question of agency and civic virtue that arose in the commonwealth model of citizenship. If the symbolic universe that contains us now derives largely from the media barrage, then shouldn't its symbols at least be held in common? Shouldn't a community's speech belong to the community?

Remember Lord Camden's 1774 commonwealth argument: created works should be *publici juris*, meaning they should belong to the public by right. *Black's Law Dictionary* currently gives two examples of how this Latin phrase is used today:

> A city holds title to its streets as property *publici juris.*

> Words that are in general or common use and that are merely descriptive are *publici juris* and cannot be appropriated as a trademark.

The first of these makes *publici juris* synonymous with *res publicae*; even—perhaps especially—in a commercial culture, city streets are republican property. The second example links the phrase to common speech.

But what is common speech? To creators like the Negativland collective, common speech must now include the "canned ideas, images, music, and text" of the "media assault" that surrounds us. Children not only watch forty hours of TV a week, they see twenty thousand commercials each year. Each advertisement they see is proprietary and (as anyone knows who has tried to write a book about the industry) it is difficult, usually impossible, to get permission to reproduce them. Which is to say, in a mass-media consumer culture, the young are taught a language that is not theirs to own.

In the early twentieth century, while most industrialized nations were building telephone networks, the Soviet Union was investing in loudspeakers. We need no better image of an antidemocratic public sphere: they speak, the people listen. In a democratic public sphere, on the other hand, the people can always speak back; they can respond to whatever comes their way as (to cite Negativland once more) a "source and subject, to be captured, rearranged, even manipulated, and injected back into the barrage by those who are subjected to it." Doing so turns passive listeners into active speakers. It brings the kind of agency to individuals that, in the republican tradition, transforms them from vassals (or, now, consumers) into true citizens. If the monopoly privileges that we've granted to "content providers" stand in the way of such citizenship, then the privileges should be called into question. After all, democracy is democracy.

5

BENJAMIN FRANKLIN, FOUNDING PIRATE

The argument: The founders believed that created works
belong largely in the commons so as to support
and enliven creative communities.

"THE INVENTIONS OF OTHERS"

Benjamin Franklin's interest in electrical phenomena began during a 1743 trip to Boston where he saw an itinerant natural philosopher from England demonstrate a series of scientific curiosities.
In a typical display, the man suspended a boy on a platform hung
from the ceiling by silk ropes, rubbed his feet with a glass rod,
then made sparks of static electricity jump from his hands and
face. Parlor tricks like these were amusing and curious, but little
understood and so fleeting as to elude empirical study.

An invention that came from the Netherlands in 1745 changed
all that. The Leyden jar was the first capacitor, a device for storing
an electrical charge, and with it came the possibility of conducting
actual experiments. It made its way to Philadelphia about the same
time that Franklin retired from his printing business in hopes, he
wrote, of spending some years "enjoying . . . Leisure to read, study,
make Experiments, and . . . produce something for the common
Benefit of Mankind."

Franklin has come down to us in American history as the quin-
tessential self-made man. A remark in Emerson's "Self-Reliance" is

typical. "Insist on yourself; never imitate . . . ," Emerson counsels. "Where is the master who could have instructed Franklin . . . ? Every great man is a unique." In fact Franklin took instruction widely, as we shall see, and as unique as he might have been, his work in science was a highly collaborative and social affair. Friends in England sent him the equipment needed for generating and storing electrical charges, and at home in Philadelphia three other men—Philip Syng, Thomas Hopkinson, and Ebenezer Kinnersley— joined him in setting up a workshop to play with this apparatus. Franklin was the theoretician in this group, but each man made contributions. Syng constructed a device for generating an electric charge, a glass ball that could be turned like a grindstone. Hopkinson demonstrated that pointed conductors can deliver a spark as well as attract one. Kinnersley showed that the charges inside and outside of a Leyden jar could be reversed. Franklin, in addition to theorizing, did what he always did: he wrote and published the results. His fame as an *individual* researcher is partly a consequence of the shorthand by which, when one person writes about a group's discoveries, we sometimes grant singular credit for collective effort.

However the credit is eventually apportioned, the fact is that in the late 1740s these four men set up a laboratory in an upstairs room at the Pennsylvania State House and began to experiment with the circumstances under which sparks could be generated, stored, discharged, and passed from object to object. The results were a series of foundational contributions to electrical theory, including:

- describing "the action of points," the fact, that is, that sharp objects attract and give off sparks better than blunt ones;
- conceiving of all electrical effects as arising from the action of a single "fluid";
- imagining that objects can accumulate this fluid, or lose it, and assigning the terms "plus" and "minus" to these states;

- proving that charges always occur in equal amounts of "plus" and "minus" and, when neutralized, disappear in equal amounts;
- and formulating from this observation the law of conservation of charge.

If your car battery should die on a cold winter day, and if you use another car's battery to get a jump start, taking care to respect each battery's polarity (connecting plus to plus and minus to minus), when the engine finally jumps to life you stand indebted to the team of Franklin, Syng, Hopkinson, and Kinnersley. Not only were they the first to describe electrical polarity, they were the first to make a battery in the modern sense, and they gave it its name. ("We made what we called an *electrical-battery*," Franklin wrote in 1748, "consisting of eleven panes of large sash-glass, armed with thin leaden plates, pasted on each side.") Large parts of the theory still organize scientific thought about electricity, and the English language is shot through with terms that first found their modern usage in that upstairs room in the State House, not just "battery" but also "armature," "brush," "charged," "conductor," "nonconductor," "electrical shock," "electrician," "electrified" . . . All these and more belong to the public domain of "common Benefit" that the Philadelphia group helped create.

As for Franklin's famous experiment with the kite, it should first be said that the observation that electric sparks resembled lightning was a commonplace long before Franklin turned his attention to electricity. Typical is this 1716 remark by Isaac Newton: "I have been much amused by the singular *phaenomena* resulting from bringing a needle into contact with a piece of amber or resin fricated on silke clothe. The flame putteth me in mind of sheet lightning on a small—how very small—scale." Franklin's contribution lay not in making the connection but in suggesting an experiment to test it. In a 1749 scientific notebook, he listed the various ways in which "electrical fluid agrees with lightning" (e.g., "crack or noise in exploding"), and concluded simply, "Let the experiment be made."

The experiment he went on to suggest appeared in print a few years later. Franklin imagined that a shed protected from the weather—a "sentry-box," he called it—might be set on some high place with an iron rod "pointed very sharp at the end" rising twenty or thirty feet above it; regardless of whether or not lightning struck, he thought, electrified storm clouds would charge the rod and that charge would in turn produce sparks when given a path to ground.

Franklin outlined this experiment in a 1749 letter to a friend in London, who published it two years later in a pamphlet reporting on the Philadelphia experiments. A year later, a French translation of this London pamphlet appeared, and within a few months the man who had made the translation successfully carried out the lightning experiment in a garden at Marly, about twenty miles from Paris. Sparks leaped from an iron rod with a cracking sound during a thunderstorm as Franklin had predicted. This was in May 1752; Franklin himself—unaware of what had happened in France—tried the experiment about a month later in Philadelphia. In order to get the needed elevation, he substituted a kite with "a very Sharp pointed Wire" for the metal rod, and managed to get sparks to jump from a key on the kite string to his knuckle. (No lightning struck, by the way; the current resulted from the wet kite string giving the atmospheric charge a path to ground.)

There may have been many who made the inference that lightning and electricity were one and the same, but as the historian of science I. Bernard Cohen notes, the Philadelphia group's earlier studies left Franklin in a unique position when it came to suggesting a proof:

The experiment depended on the "power of points," which had not been fully investigated nor understood prior to his work. Then, too, the experiment was but one of the results of his theory of a single fluid. The electrified cloud had a positive charge, he thought. In other words, it had an excess of the electrical fluid.

A point could draw off this excess fluid and, if it were attached to the ground in a moist spot, could transmit that fluid into the earth. Thus the experiment depended on Franklin's theoretical and experimental results. The discovery must certainly be deemed his.

From this discovery came the lightning rod, one of Franklin's most useful inventions. Soon after the kite experiment, in June or July 1752, lightning rods were erected on two public buildings in Philadelphia. Immediately thereafter Franklin published both the results of the kite experiment and detailed instructions for how to make a lightning rod, the former in the *Pennsylvania Gazette* in October and the latter about the same time in the fall printing of *Poor Richard's Almanack* for the following year, 1753.

Franklin's work on electricity was to make him famous around the world, but in these announcements there is little self-promotion. The description of the kite flying merely says that the European success of the sentry-box experiment had been reported in the newspapers and that therefore the curious might like to know "that the same Experiment has succeeded in Philadelphia, tho' made in a different and more easy Manner, which any one may try, as follows." The article then describes how to make a kite with a metal point, when to fly it, where to stand when doing so, and so forth. Franklin never mentions that the experiment was proof of a theory, nor, for that matter, does he say that he was the experimenter, nor even that he is the author of the note.

He is similarly absent from the second publication, the instructions for "securing . . . Buildings from Mischief by Thunder and Lightning." The notice begins by saying that "It has pleased God in his Goodness to Mankind, at length to discover to them" how to avoid damage from lightning, and it then gives clear instructions for making the device. ("Provide a small Iron Rod . . . of such a Length, that one End being three or four Feet in the moist Ground, the other may be six or eight Feet above the highest Part of the

Building," etc.) No mention is made of Franklin himself as either inventor or author. Both publications read not unlike the descriptions that would later be required of anyone seeking to patent a useful invention; they disclose to the public exactly how the thing is made such that any competent practitioner can reproduce it. In this case, however, Franklin was not seeking any patent; he was merely delivering on his expressed intention to "produce something for the common Benefit."

In the *Autobiography*, Franklin tells us that he was offered a patent for his woodstove and that he declined it on principle. What that principle was is nicely illuminated by these accounts of how he actually worked. In none of the electrical researches did he proceed unaided, and by that I don't mean to speak only of his collaborators in Philadelphia. Franklin was born into the early flowering of an international scientific culture. Much of the language of the Philadelphia group's theorizing was easily at hand to be borrowed from other branches of inquiry. William Harvey's seventeenth-century demonstration of the circulation of blood in the body, for example, had so struck the public imagination that soon many things—heat, water, air, money—were figured as circulating fluids (Franklin himself owned a glass apparatus for demonstrating Harvey's theories). The part of Newton's physics that explained how balanced forces come to equilibrium had also taken on wide explanatory force, as may be seen in the "balance of power" that John Adams built into his political theory. For Franklin and his collaborators, to conceive of electricity as a circulating fluid whose charges always balanced was to draw upon and replicate commonplace patterns of thought.

Newton's published work provided the Philadelphia group with even more specific pointers. Franklin had read Newton's *Opticks*, for example, which contains a set of experimentally proven propositions and ends with a group of "queries," unsolved questions for further study. Query 21 offers the idea that "aether (like our air) may contain particles which endeavour to recede from one another," a brief enough remark but one that, when combined with Newton's atomism, encouraged the group to assume an elastic electrical fluid that could spread out on any conducting body because it consisted of mutually repelling particles.

The early eighteenth century also saw the rise of proto-scientific journals. Specifically in regard to electricity, a group of German academics had experimented with static electric sparks, their investigations being subsequently published in the early 1740s in the *Bibliothèque raisonnée des ouvrages des savans de l'Europe*; that article was in turn translated into English and printed in both the *Gentleman's Magazine* (London) and the *American Magazine and Historical Chronicle* (Boston). Franklin knew of these reports, and they gave him several useful terms: the Germans spoke of things becoming "electrised" and they supposed a charged body to be surrounded by an electrical "atmosphere."

The report out of Germany also described an experiment in which sparks were made to pass from a man standing on an insulated platform to another man standing, grounded, on the floor. Franklin, Syng, Hopkinson, and Kinnersley modified this by having *two* men stand on insulated platforms and one on the ground. It was in this instance, by watching carefully when sparks could be made to pass among them, and how strong the sparks were, that they began to think of electrical polarity. Franklin ends his description of the experiment thusly: "Hence have arisen some new terms among us: we say B . . . is electrised *positively*; A *negatively*. Or rather, B is electrised *plus*; A, *minus*."

By altering the German experiment, Franklin and his friends were able to demonstrate something then unknown, the existence of contrary electricities. As I. Bernard Cohen writes, the slight alteration of adding a third man to the experimental chain makes for "a striking illustration of the doctrine that the most original, and even revolutionary, innovations in science are apt to be brilliant intellectual 'transformations' of existing ideas, concepts, laws, theories, or experiments."

Everything I've just outlined adds to that point, for it is the recombination and alteration of a host of elements that leads to "B is . . . *plus*; A, *minus*." Before that simple statement can be made, there had to be the culture of scientific experimentation brought into being by Bacon, Newton, and others; there had to be Newton's theories themselves and the queries in his *Opticks*; there had to be terminology in place for imagining natural phenomena. It also helped to have local collaborating friends and itinerant lecturers demonstrating curiosities; it helped to have inventions like the Leyden jar, and an international circulation of books and journals. Finally, of course, it helped to have Franklin himself, who read widely, corresponded constantly, published quickly, and had a mind capacious enough to absorb the ambient science and to theorize experimental results.

But note how far we are from Emerson's bizarre declaration that no master could have instructed Franklin. What Franklin's ranging intelligence contained, first and foremost, was a great store of other people's. work. The Philadelphia electrical theory was additive, transformative, associative, cumulative . . . It built on what came before. Franklin saw further, true, but he did so by standing on the shoulders of those who came before. His is not the genius of the untutored "unique" but of the commoner who seeks and absorbs the wisdom of many masters.

In such a context, how shall we figure the ownership of ideas, and how shall we figure the "self" that claims them? John Locke assumed that "every man" acquired property through "the labor of his body, and the work of his hands." Whatever a man "removes out of the state of nature" and "mixe[s] his labor with" becomes his to own. Fair enough, perhaps, but how are we to translate such notions into the cultural realm, where there is no "state of nature," where all materials already come from the hands and minds of others? Franklin adds his part to the whole, yes, but the whole is not his creation. "If I own a can of tomato juice and spill it in the sea . . . , do I thereby come to own the sea . . . ?"

This is the context within which to read Franklin's explanation of why he refused a patent on his woodstove. That invention itself is yet another case of Franklin's genius being cumulative and associative rather than "unique" and independent. It is commonly said that Franklin's innovation was to make a freestanding stove, one that sat out in the room and thus radiated heat rather than letting the heat go up the chimney. It is true that the Franklin stove stood in the room, but that was not a new idea: the metal box stove (called a "Holland stove" or a "six-plate stove") was common in the Colonies for warming large rooms, and German settlers in Pennsylvania typically added open-ended cast-iron box stoves to their fireplaces. The innovation of the Franklin stove was, rather, a design based on the idea that hot air could be made to descend, an insight that Franklin took from Newton's and Hermann Boerhaave's theories of matter and heat, theories whose practical application he had seen spelled out in a 1713 book from France, *La mécanique du feu*, itself one of at least six books that Franklin drew on to compose, as it were, his stove.

The Pennsylvania fireplace was made by combining other men's stoves and other men's ideas. Franklin was a man who loved to tinker in a collective shop, and he never pretended otherwise. Thus does he explain the principle behind his refusal of monopoly privileges: "That as we enjoy great Advantages from the Inventions of Others, we should be glad of an Opportunity to serve others by any Invention of ours, and this we should do freely and generously." With the stove, those "Others" are Newton, Boerhaave, and half a dozen other writers and thinkers on several continents, not to mention those Dutch and German immigrants who already had freestanding stoves. Again, it takes a roomy mind to play host to all those others and to find new ways to combine what they have to offer, but not a mind for whom there are no masters, not a "unique." Quite the opposite—this is a mind willing to be taught, willing to be inhabited, willing to labor in the cultural commons so as to contribute to the common good.

"UNLOCKING SECRETS"

There seems to be one case in which a Franklin innovation never found its way to the public, apparently kept as a trade secret until he died, and now lost. In the 1730s, a number of colonial governments hired Franklin to print their paper currency. In order to discourage counterfeiting, Franklin's bills sported "nature prints," images of ferns, willow leaves, blackberry leaves, and other plant material. These were probably made by taking a papier-mâché impression of a plant and using that as a mold to cast a lead character that could then be used in the press. In fact, however, no one knows exactly how Franklin's nature prints were made because the method was a secret and he revealed it only to a few of his associates. These included his partner David Hall and a scientist friend, Cadwallader Colden. The latter once wrote a letter to the British printer and publisher William Strahan, in which he declines to explain how Franklin made the nature prints, saying that "as printing is this man's trade and he makes a benefit of it I do not think myself at liberty to communicate it." Silence prevailed and, as the historian Joyce Chaplin writes, "the trade secret died with its inventor, the Philadelphia master printer."

The word "benefit" in Colden's letter can usefully be taken to mark a pivot point between the world of guild secrecy that dominated the trades at the time of Franklin's birth and the world of public knowledge that emerged during his lifetime. Remember the story of Dollond's patent: two men made the same invention, but Dollond applied for a patent, thus releasing the idea to the public in return for the short-term monopoly privilege. "It was not the person who locked up his invention in his scrutoire that ought to profit for such invention, but he who brought it forth for the benefit of mankind."

The benefit of secret knowledge versus the benefit of mankind—the shift from one to the other was one of the great transformations of Franklin's lifetime and, despite this one example to the contrary, of his life as well. At the time of his birth in 1706, trades in Europe and the Colonies were still organized by guilds. Craftsmen like Franklin's father—a cloth dyer when he lived in England and a soap and candle maker in Boston—or like his brothers (a blacksmith, a printer, another soap maker) were not in the habit of revealing the tricks of their trades to the general public. They passed their skills to their apprentices, orally and directly, but they would never do what Franklin later did with his knowledge: publish it for general consumption. Craft companies themselves and the arts they imparted to their members were known as mysteries, a term that aptly connotes their ethic of public silence. Apprentices initiated into these mysteries were obliged to pay entry fees, swear oaths, and in general take on the obligation of maintaining the secrecy that protected each trade from competition.

All this said, in colonial America, Chaplin tells us, "guild structure was weak or absent," and the men of Franklin's father's generation were "losing some control over the mysteries of their trades as those secrets . . . made their way into books." The day that Franklin himself broke the contract that had apprenticed him to his brother, a printer, and ran away to Philadelphia exemplifies this loss in several ways. First of all, the law binding apprentices to their masters was there precisely to help keep proprietary knowledge from wandering—and Franklin broke that law.

Second, he was a printer and printing was the trade that betrayed all the other trades. One historian of science has argued that the early "books of secrets"—collections of craft techniques, medical remedies, household hints, and more—are the "missing link" between medieval craft knowledge and seventeenth-century experimental science. Appearing first in the sixteenth century, such books were the initial embodiments of the printer's ability to erode the exclusivity of other trades. By Franklin's day, these publications had turned craft-specific; the seamen's techniques for navigation and gunnery began to be described in print, for example, along with the needed mathematics and geometry, all of which undercut the craft monopoly of mariners. (Franklin himself learned navigation from books, one of which made a point of proclaiming that it was "unlock[ing] . . . Secrets.")

Alongside craft-specific publications, Franklin's generation also knew a series of attempts at offering encyclopedic knowledge. A book like Ephraim Chambers's *Cyclopaedia* (1728) announced itself directly as an attack on private knowledge: "To offer a thing to the Publick, and yet pretend a Right reserved therein to one's self, if it be not absurd, yet it is sordid," wrote Chambers in the introduction to his first edition.

Franklin of course belonged almost wholly to the emerging print culture that prided itself in exposing secret knowledge. When he became the publisher of the *Pennsylvania Gazette* in 1729, he announced that one thing the paper would do was publish "such Hints . . . as may contribute either to the Improvement of our present Manufactures, or towards the Invention of new Ones." His 1743 proposal for establishing an American Philosophical Society stressed the need for open and public communication of ideas so as to "improve the common Stock of Knowledge." The story about the lost method for making nature prints is in fact the exception that highlights Franklin's general rule, a wholehearted dedication to public access to knowledge.

But of course, one nation's access to knowledge may be another's trade piracy. In the eighteenth century, the "theft" of industrial and craft knowledge commonly took two forms: the smuggling of manufacturing machines from one country to another and the emigration of skilled workers. All European governments passed anti-emigration laws, the English for example regularly forbidding craftsmen to leave the country, knowing that in their heads and hands lay the skills that made the nation rich. British law prohibited the movement of a whole range of artisans, from clock makers to potters, from glassblowers to weavers.

This being the case, a good sense of the mature Franklin's relationship to the ownership of knowledge—and thus to so-called piracy—can be gleaned from his position on the free movement of skilled artisans across national boundaries. An illustrative case arose in 1781, a time when Franklin was living in Paris as the diplomatic representative of the newly independent nation. As such, he found himself regularly petitioned by artisans with emigration schemes both useful and foolish. One such came from Henry Royle, a skilled calico printer from England. Knowing that his talents would be useful to the new nation, Royle proposed on behalf of himself and some friends that the United States agree to support them while they prepared to emigrate, pay for their transportation, exempt them from military service, and give them a seven-year monopoly on the silk and cotton goods they produced once they arrived.

Franklin had neither the authority nor the funds to enter into such a scheme, but he wrote encouragingly to Royle nonetheless, saying that "a special Law might easily be obtain'd to give you a Property for seven Years in the useful Inventions you may introduce." At the end of the letter, he turns his attention to anti-emigration laws, naming them "tyrannical." Such laws "make a Prison of England" and "confine Men for no other Crime but that of being useful & Industrious." (In another letter protesting trade protection, by the way, Franklin has this to say about publishers: "If Books can be had much cheaper from Ireland, (which I believe for I bought Blackstone there for 24s. when it was sold in England at 4 Guineas) is not this an Advantage, not to English Booksellers indeed, but to English Readers, and to Learning?")

As for Henry Royle and his friends, Franklin's suggestion that they might receive a seven-year monopoly is an almost unique

assent on his part to such a privilege, and thus worth pausing over.*
The first thing to say is that Franklin was clearly not a "common
stock" purist; the new nation needed calico printers, and if this
was how to get them, so be it. But the second thing to say is that
in order for Royle and his friends to do what they proposed, they
would have to smuggle the needed machinery out of Britain. From
the British point of view, the emigration of the workers and the
transport of their machinery were what would now be called the
piracy of intellectual property. To Franklin, however, it wasn't piracy at all; it was the diffusion of useful knowledge brought about
by underwriting the liberty of ideas with the liberty of citizens.
That is also, I suspect, how the elder Franklin might have wanted
us to think of the printing skills that the young Franklin carried
in his head and hands when he stole away from his apprenticeship
contract. Seen in this light, the young man's flight from Boston
was a foundational act of American piracy.

Or, rather, it is a foundational act in the creation of a Republic
of Letters, and that commonwealth is not just "American," but international. It is tempting to see Franklin's offer of a monopoly
privilege to Royle as befitting a nationalist trade policy, "America"
still fighting "England" by encouraging emigration. That is not a
misreading of the case, but it doesn't take into account Franklin's
much more pronounced disregard of national identity. Take, for example, the remarkable letter that he wrote while serving as "Minister
Plenipotentiary from the Congress of the United States at the Court
of France" during the Revolutionary War. Addressed to "All Captains
and Commanders of American Armed Ships," it reads:

> Gentlemen, A Ship having been fitted out from England before
> the Commencement of this War, to make Discoveries of new

*What Franklin offered Royle used to be called a "patent of importation," a
monopoly privilege given to the first importer of a useful form of manufacture
rather than to the inventor of one.

Countries, in Unknown Seas, under the Conduct of that most celebrated Navigator and Discoverer Captain Cook; an Undertaking truly laudable in itself, as the Increase of Geographical Knowledge, facilitates the Communication between distant Nations, in the Exchange of useful Products and Manufactures, and the Extension of Arts, whereby the common Enjoyments of human Life are multiplied and augmented, and Science of other kinds encreased to the Benefit of Mankind in general.

This is therefore most earnestly to recommend to every one of you; that in case the said Ship which is now expected to be soon in the European Seas on her Return, should happen to fall into your Hands, you would not consider her as an Enemy, nor suffer any Plunder to be made of the Effects contained in her, nor obstruct her immediate Return to England, by detaining her or sending her into any other Part of Europe or to America; but that you would treat the said Captain Cook and his People with all Civility and Kindness, affording them as common Friends to Mankind, all the Assistance in your Power which they may happen to stand in need of.

Doron Ben-Atar, a historian who has written on trade secrecy, has used the Captain Cook letter as part of his evidence for the claim that "Franklin never became an intellectual property nationalist or tried to prevent the diffusion of American know-how back to Europe." To give just one of Ben-Atar's concrete examples, when Franklin lived in Paris he developed a new method for casting printer's type. The idea of owning the innovation, or of preserving it for American use only, never occurred to him: he immediately showed his method to the king's printer, and soon after the peace accord with Britain was signed, he shared it with British printers.

All of which harks back to that 1748 letter in which Franklin declares that he hopes to "produce something for the common Benefit of Mankind." There are cases in which Franklin supported

local and limited monopoly rights to ideas, but they are the exceptions that prove the rule, and the rule, as Ben-Atar puts it, was
that "humanity, regardless of national boundaries, was entitled
to enjoy the fruits of innovation." Franklin's life is a standing
illustration of the point. In public affairs, his expressed opinions
and concrete actions argue for an end to craft secrecy and attack
directly any "tyranny" that would inhibit the free movement of
science and technology. All of which is of a piece with his own
practice as a scientist and inventor. The unimpeded travel of artisans and industrial knowledge across national boundaries is the
equivalent in political economy of the uninhibited international
conversation that allowed Franklin and his friends to theorize so
fruitfully about electricity and to share so widely what they had
discovered.

"IMPROVEMENT FLASHED UPON IMPROVEMENT"

In Franklin's own expressed opinions about knowledge and print,
he concerns himself never with what craft guilds might lose
when their secrets are published but always with what the public
might gain. Print, he liked to point out, can overcome distances
separating scholars from one another; it provides a stay against
the assaults of time and death; and it had proven to be the ideal
medium for increasing the reach of associative and cumulative
innovation. If only the ancients had possessed the arts of "copper
plate and letter printing," much of their knowledge would not have
been "lost to posterity," Franklin wrote to a friend. Even in his
own day, "many useful Particulars remain uncommunicated, die
with the Discoverers, and are lost to Mankind," he cautioned in
a Philadelphia broadside, going on to propose the antidote: the
Colonies should have an "American Philosophical Society," a community of scholars whose simple charge would be to correspond
with one another and to annually put into print "such Experiments,

Discoveries, Improvements, &c. as may be thought of publick Advantage." Thus would far-flung scholars be in close conversation, and thus might foundations be laid such that future generations could build on present insights, however fragmentary those might be. As the letter about "copper plate and letter printing" goes on to say, "the Knowledge of small Matters being preserv'd, gives the Hint and is sometimes the Occasion of great Discoveries, perhaps Ages after."

It is not hard to find cases in which we see Franklin acting on his own advice. Take the map of the Atlantic Gulf Stream that he published in 1768: living in London and serving as postmaster for the northern American colonies, Franklin had been asked to address the odd fact that mail packets sailing from London to Boston made the trip two weeks faster than those sailing from Falmouth to New York, despite the approximately equivalent distances. He quickly surmised that the Gulf Stream gave rise to the difference, westbound ships that entered it being carried backward at the rate of sixty or seventy miles a day.

Mariners had known about the Gulf Stream for a long time. Norse sailors seem to have been aware of it; Christopher Columbus knew about it; colonial fishermen and whalers knew about it. All this knowledge was, however, imprecise and fragmentary; no map showed where the stream lay and no common methods were available to help sailors determine if their boats lay in the stream or out of it.

This spotty understanding was partly a result of a general absence of North Atlantic hydrography—maps simply showed an empty ocean—but it was also a consequence once again of craft secrecy, in this case on the part of coastal fishermen and whalers who actually benefited from what they knew about the currents. When Captain Cook tried to chart the shores of Newfoundland in 1765, he found the local fishermen closemouthed about currents in the coastal waters. Why tell a stranger the hard-won expertise by which you earn your living?

Franklin's luck was better than Cook's, for he happily found a fisherman who felt no need to guard his knowledge. Living in London when Franklin sought to say something precise about the Gulf Stream was his Nantucket cousin, Captain Timothy Folger, a mariner well acquainted with the whaling industry. In the 1750s, Nantucket whalers working in the North Atlantic had come to know a lot about the Gulf Stream; by the late 1760s, they had turned to southern and to Arctic waters, so Folger had no reason not to share his know-how with Franklin.

What he knew, Franklin wrote to his superior in the British postal system, was "that the Whales are found generally near the Edges of the *Gulph Stream*," and that whaling vessels consequently "Cruise along the Edges of the Stream in quest of Whales," and thus "become better acquainted with the Course, Breadth, Strength and extent of the same, than those Navigators can well be who only cross it in their Voyages to and from America." Franklin asked his cousin if he could mark the stream on a map and Folger did so, indicating its course, size, and speed, and including directions whereby ships traveling from Newfoundland to New York could avoid both the Gulf Stream on the one hand and the coastal shoals and banks on the other. Franklin then had Folger's map and directions printed so that they might "be of use to our Packets." This map, published in 1768 by Mount & Page in London, is the first-ever chart of the Gulf Stream.

What Franklin does in this and other cases is to use "copper plate and letter printing" not so much to create *new* knowledge as to create *public* and *durable* knowledge. By the simple act of printing, he moves proprietary, secret, local, and potentially ephemeral information—something known to fishermen and whalers (and to whales, for that matter) but not to the majority of navigators, packet boat captains included—into the public sphere, the cultural commons, so that it can widely "be of use" and so that it will not "die with the Discoverers."

As for print's ability to "give . . . the Hint" that might lead to discoveries "Ages after," at the end of his life Franklin recorded one other contribution to our understanding of ocean currents, in this case creating new knowledge, albeit fragmentary and little understood at the time. All his adult life, Franklin had puzzled not just over where the Gulf Stream lay, but over what caused it. Was it the rotation of the earth? Temperature changes in seawater? The trade winds? Beginning in 1775, when he left London in a hurry as the war broke out, each time he crossed the Atlantic he carried along a thermometer and took repeated measurements of surface temperatures, a simple application of his old dictum "Let the experiment be made." In one of his last scientific papers, the "Maritime Observations" of 1785, he published three pages of data on ocean temperatures gathered during the previous decade. Our understanding now is that the Gulf Stream is a typical "density current," kept in motion by the force of gravity acting on small differences in the weight of seawater, these caused in turn by variations in salinity and temperature. Though he never came to it himself (in his last writing on the topic, he names trade winds as the current's likely cause), it was Franklin who initiated the experiments from which others would eventually draw the right conclusions.

To return, then, to the connections between print and the advancement of knowledge, and to Franklin's practice of his own ideas, the map that he printed in 1768 is as good an example as any of the erosion of trade secrecy in favor of a less ephemeral and fragmented public domain, and the fact that Franklin's ocean temperature records might be read in Philadelphia or in Paris, that they might be read by his own generation or by ours—that they might give "the Hint" for "Ages to come"—stands witness to the power of print to enable conversation across the divides of space and time.

It should also be said that with these assertions about print's ability to create a generative public domain, a commons of knowledge, we come to one of the many places where eighteenth-century practice in natural science and the useful arts overlaps with civic republican politics. In the political realm, Franklin's print ideology was kin to the one we saw expressed by John Adams in the last chapter. In a letter written after the Revolutionary War, Franklin asserts that "the art of printing . . . diffuses so general a light . . . that all the window shutters despotism and priestcraft can oppose to keep it out, prove insufficient." The claim might be hard to support in all times and places (there are enough examples of print used as the tool of tyranny), but it nonetheless reflects how writers in the early Republic saw the matter.

An oration on the history of inventions given by the clockmaker Owen Biddle in Philadelphia in 1781 makes for an expanded example. For Biddle, the invention of printing was not only a watershed in the progress of science; it became the art that freed all other arts from dominion by "the powerful and opulent." Print culture's capacity to distribute books to people of all ranks "has made every invention of art, or improvement of science, as universal as the influence of the sun . . . This art is of a perfect republican nature; without respect of persons, it diffuses its benefits alike to all."

Note that for both Franklin and Biddle, sunlight is the obvious analogue of print. The shutters of despotism cannot contain it; it shines on rich and poor alike; it is spread throughout the world. The "light" of printing is, moreover, additive, cumulative. As soon as the printing press appeared, "improvement flashed upon improvement," Biddle told his audience, "and one ingenious invention succeeded another with such rapidity, that greater progress was made in one age, than had been before from the foundation of the world."

Such lucubrations nicely prefigure the way Jefferson was to describe the nature of shared ideas—"he who lights his taper at mine receives his light without darkening me"—and offers a chance to read that image more deeply: Who are these who light their candles one from another? Why are they doing so? For Franklin and Biddle, they are the citizens of an egalitarian republic. They are those who have access to knowledge without regard to rank (such that a chandler's son might theorize about electricity). And they are engaged in the modern form of associative creation, having found a way to pass the light of learning from generation to generation without its being extinguished. The poet Edward Young once wrote, "Our Birth is nothing but our Death begun; / As Tapers waste, that Instant they take Fire." Tapers waste, it is true, and human beings die. But the fire of knowledge need do neither so long as it burns in the cultural commons.

Here I should say that nothing in this line of thought, from Franklin's Gulf Stream map to Biddle's succession of ingenious inventions, is necessarily at odds with grants of limited monopoly privilege. On the contrary, as we've seen, patent was a useful tool for helping to move craft knowledge into the public domain; and copyright, to the degree that it freed writers from old forms of patronage, was instrumental in the rise of the public sphere. That said, in each case, monopoly privilege was a means to larger, public ends, and for those ends it mattered that monopoly be strictly limited. The outlying conceptual frame for men like Franklin and Biddle was always the public benefits that follow from creativity in science and the useful arts. It was never individual property rights; it was always the common good. They never concerned themselves with questions of "theft" or "piracy," creativity being, after all, creativity.

Here then a word is in order about Franklin's views on property rights in the conventional sense. These probably found their fullest expression in his response to a proposal that the Constitution establish a legislative upper house to represent the rich ("Freemen possessing in Lands and Houses one thousand Pounds"). To this Franklin asked, "why is Property to be represented at all?" Under the assumption that there is no natural right to property, Franklin believed that property should not command society, society should command property: "Private Property . . . is a Creature of Society and is subject to the Calls of that Society whenever its Necessities shall require it, even to its last Farthing." The contributions that private property makes to public needs are not, therefore, "to be considered as conferring a Benefit on the Public . . . , but as the Return of an Obligation previously received or the Payment of a just Debt."

In explaining this position, Franklin regularly contrasted European property rights with those of the "Indian Nations," noting that Native Americans considered themselves to have a "common Right" to nature's bounty, especially "whenever they want provision." A family with many deer should not deny food to a family with none. Built into this line of thought is a distinction between "necessary" property and "superfluous" property, the latter especially being "the Creature of Society." Superfluous property is always social property to Franklin: "what we have above what we can use, is not properly *ours*, tho' we possess it." Superfluous property belongs ultimately to the community, not to the individual, society having secured the conditions that allow it to exist, and society having protected it. Communities thus have a right to tax their members, and a right to resist gross disparities in the distribution of wealth.

If we superimpose these ideas over Franklin's practice in regard to what is now called intellectual property, we find them fully congruent. While Franklin never opposed limited monopoly privileges for other men and women, his own practice in regard to the ownership of inventions and his conviction that property in excess of need is a "creature of society" make him a commonwealth man in the style of Jefferson. When delegates to the Constitutional Convention debated copyright and patent, Franklin—the delegate most famous for his inventions—apparently remained silent, and silence is always hard to read. Nonetheless, his actions and his positions elsewhere expressed make it clear that he would have understood the Constitutional language the way others then understood it, as a balance between a short-term monopoly and a long-term grant to the public. That the clause might become the ground for creating a perpetual property right for individuals and private corporations would have astounded him. After all, to revise his own language only a little, "intellectual property is a creature of society and is subject to the calls of society whenever necessity requires it, even to its last nickel; the contributions of intellectual property to the public good are not to be considered as a favor to the public but as the recognition of an obligation previously incurred, or the payment of a just debt." Knowledge is a republican, not a private, estate.

6

LIBERTY TO COMMUNICATE

*The argument: In the civic republic, a play
of self-possession and self-negation produces
a comedy in whose final act common wealth appears.*

TRUTH HAS NO THINKER

When Benjamin Franklin first communicated the Philadelphia studies on electricity to a friend in London, he claimed to be doing so partly from a sense of their *lack* of completion. The modesty of this declaration—real or pretended—offers a way to begin looking at how Franklin conceived of himself as a scientist and inventor. He understood, first of all, that scientific claims do not depend on particular scientists; the more personal the origin of the claim, in fact, the more likely its errors. His letter to the London colleague ends as follows:

> These Thoughts, my dear Friend, are many of them crude and hasty, and if I were merely ambitious of acquiring some Reputation . . . , I ought to keep them by me, 'till corrected and improved by Time and farther Experience. But since even short Hints, and imperfect Experiments in any new Branch of Science, being communicated, have oftentimes a good Effect, in exciting the attention of the Ingenious to the Subject, and so becoming the Occasion of more exact disquisitions . . . and more compleat Discoveries, you are at Liberty to communicate this Paper to

whom you please; it being of more Importance that Knowledge should increase, than that your Friend should be thought an accurate Philosopher.

Collective inquiry is less prone to error than is solitary inquiry, individualism in this case being an impediment to knowledge. The phrase to mark in Franklin's letter is *liberty to communicate*: the breeding ground of truth lies in the conversation of the ingenious, not (or not only) in the ambitions of individuals. The spirit here embodied is, once again, civic republican: where truth requires community, individuals should be willing to sacrifice any concern they have for private reputation.

Here also lie the seeds of Franklin's lifelong refusal to defend his own ideas. A letter written during the Revolution contains a typical explanation of his position and goes on to connect it tellingly to the question of the ownership of ideas.

I have never entered into any Controversy in defence of my philosophical Opinions; I leave them to take their Chance in the World. If they are right, Truth and Experience will support them. If wrong, they ought to be refuted and rejected. Disputes are apt to sour one's Temper and disturb one's Quiet. I have no private Interest in the Reception of my Inventions by the World, having never made nor proposed to make the least Profit by any of them.

This last sentence gives a second principle by which Franklin declined to patent his inventions. Here the issue is not indebtedness to past inventors but something closer to care of the soul. To patent an invention for profit confers "a private interest"; such interest will, the letter implies, prompt a man to defend his ideas, right or wrong; and disputes that do not care for right or wrong will sour the temper. This line of thought grounds the civic republican ideal not so much on obligations of public service as on a sense of how one wants to live and be in the world. Disidentifying with one's ideas—and thus declining to own them—leads to a valued way of being, one where quiet and sweet temper arise from associating with truths that lie outside the self.

The values here expressed have implications for politics and property, but the point of departure lies more in spiritual or psychological territory and may be usefully illuminated by turning in that direction. The British psychoanalyst Wilfred Bion once addressed himself to the puzzle of how to psychoanalyze a liar and at one point in his argument he makes this striking claim: "The lie requires a thinker to think. The truth, or true thought, does not require a thinker—he is not logically necessary." What can this mean?

Bion compares the working psychoanalyst to a scientist, and in the case of science the point would seem to be that truths of the natural world are independent of the particular people who conceive of them. If Franklin and his friends were right that electrical charges always appear in equal and opposite amounts, the correctness of the insight would still exist had they never been born. Once the Leyden jar had been invented, someone else would have soon come upon this truth. Similarly, once Franklin declared his idea, anyone else could do the experiments in question and arrive at the same conclusion. Of "work that corroborates the discovery of others," Bion writes, "even if it requires a thinker it does not require a *particular* thinker and in this resembles truths—thoughts that require no thinker." Human minds in general are where such thoughts appear, but these thoughts do not depend on any one such mind.

The point gains clarity by way of its opposite: "The lie and its thinker are inseparable," Bion writes. "The thinker is of no consequence to the truth . . . In contrast, the lie gains existence by virtue of the epistemologically prior existence of the liar." Lies require a liar, and as such they say something about the liar; they are thus better fitted than truths to the task of gratifying the self-regard or narcissism of the individual who makes them. Any work that simply replicates a truth known to others lacks narcissistic appeal.* No "I" can get much from it. When it comes to truth, however, as the poet Rimbaud wrote, "it is wrong to say: I think. One should say: I am thought."

Eighteenth-century thinkers might have framed ideas such as these not so much in terms of truth versus lies as of truth versus opinions. Opinion, in Franklin's day, acted as a sort of middle term between truth and error, denoting any belief that was not yet, or could never be, confirmed by sense experience, experiment, and reason. Like lies in Bion's view, opinions reside with particular peoples in particular places. Englishmen in London observe the first day of the week as their day of worship, Turks in Constantinople observe the sixth: there may be truth in one case and error in the other, but no experiment or line of logic will tell us which is which. True knowledge, on the other hand, does not suffer the contingency of opinion. Lightning is electricity no matter if it is described by Dalibard in Paris or by Franklin in Philadelphia. As Newton suggested in his "Rules of Reasoning in Philosophy," the cause of the falling of stones should be the same "in Europe and in America"; the cause of "the reflection of light" should be the same "on our earth and the planets."

Opinions can never be detached from persons and places in that way. More to the point, because they require a thinker, as Bion says of lies, opinions are potentially divisive. Truth, needing no particular embodiment, can lead to concord; opinion, on the other hand, produces sects and factions, and makes it difficult to move from any group of private selves to "the public good."

Much of Franklin's wit in public affairs was directed at this potential sticking point, at the self-importance and assumed infallibility by which individuals allow their opinions to trump the

---

*Claims to priority, not to truth, are what is available to satisfy scientific self-regard.

common good. By way of example, let us move from science to politics and consider how Franklin persuaded the delegates to the 1787 Constitutional Convention to lay aside their differences and approve the document they had produced. The speech is a rhetorical tour de force. Franklin begins by saying that although he himself has doubts about the Constitution, he is disposed to doubt his doubts. A long life has shown him how often he has been "obliged . . . to change Opinions even on important Subjects." He then contrasts the professed instability of his own beliefs with the stubbornness of those who do not even realize that their opinions are opinions: "Most Men indeed as well as most Sects in Religion, think themselves in Possession of all Truth, and that wherever others differ from them it is so far Error." Error, truth, and opinion: with these key terms in play, he begins to joke:

> Steele, a Protestant in a Dedication tells the Pope, that the only Difference between our two Churches in their Opinions of the Certainty of their Doctrine, is, the Romish Church is infallible, and the Church of England is never in the Wrong. But tho' many private Persons think almost as highly of their own Infallibility, as of that of their Sect, few express it so naturally as a certain French Lady, who in a little Dispute with her Sister, said, I don't know how it happens, Sister, but I meet with no body but myself that's *always* in the right.

Franklin's self-deprecation and humor are meant, of course, to prod his fellow delegates into relaxing their attachment to their own opinions. The Constitution surely has faults, he tells the assembly, but it is also astonishingly good, and it isn't likely that some later convention will produce a better one: "For when you assemble a Number of Men to have the Advantage of their joint Wisdom, you inevitably assemble with those Men all their Prejudices, their Passions, their Errors of Opinion, their local Interests, and their selfish Views."

If the negatives in this argument are "local" and "selfish" errors, the positive is the kind of truth supposedly offered by empirical science, something neither local nor personal. And though the document in question is political rather than scientific, Franklin is borrowing on the authority of science to suggest a path by which the Convention might rise above its potential factions. In the key turn of the speech, he declares: "I consent . . . to this Constitution . . . The Opinions I have had of its Errors, I sacrifice to the Public Good." Thus does he perform for others the requisite ritual by which a group of opinionated private citizens might be converted into the founders of a republic.

I began this chapter saying that we would be looking at how Franklin conceived of himself as a scientist and inventor; now the focus has widened to include his self-presentation in politics. In all cases, the implication has been that self-negation is somehow central: in seeking to serve nature's truths and the public good, Franklin first tries to remove his own "Errors of Opinion," "local Interests," and "selfish Views."

I think that's right, but only partially so. It misses Franklin's complexity, a key to which may be found if we back up and look again at the part of his Convention speech where he jokes about conflicting opinions. The passage is representative of a strand of humor everywhere present in Franklin's writings and it is in his humor, I think, that we will find Franklin's true relationship to his own creations, be they political achievements, scientific theories, or useful inventions.

"I'M NOBODY!"

In the spring of 1784, while living in Paris, Franklin proposed that the French adopt what's now called "daylight saving time" so as to economize on candles and lamp oil. In a satiric letter to the *Journal of Paris*, he recounted how he had spent an evening during which "the new lamp of Messrs. Quinquet and Lange was introduced," followed by a discussion of "whether the oil it consumed was not in proportion to the light it afforded" and the general problem of "the expence of lighting our apartments." Franklin went home to bed at three in the morning, his head "full of the subject," only to be awakened by "an accidental sudden noise" a few hours later. To his great surprise, he found that his room was filled with light; at first he imagined that a number of Quinquet and Lange lamps had been lit, but soon realized that the sun had simply risen and begun to shine.

The simultaneity of the sun shining as soon as it rises Franklin presents as a great discovery:

> Your readers, who with me have never seen any signs of sun-shine before noon . . . , will be as much astonished as I was, when they hear of his rising so early; and especially when I assure them that he gives light as soon as he rises; I am convinced of this. I am certain of my fact. One cannot be more certain of any fact. I saw it with my own eyes. And having repeated this observation the three following mornings, I found always precisely the same result.

Struck by the way the French, lacking empirical evidence of sunrise, sleep until noon and then stay up late worrying about lamplight, Franklin goes on to offer a detailed accounting of how much might be saved each summer simply by shifting the hours of sleep (the answer being 64 million pounds of "wax and tallow"). The utility of the time shift proven, Franklin closes with a remark on "antients and moderns," saying:

> I know there are little envious minds who will . . . say that my invention was known to the antients . . . I will not dispute with these people that the antients might know the sun would rise at

certain hours . . . ; but it does not follow from thence that they
knew he gave light as soon as he rose. This is what I claim as my
discovery. If the antients knew it, it must have been long since
forgotten, for it certainly was unknown to the moderns.

Franklin is teasing the French in terms of the century-old *que-
relle des Anciens et des Modernes*, a debate that had been carried
on mostly in London and Paris about each age's accomplishments
in science, religion, and the arts. Was it possible for a modern poet
to equal an ancient like Homer? Were Aristotle's rules the last
word in drama? Were classic languages sweeter and more elevated
than vernacular French or English? As for knowledge about the
natural world, Sir Francis Bacon in London and René Descartes in
Paris had assaulted the ancients with a new empirical method of
truth-seeking.

The ancients/moderns quarrel was about many things, not
least of which was the tension between progress and tradition, or
between individual innovation and inherited knowledge. As we've
seen, one common way of figuring that tension is found in the
aphorism first offered by the twelfth-century Christian Platonist
Bernard of Chartres: "In comparison with the ancients, we stand
like dwarfs on the shoulders of giants." The aphorism is of course
ambiguous as to the rank described: are the ancients mere foot-
stools for elevated moderns, or are moderns the shrunken children of earlier, more large-limbed generations?

It is in fact the ambiguity I want to mark, and the humor arising from it. I am aware that the humor may not be immediately
apparent, so let me highlight it by way of a few more obvious jokes,
beginning with an old Hasidic story:

A rabbi one day, passing by the ark in the synagogue, falls into
a frenzy of religious passion and drops on his knees, beating his
breast and crying, "Lord, I'm nobody! I'm nobody!" The synagogue's cantor, impressed by this example of spiritual humility,

joins the rabbi on his knees and also prays in a loud voice: "I'm nobody! I'm nobody!" The janitor, watching from the corner, cannot restrain himself either. He joins the other two on his knees: "I'm nobody! I'm nobody!"

Whereupon the rabbi nudges the cantor and whispers: "Look who thinks he's nobody!"

The same humor animates a quip that Winston Churchill once made about a member of his cabinet: "What has he done that he is so modest about it?"

With these in mind, note the exemplary deftness with which Sir Isaac Newton managed the boundary between pride and humility in that famous letter to Hooke that I touched on in an earlier chapter: "If I have seen further it is by standing on the shoulders of Giants." The sentence has a neatly compact doubleness, humble enough to acknowledge the giants, proud enough to claim greater sight, and proud enough as well to evict the dwarf who'd been a tenant in that commonplace for four hundred years.

Pride would seem to be the precondition of humility; you can't be a nobody until you're a somebody. Like the rabbi and the cantor, like Churchill's friend, Newton knows he's a somebody and so he can afford the modesty of his letter to Hooke. His version of the aphorism is not an overt joke, of course, but it embodies the wit of preserved ambiguity.

That wit I take to be the key to understanding the tone of much of Franklin's writing, a tone that Herman Melville once named "philosophical levity." We see that tone in his joking at the Constitutional Convention or in his teasing of the French over their advances in lighting; we see it, that is, in his constant play with the problem of humility and pride, the soul's version of community and individualism, ancients and moderns. In the *Autobiography*, describing his attempts to develop an art of virtue, Franklin names pride as the "natural Passion" hardest to subdue, and ends by saying: "You will see it perhaps often in this History.

For even if I could conceive that I had completely overcome it, I should probably be proud of my Humility."* The book is full of the same joke, as when Franklin says, "I scarce ever heard . . . the introductory Words, *Without Vanity I may say*, etc. but some vain thing immediately follow'd," and then begins the very next paragraph by saying, "I desire with all Humility to acknowledge . . ."

To my way of thinking, this sort of joking is also hidden in much of the ground we have already covered. In the last chapter, I described, for example, the way that Franklin absents himself from his own publication of the invention of the lightning rod. He never names himself as inventor nor does he sign the announcement. And yet he opens by saying, "It has pleased God in his Goodness to Mankind, at length to discover to them the Means of securing their Habitations . . . from Mischief by Thunder and Lightning." There's a touch of that proud rabbi here, the somebody who's free to be a nobody. God may have revealed the secret of lightning to "Mankind," but he chose to do so through his prophet in Philadelphia. "What has he done that he is so modest about it?"

It seems to be a difficult task for the grand, to share their work with the world and at the same time avoid the pride that grandeur brings. Witness Jonas Salk: asked if he was going to patent the polio vaccine, he famously replied that he would not, saying, "Who owns my polio vaccine? The people! Could you patent the sun?" There's a nice parallel here to Franklin: he declined to patent his Pennsylvania fireplace, but his design for the front plate of that stove displayed an image of the sun with the motto ALTER IDEM ("another one"). Both cases display an exemplary self-sacrifice even as they suggest that the creations involved are of the sort usually reserved for the book of Genesis.

---

*As a boy, Franklin read John Checkley's *Choice Dialogues*, which contains this observation: "There is none so *proud* as the *proud-humble man*, who is *proud* of his *Humility*!" Many are the shoulders on which Franklin stood.

In any event, the struggle between, or rather the play of, pride and humility followed Franklin all his days. One gathers that he was an exceedingly proud man, as well he might have been considering his accomplishments, but that he also believed deeply that pride was a vice and humility a virtue or, to put it another way, he also knew that his accomplishments were never his alone, that all pretensions to being self-made hide the reciprocal truth, that we have unpayable debts to the world around us, to our community, to our forebears, to the ancients, to nature, to the gods. When I earlier spoke of a "preserved ambiguity," I meant to indicate a way of speaking that declines to choose between ancients and moderns, tradition and progress, community and individualism, humility and pride. What is preserved is the useful truth that trying to eradicate the supposed darker side of these pairings only makes it grow stronger in secret.

Franklin's philosophical levity is a sign of respect for that truth. He never quite stifles his pride; it's always there, and he lets it speak. But it is a regular reflex in his work to mark it when it appears, and to perform beside it some ritual of humility. I don't mean "ritual" to imply an empty gesture, either; the wholly proud will either present their pride and never notice it, or pretend to a humility they do not in fact have ("I'm nobody!"). Feeling both pride and humility, Franklin declines to choose. He has it both ways, thus, which seems to me more wisdom than duplicity, better than pretending to be a nobody when in fact he's a somebody and better than pretending to be self-made when in fact his debts are legion.

A single example of Franklin entertaining his scientific pride will lead us into the wider issue of how selfhood might be put in play in a civic republic. When Franklin's theory about lightning was confirmed in France in 1752, King Louis XV himself praised the American by name in a message sent to the Royal Society in London. Franklin heard of this a year later in Philadelphia by way of a letter from his friend Peter Collinson. It pleased him deeply and in a letter to another friend he reproduced a long section of Collinson's letter. He introduces the news of royal praise, however, thus:

> The Tatler tells us of a Girl who was observ'd to grow suddenly proud, and none could guess the Reason, till it came to be known that she had got on a pair of new Silk Garters. Lest you should be puzzel'd to guess the Cause when you observe any thing of the kind in me, I think I will not hide my new Garters under my Petticoats, but take the Freedom to show them to you, in a Paragraph of our Friend Collinson's last Letter viz.—But I ought to mortify, and not indulge, this Vanity; I will not transcribe the Paragraph.—Yet I cannot forbear.

Truly he cannot, and the praising paragraph follows, whereupon Franklin returns to his framing theme, humility; Collinson had called the news a feather in Franklin's cap, and Franklin ends by saying:

> On reconsidering this Paragraph, I fear I have not so much Reason to be proud as the Girl had; for a Feather in the Cap is not so useful a Thing, or so serviceable to the Wearer, as a Pair of good Silk Garters. The Pride of Man is very differently gratify'd.

Surely it is, as we shall see. In a civic republic, the proud man cannot become a somebody through his own efforts; others must do it for him.

SPECULATIVE STATESMEN AND THE COMMON HIVE

Franklin's declaration at the Constitutional Convention that he would sacrifice his own opinions in favor of the common good may seem unusual to modern ears, but it would have been familiar to his fellow delegates. In the eighteenth century, the willingness to erase the personal in favor of the public was an ideal regularly expressed in political debate. It was part of the rhetoric by which private citizens made themselves into public citizens; it was, in fact, part of the rhetoric by which something new under the sun, "the public," came into being, and with it what we call in retrospect "the public sphere."

It is worth trying to understand the origins of this way of speaking because, in regard to the ownership of ideas, it will return us by another path to the way in which the founders resolved the tension between commonwealth and monopoly. Looking at Franklin's life is useful in this regard, as it was exactly synchronous with the rise of the public sphere in British North America. At the end of that life lies what we've just seen: Franklin's participation in the convention that produced a written Constitution, a document that was ratified only after much pamphleteering and public debate. At the beginning of that life, eighty years earlier, nothing of the sort could have happened.

In 1706, when Franklin was born, Boston's first-ever newspaper was only two years old and, as I mentioned earlier, it bore the obligatory notice of a state-controlled press, "Published by Authority." By the time Franklin was fifteen, there were three newspapers in Boston and one of these, the *New-England Courant*, published by his brother James, was the first to appear *not* by authority. It was in his brother's shop that Franklin learned the printer's craft; it is no exaggeration to say that there he literally helped to hand-set the emerging public sphere in Boston.

He also literally helped to import its norms from their breeding ground in London. Before he began working in the print shop, he had used a volume of Addison and Steele's London journal, *The Spectator*, as a model for self-expression in prose. "I took some of the Papers," he writes in the *Autobiography*, "and making short Hints of the Sentiment in each Sentence, laid them by a few Days, and then without looking at the Book, tried to complete the Papers again, by expressing each hinted Sentiment at length and as fully as it had been express'd before."

As for that London journal itself, in its first issue Joseph Addison had created its eponymous character, the Spectator, an early prototype of the kind of citizen who erases the private in favor of the public. Addison had opened the initial issue by having this fictive gentleman offer to tell the readers all about himself: "I have observed," he writes,

> that a Reader seldom peruses a Book with Pleasure 'till he knows whether the Writer of it be a black or a fair Man, of a mild or cholerick Disposition, Married or a Batchelor, with other Particulars of the like nature, that conduce very much to the right Understanding of an Author.

Thus he promises "to open the Work with my own History" and begins in a conventional manner. "I was born to a small Hereditary Estate . . ." The more he tells us, however, the less we seem to know. He describes himself as remarkably unforthcoming:

> I had not been long at the University, before I distinguished myself by a most profound Silence: For, during the Space of eight Years . . . , I scarce uttered the Quantity of an hundred Words; and indeed do not remember that I ever spoke three Sentences together in my whole Life.

He declines to reveal his name, his age, or his place of lodging. He will tell us nothing of his dress or his complexion. He lives, he says, "rather as a Spectator of Mankind, than as one of the Species," and

> I have been taken for a Merchant upon the Exchange for above these ten Years, and sometimes pass for a Jew in the Assembly of

Stock-Jobbers at Jonathans. In short, where-ever I see a Cluster of People, I always mix with them, tho I never open my Lips but in my own Club.

He is the "Silent Man," the "Speculative Statesman," whose particularity has been sacrificed to ubiquity. An everybody in consequence of his being a nobody, he has no substance except for the substance of print. "I have neither Time nor Inclination to communicate the Fulness of my Heart in Speech," he writes, and so resolves instead "to Print my self out, if possible, before I Die."

There will be more to say about "spectatorship," but before getting to that let us return to the image of young Franklin acquiring a prose style by imitating essays such as these. As is well known, when he was sixteen and apprenticed in the print shop, he began to submit anonymous essays to his brother's newspaper. Signed "Silence Dogood," the first of these missives opens with a direct lift from Addison:

> Since it is observed, that the Generality of People, now a days, are unwilling either to commend or dispraise what they read, until they are in some measure informed who or what the Author of it is, whether he be poor or rich, old or young, a Schollar or a Leather Apron Man, &c. and give their Opinion of the Performance, according to the Knowledge which they have of the Author's Circumstances, it may not be amiss to begin with a short Account of my past Life and present Condition.

In what follows, the reader learns that Silence Dogood is a woman and an orphan but not much else, for she is reluctant to abuse her readers "with a tedious Recital of all the frivolous Accidents of my Life." The exception, the one "accident of life" that we do learn, is that Silence has "a more than ordinary Delight in reading ingenious Books," that books make "the best of Company," and that her favorite retreat has been a minister's library.

Franklin alters Addison, of course (putting a skirt on Silence is a nice touch), but Addison's model animates the piece, from the promise of particulars offered and then withdrawn to the way the "person" we get to know is Silence, the silence of print.

The Spectator and other such publications out of London offered Franklin more than a prose style; they gave him as well a model of republican citizenship. The Dogood letters show the beginnings of that, but witness as well a series of events that took place soon after the first of those letters appeared. James Franklin's newspaper had been at odds with colonial authorities ever since it began in 1721; matters came to a head the following summer, when the authorities took offense at the publication of a hoax having to do with pirate ships supposedly sighted off the coast. The elder Franklin was arrested and spent a month in jail. While he was incarcerated, young Benjamin took over the newspaper and published his eighth Dogood letter, this one reprinting (in quotation marks but without attribution) one of the radical Whig "Cato's Letters" that had recently appeared in London.

The letter in question was a defense of the citizen's right to know and speak freely about the operations of government. It set such freedom in opposition to the British royal habit of forbidding publication of the proceedings of Parliament (the assumption being, in the words of a 1620 proclamation, that matters of state were "not themes or subjects fit for vulgar persons or common meetings"). Such press control, the letter declared, "is only the Prerogative and Felicity of Tyranny." Free nations assume a different standard: "As it is the . . . Business of the People . . . to see whether they be well or ill transacted, so it . . . ought to be the Ambition of all honest Magistrates to have their Deeds openly examined, and publickly scann'd."

To see, to examine, to scan: these are the active verbs in Franklin's appropriated text and the actor to whom they belong is kin to Addison's "Speculative Statesman." The Spectator who "prints himself out" has a civic role to play: he watches and reports on those in power—as soon, that is, as power has agreed to open itself to scrutiny. Transparent government and the citizen spectator: these are the fraternal twins of the early public sphere, one mark of their birth being the simple innovation of reversing the tradition of keeping legislative proceedings hidden from the public.

That tradition of secrecy was not only British; it had been reproduced in the Colonies, where the assemblies had long enforced their own code of obscurity and silence. In Maryland in 1693, for example, we find a printer thrown in jail for publishing the proceedings of the legislature. By the time young Franklin printed his Dogood letter on open government, however, such press control was under assault and slowly dropping away on both continents. In the Maryland case, by 1725 the assembly itself decided to print its proceedings, explaining that doing so would allow citizens the "Opportunity of Judging . . . their Representatives," "judging" being shorthand for the range of civic actions (publishing, debating, voting, etc.) available to citizens once transparency has made active spectatorship a possibility.

It may be worth pausing here to point out the contrast between this active spectatorship and the passive form of feudal times. Feudal rulers made their power evident by display, by pomp. As Jürgen Habermas has argued, the public realm then consisted of show, not debate; publicity—in the old sense of "being open to public observation"—involved no real politics but rather the staging of authority, the performance of majesty by way of dress, courtly behavior, special ways of speaking, and so forth. In the French court at Versailles, even the royal bedroom was a stage, the bed raised on a platform for the ceremonial enacting of getting up in the morning and going to bed at night, the *lever* and the *coucher*.

As for our own age, Habermas speaks of "a refeudalization of the public sphere," what with the fusion of news and advertising, the corporate ownership of media, the return of government secrecy, the intrusion of celebrity into politics, and the conversion of citizens into consumers. Peter Drahos and John Braithwaite have made a similar argument in their 2002 book, *Information Feudalism*, which tells of the appalling lack of transparency that allowed corporations and the developed nations to promulgate the TRIPS accord that now governs all international "intellectual property" disputes. (TRIPS stands for Trade-Related Aspects of Intellectual Property Rights.)

To come back to the eighteenth century, however, and to the idea that transparency in government is linked to spectatorship, we've seen that Franklin's acquaintance with that mode can be traced all the way back to his days as a leather-apron boy in Boston. The Dogood letters, his first-ever published prose, were modeled on a spectator who was not only a civic actor but one whose public presence was of a piece with his self-erasure. The anonymity of those letters is always explained as a ploy to fool Franklin's brother, and it was surely that, but his mentor Addison had no such motive when he published the *Spectator* essays anonymously, and if Franklin follows suit, we may say there are plausibly other reasons that he did not advertise his name.

Whatever the case in that first instance, the fact is that a self-effacing use of pseudonyms and anonymity became a lifelong practice for Franklin. The *Autobiography* gives many examples. Of his efforts to establish a public library, Franklin writes: "I . . . put my self as much as I could out of sight, and stated it as a Scheme of a *Number of Friends*, who had requested me to go about and propose it to such as they thought Lovers of Reading." Of a 1749 pamphlet proposing an academy to educate youth, he explains: "In the Introduction to these Proposals, I stated their Publication not as an Act of mine, but of some *publick-spirited Gentlemen*."

This mode was not Franklin's alone; it belonged to the age. A 1729 Maryland debate over tobacco policies offers a typical case. The debate was carried on by anonymous pamphleteers, one of whom made the norms of publication explicit, saying that those who care for the good of their country have a duty to publish and that in doing so no one should allow "any private Views or Ends (inconsistent with the common Good) to bias or influence him." Or consider these lines from a later, unsigned, but more famous pamphlet:

> In the following sheets, the author hath studiously avoided every thing which is personal . . .
>
> Who the Author of this Production is, is wholly unnecessary to the Public, as the Object for Attention is the *Doctrine itself*, not the *Man*. Yet it may not be unnecessary to say, That he is unconnected with any Party, and under no sort of Influence public or private, but the influence of reason and principle.

The lines are from Tom Paine's *Common Sense*, published January 1776 in Philadelphia. The demand that Paine makes of himself at the start—to avoid "every thing which is personal"—he soon extends to his reader, asking "that he will divest himself of prejudice and prepossession," and "that he will put *on*, or rather that he will not put *off*, the true character of a man, and generously enlarge his views beyond the present day."

Both reader and writer must lay aside present circumstance, prejudice, party, and so on, and make themselves civic rather than private persons. They are made so by acting so, by which I mean to say that the claimed protocols of publication are cultural norms for a civic republic: its citizens appear if these norms are followed and disappear if they aren't. Said conversely, where this sort of self-erasing speech has no standing, where for example all writers claim their work as their own, take pride in its individual voice, and guard it against appropriation, it will be more difficult to create a lively public sphere and to call its occupants into collective being as a "people."

A model of how "the good" is to be found lies behind these ways of speaking, one that borrows on the developing scientific norm for how to find "the true." In both cases the assumption is that individuals alone are unlikely to have access to either the good or the true. Each man and woman will always have a "partial view"— partial in the double sense of incomplete and biased. No one, no matter how self-made, self-taught, or self-reliant, can escape this partiality. Thus the call to sacrifice private opinion, to studiously avoid the personal, to focus on "the *Doctrine* . . . , not the *Man*" in favor of something less partial, more common. The 1729 Maryland pamphlet cited earlier offers an analogy to describe the move from partial to common: "The Bee gathers honey from all sorts of Flowers to encrease the common Stock, and our Assembly is the common Hive into which every Man's Thoughts and Sentiments ought to be carried." Be it "our assembly" or be it more broadly "the public," the point is that the good appears not by proclamation but by conversation. In this new world of self-abnegating postures, appeals to individual authority ("I'm Lord So-and-So, and my family for generations has . . .") will weaken an argument rather than bolster it. Better to be one of the nobodies, one of the spectators; better to take one's place in the Republic of Letters, an impersonal commons of print where the good can arise without a do-gooder.

I AM OTHER BIRDS

But here I feel myself being drawn into the idealism of the age and forgetting not only the salt of Franklin's humor but also the contingencies of history, as if the founding of the nation occurred somewhere outside of time. As the joke about the rabbi makes clear, self-abnegation is a privilege of the self-important; in politics it is the privilege of those with civic presence, and in 1787, that would mean almost exclusively white, propertied men. As if to point this out, many of the authors of eighteenth-century anonymous pamphlets don't begin their self-erasure until they've given a hint about their social status. The title often does the trick, as with this pamphlet from 1727: *A Letter from a Freeholder, to a Member of the Lower House of Assembly.* We never get to know who the freeholder is, but we surely know that he is a freeholder and that presumably means not a black sharecropper, say, or a housewife, or a Penobscot Indian. These others, having no civic self to begin, never get to join the happy republican game of public humility.

In retrospect it should be no surprise, then, that as the next century unfolded, abolitionists, feminists, and others made it clear that the Constitution was no text "without a thinker"; containing a clause dealing with fugitive slaves, for example, it was quite adequately marked by the partial views of those who wrote it. As for anonymity in public discourse, an African-American patriot like Frederick Douglass makes a good contrast to someone like Tom Paine. Paine, it should be said, was hardly a freeholder in the literal sense; in England he had been a customs officer but lost his job and emigrated with little but a letter of introduction from Franklin. In Philadelphia he was a man of property only in the sense that white men always had gratuitous "rights of action" in the world. Beyond that, his sense of political agency, the confidence with which he wrote, derived from his taking to heart and deploying the rhetoric of republican governance. He was a freeholder not in land but in the Republic of Letters, where he had large holdings inherited from the ancients and from the European Enlightenment.

Frederick Douglass, on the other hand, when he escaped from slavery in the 1840s, could claim no such rights of action and no such estate. In Baltimore he had been obliged to steal literacy and literacy's fruits, especially the Enlightenment arguments about liberty and servitude. In the North, once he began to have a voice of his own in print, he was hardly a self-effacer. He almost always included his name in the titles of his books; in the late 1840s, he began to publish his own newspaper, and he didn't call it *The Freeholder's Journal* or something like that; he called it *Frederick Douglass' Paper.* Self-erasure is a republican ideal, but civic presence is its prerequisite. There's no virtue in anonymity for those who have no name.

At the nation's founding, the legions of disenfranchised surely outnumbered those with political agency. Should we think of this as a fatal flaw in the early republican ideal? The next century almost answered in the affirmative, the Union breaking into civil war partly over some of the very "errors" that Franklin had urged his fellow delegates to ignore. But to speak of "early" and "next" is to indicate that historical contingencies are themselves set in history; the Constitution, after all, was designed to be amended and has been. Lightning may be the same in Paris and Philadelphia, in 1753 and 1953, but the substance of civic virtue has been open to revision by each succeeding generation.

To speak of how such virtue was made in the eighteenth century, we shall have to return to Franklin's humor, and enter the story once again on terms that he might recognize. I earlier spoke of Franklin's wit as arising from a preserved ambiguity, his sense that human beings are inexorably doubled, always individual and always social. Himself both a striding egotist and a public servant ("God gave me the lightning rod, and I give it to you"), he jokes at the Convention about those who cleave to their opinions, then offers to sacrifice his own to the public good, but that does not mean that the good, should it appear, won't bear traces of his name. We have the text of his speech, after all. Among the pleasures of philosophical levity was the way it let the philosopher eat his pride and have it, too. Consider what follows the remarks cited earlier about Franklin's putting himself "out of sight" when he proposed the public library. After recommending that his readers try the method themselves, Franklin comments:

> The present little Sacrifice of your Vanity will afterwards be amply repaid. If it remains a while uncertain to whom the Merit belongs, some one more vain than yourself will be encourag'd to claim it, and then even Envy will be dispos'd to do you Justice,

by plucking those assum'd Feathers, and restoring them to their right Owner.

Here in capsule is a plot outline for the creation of public virtue in a fallen world. It has three acts: the protagonist must begin as a somebody; then he makes himself a nobody; then he becomes a somebody again, although in the last instance he cannot act on his own behalf, but must let others do the work for him.

Franklin's avian metaphor nicely indicates how the process works, perhaps more accurately than he could have known. Among those who currently study actual birds, the house sparrow has become a stock species for investigating the fate of birds with falsely "assum'd Feathers." Male sparrows indicate their status as aggressors for food and nesting sites by the size of a black patch on their throats. Other sparrows, however, regularly test the truth or falsity of the advertisement by picking fights, and any sparrow with false feathers soon finds himself in trouble. No sparrow gets to create his own reputation merely by assuming more dark feathers; each can make a claim in that line, but it is the sparrow community that determines if the claim is a social truth or not. Similarly, civic virtue in the Republic of Letters is a quality bestowed by the community, not created by the individual citizen. There is no such thing as self-made virtue. In this three-act play, you first need sufficient agency to propose a library; then you attribute the plan to "a Number of Friends"; then, if merit arises from the work, others attach it to your name. They may call it the Franklin Library, but it is the public that signs your name, not you.

Note that Franklin's description of the process by which "Sacrifice of . . . vanity" might "afterwards be . . . repaid" hardly idealizes the human character; the harnessed forces he mentions are vanity and envy. Contrast that social psychology with the way John Adams imagined the creation of public virtue. A 1776 letter to Mercy Warren contains a typical assertion: "Every man must seriously set himself to root out his Passions, Prejudices and

Attachments, and to get the better of his private Interest." To this model of human development, Franklin might have said, "Good luck." He himself had tried to "root out" vanity and had failed, leading him to conclude, I think, that if others were like him, then the public good would not be found out simply by "purity of heart and greatness of soul" (Adams again). Some middle road was needed, one that directed self-interest rather than one that tried to transcend it.

What was needed, in short, were systems of public virtue more than citizens of public virtue. Franklin's idea that "Envy will be dispos'd to do . . . Justice" points in this direction, though it's not yet a real system, relying as it does on gossip and happenstance. Better to create actual laws or norms or structures of governance by which private interests might be channeled toward the public good. Under one view at least, such was the achievement of the U.S. Constitution. As one of Virginia's early senators, John Taylor, wrote long after the Constitution was framed, the United States had demonstrated that "the principles of a society may be virtuous, though the individuals composing it are vicious." For Taylor, the virtue of republican government resided not in the individual players but in the rules of the game, in the design of the thing. "The interest of vice" cannot be eradicated, he wrote, but it can be "enlisted on the side of virtue." Even "an avaricious society can form a government able to defend itself against the avarice of its members."

National governance is a complicated matter, however, and rather than try to illustrate Taylor's point in any detail, let us here ask more simply if this idea—that "the principles of a society may be virtuous"—can be applied to creative communities. When it comes to "science and the useful arts," are there structures by which individuals will end up contributing to the commonwealth without being required to root out self-interest along the way? Can the wit of preserved ambiguity be joined to the comedy of the commons?

Yes, of course, the early patent and copyright systems being prime models, as we've seen. If virtue arises from enriching the cultural commons, then those systems embodied virtuous principles: both of them respect and gratify self-interest in exchange for two things—in the near term, the work must be revealed to the public, and in the long term it must pass fully into the public domain.

But even this reward structure does not really translate the pattern implicit in Franklin's remark about how present sacrifice might afterward be repaid. In Franklin's model, public recognition appears at the end of the story, not private reward at the beginning. For principles that are virtuous in that mold, one need look not to patent or copyright law but to institutions like those governing status and reward in the academy. In U.S. higher education, at least, professional advancement is typically keyed to the quality of one's scholarship, teaching, and service to the institution. Any ego who wishes to move forward must render service to others in order to do so; he or she must contribute to knowledge, educate the young, and attend to the community. The quality of work in each of these spheres, moreover, is judged by the community, by other birds. Only at the end of that process—after all the letters have been written by colleagues and students, after the tenure and promotion committee has met, after the dean of faculty has read the file, and so forth—only then can professional advancement, both in rank and in salary, come. As in Franklin's model, if merit belongs to the work, the community assigns it, not the scholar.

There are two things to note about this and other such norms-based reputation systems. First of all, they contain incentives. The claim is often made that without the near-term rewards of monopoly privilege, knowledge would not advance. This assumes a strikingly narrow notion of what motivates people to do creative work. Sometimes we work merely for gain, to be sure, but we also work out of simple curiosity (think of Franklin fascinated by electricity), or for the fun of it, or for the aesthetic pleasure of finding an elegant solution, or to while away the idle hours, or out of gratitude, spite, or patriotic zeal. In reputation systems, we may work for any of these and for status as well, or for the delayed gains that status can bring.

In fact, once we have a list of possible driving forces before us, we can also say that any incentive system that emphasizes only present financial reward may have the side effect of crowding out these others. This is one of the insidious consequences of the recent push to have academic researchers patent their discoveries; it undermines the presumption of a knowledge commons and cheapens the traditional, carefully designed deferred rewards that allow reputation systems to put egotism in the service of altruism.

The second thing to say about such "systems of virtue" is that the public benefits they produce do not arise from the workings of any invisible hand. These are not systems by which the summed results of blind self-interest magically produce the good; these are systems in which the good is pronounced ahead of time, and self-interest directed toward it. It is a good, for example, that useful inventions be published rather than kept as trade secrets; it is a good that we have a public domain; it matters that the young get educated, and that scholars contribute to the commons upon which all work depends in the first place.

Such are typical positive liberties in the Republic of Letters. Positive liberty, wrote Isaiah Berlin, means "not freedom from, but freedom to—to lead one prescribed form of life." Negative liberty—freedom from coercion—has little to say about how citizens should live; positive liberty is less reticent. If the progress of science requires "liberty to communicate," then the term of monopoly privilege must always be limited; if scientific truth belongs to communities, not to individuals, then research is better motivated by reputation systems than by private reward; if the creation of a commonwealth requires detachment from opinion, then virtue must be accorded to those willing to stand down from partial views. In each of these, liberty itself demands that there be certain conventions widely valued. For those who care about these, the goal of any debate about liberty is to render a "form of life" possible. In the cases at hand, the goal is to create *freedom to*: the freedom to be co-creator of the cultural commons and, if others feel the merit is deserved, the freedom to be somebody in a commonwealth of art and ideas.

7

THE COMMON SELF

The argument: Cultural properties belong largely in
the commons so as to enable certain kinds of collective
being—civic, creative, and spiritual—
valuable in their own right.

·

The mind / Is so hospitable, taking in everything / Like boarders . . .
—JOHN ASHBERY

The *polis* was for the Greeks, as the *res publica* was
for the Romans, first of all their guarantee against
the futility of individual life.
—HANNAH ARENDT

"DIGNITY"

The Declaration of Independence famously names "Life, Liberty
and the pursuit of Happiness" as being among the "unalienable
Rights" bestowed upon human beings by their Creator. There are
some things, the Declaration asserts, that cannot be taken from
us, and that we ourselves should not surrender if we are to be true
to ourselves. Such things are foundational, essential, substantive.
They make us who we are; they give us our identity.

Nature itself gives rise to some inalienable things, and culture
to others. No human being can do without air and water; these at
least belong on a list of the natural inalienables, required by our

being in so obvious a way that no previous generation would have thought it necessary even to make the list, though some of us now must. In an age when potable water commands a price and real estate values fluctuate with the smog, declarations will appear asserting inalienable rights to clean water, clean air.

The Declaration of Independence was not concerned with natural inalienabilities, but with spiritual or cultural ones, ones derived from God or from consensus. What belongs on that list is open to debate. British critics of the Declaration happily pointed out that states throughout history have deprived their citizens of life, liberty, and happiness, despite what the colonists thought. But the point of departure for the colonists was not empirical. The Declaration and other foundational documents are idealist expressions; they name their rights as "unalienable" to indicate what their authors mean to be, ideally. We announce our sense of ourselves by saying what we cannot be parted from and still be ourselves. Throughout I have been using the right to vote as an example of the link between identity ("a citizen" in this case) and inalienability. Depending on how a nation imagines itself, there will be other such "civic inalienabilities": the right to trial by jury, the right to bear arms, the right of free speech and assembly, and so on.

A pamphlet that Noah Webster published in 1787 in defense of the proposed federal Constitution gives a further example of this link between identity and inalienability, only it does so by inverting the proposition I've been making. At one point in his "Examination" of the Constitution, Webster argues that traditional theorists of government were wrong to suppose that a republic could be founded on the virtue of its citizens. "The whole basis of natural freedom," Webster writes, is an "equal distribution of landed property"; the old theories "will ever be erroneous," therefore, until every use of the word "virtue" is replaced by the phrase "lands in fee simple."

In the background for Webster, as for others at the time, lay the European aristocracy's ability to hold power over time by holding

land over time. Thus for Webster "the very *soul of a republic*" was to
be found in "an equality of property, with a necessity of alienation,
constantly operating to destroy combinations of powerful families."
Rather than preserve something through inalienability, Webster
here wishes to wipe something out ("powerful families") and to
that end demands "a necessity of alienation" for the otherwise enduring properties by which such families know themselves.

The inalienability Webster would do away with was typically
ensured in England through *entail*, the legal device by which an
estate could be bestowed on a particular line of descendants, none
of whom would ever be free to give or sell it to someone else. Put
positively, the family that owns entailed real estate has inalienable
possessions and thus a good chance of preserving its place and
name generation after generation. Put negatively, as Webster does,
entail perpetuates feudal power and is thus "dangerous to liberty
and republican government." The new nation ought therefore to
make "irrevocable laws . . . destroying and barring entailments."
It ought to "leave real estates to revolve from hand to hand, as
time and accident may direct" so that "no family influence can be
acquired and established for a series of generations."

Fair enough, but there is a paradox in Webster's placing "a necessity of alienation" at the root of the new government. As we've
seen, in its classical root the word "republic" points toward a class
of properties no citizen ever owned in fee simple—not simply the
tangibles of public life (roads, waterways, harbors, bridges) but especially the intangibles of self-governance, the civic inalienabilities of the Declaration and the Bill of Rights. The soul of a republic
must thus be somewhat more layered than Webster at first allows;
it must have in it a combination of properties, some of which can
be bought and sold and some of which can't.

To read this point back into my earlier image of the Republican
Two-Step: once citizens have been freed from "powerful families,"
we are still left to wonder, freed to what end? And if the answer
points toward the very things that Webster's pamphlet finds worth

defending in the Constitution—from self-governance to "the progress of science"—then the private selves allowed by alienation will need to become public selves as well, inheritors of the inalienables of civic life. Lands held "in fee simple" are not sufficient to create a republic, especially not a Republic of Letters. For that we also need a commonwealth of knowledge and citizens whose public virtues will not regularly be overwritten by everyone else's private freedoms. Figuratively, we need the kind of allodial holdings by which freeholders can mature into civic republicans.

In Webster's ideal republic, then, while citizens do not necessarily have inalienable rights to landed property, on the more abstract level of cultural property the opposite would have to be the case. Webster says so himself: his "Examination" of the Constitution lists among the "auxiliary supports" of democratic freedom "the information of the people," especially their access to education and knowledge. The point echoes the stock opinions of Jefferson, Madison, Adams, and Franklin, of course, whose support for open discourse occasioned their regular caution in regard to monopoly and their warnings against perpetuities. To restate at the cultural level Webster's point about land, then, and to join it to his assumption that freedom depends on access to knowledge, we might say that families (and corporations) with exclusive rights to cultural property must eventually face "a necessity of alienation," lest their holdings turn into a new form of entailed estate, "dangerous to liberty and republican government." Only then, only when we have refrained from entailing expression, can the public domain arise, that realm in which public citizens can know themselves as such by their inalienable right to "information."

To say this another way, it is difficult to know who you are, to establish and hold on to identity, if all your properties are fungible. Things are said to be fungible when any member of a class can substitute for any other. Grain and coin are the traditional examples: if I buy a bushel of wheat, I do not care about the particular grains in the bushel, for I am buying a generic thing. And if I pay with dollar bills, the seller does not care about the particular bills; all dollars are equivalent.

Market economies potentially turn all alienable goods into fungibles, cash being a sort of universal solvent, the mother of all fungibles that allows for endless substitution. Once all things can be converted into cash, a class of goods arises whose essential trait is their market price. All goods then become commensurable, each and every thing available as a substitute for each and every other. You can sell your chickens to buy some cloth, sell the cloth to buy some wheat, sell the wheat to buy some shoes, and sell your shoes to buy some eggs. Every market-alienable thing is fluid in regard to every other and consequently none is of much use in establishing identity—except, it should be said, the set of in-fact fluid identities that arise from fungibility itself (merchant, speculator, wanderer, consumer . . .).

Less fluid identities require some limit, some edge, some place where substitution and conversion are resisted. As long as the law permitted entail, feudal families were not subject to what Webster calls "time and accident." Once "Life, Liberty and the pursuit of Happiness" are declared inalienable, "America" can appear. "As a man is said to have a right to his property, he may be equally said to have a property in his rights," James Madison wrote: once a Bill of Rights has been adopted as a catalog of inalienable properties, a democratic citizenry may know itself as such.

We know such things—"America," "a citizen"—by the properties from which they cannot be parted. Alienating those properties changes or harms the identity of their "owners." There are cases in which we welcome such change (as in Webster's attack on feudal land tenure), but in other cases, those in which the harm matters, we resist. Some identities should not be dissolved in the flow of fungibles. Our bodies, our sense of personal integrity, and our immediate families often provide the boundary cases that make this clear. We resist, for example, allowing a market to arise in which the poor sell their kidneys to the rich. We resist the kind of analysis that would judge a case of rape in terms of costs and benefits. *Uncle Tom's Cabin* is a tearjerker because familial roles—mothers, fathers, children—get stripped of meaning by the substitutions of chattel slavery.

Asked once if the United States invaded Iraq to control its oil, Secretary of Defense Donald Rumsfeld dismissed the charge as "utter nonsense." Oil, he said, "is fungible. People that have it will want to sell it, and it doesn't matter who they sell it to." Though one could tease out complexities here, Rumsfeld is more or less right: a barrel of oil is a barrel of oil. His response to a later question asking why twenty thousand American soldiers had to stay three extra months in Iraq was less convincing. "Oh, come on," came the irritated reply. "People are fungible. You can have them here or there."

From kidneys to soldiers, the harm that we sense in each of these cases arises from an injudicious confusion of categories. There are, on the one hand, things constitutive of identity, properties that are essential attributes of the individuals or communities that have them, and on the other hand, there are things accidental to identity, things that can be alienated without meaningful change or injury. Immanuel Kant's way of describing these categories adds the useful term "dignity": "In the kingdom of ends everything has a *price* or a *dignity*. Whatever has a price can be replaced by something else as its *equivalent*; on the other hand, whatever is above all price, and therefore admits of no equivalent, has a dignity."

It is one thing to accept these categories—things with prices and things with dignity; it is another to decide what belongs to each. When it comes to marking where dignity matters, where identity itself demands a limit on alienability, the easier cases are those, as I say, having to do with persons, their bodies, and their immediate families. The harder cases are legion, and debates about them are the work of politics or philosophy. For now the point is that these debates have to do with our sense of who we are or wish to become. Arguments over the commons, cultural or otherwise, are never simply about efficiency and maximizing wealth, therefore, as they sometimes seem to be; they are also about ways of living, the claim being that human dignity itself demands there be limits to the commodification of the many things that the commons movement has yoked together. That movement aspires to a world of commoners with inalienable rights to clean air and fresh water, a world where an essential portion of the commons of nature (from the human genome to the atmosphere) and the commons of culture (from nursery rhymes to medicinal herbs) cannot be enclosed, priced, and entered into the endless flow of commercial substitution.

The citizens of such a world have a kind of freedom distinct from the freedom derived from Webster's "necessity of alienation." It should be acknowledged at the outset that this is a freedom that depends on the constraint of other freedoms. A commons is a stinted thing; it requires limits (such as the limit on alienation in the line of thought I am developing here). If you want a viable democracy, you cannot sell your vote. If you want a lively cultural commons, you can't allow corporate media to enclose the public domain. If you and your neighbors own land over an aquifer, none of you should be allowed to sink a well and sell the water to some thirsty distant metropolis. Each of these is a constraint on some freedoms but at the same time each is the foundation of others: the freedom to live in a democracy, to partake of cultural inheritance, to enjoy a constant flow of potable water. Inalienabilities of this sort will frustrate the formation of private, choosing, subjective selves, but at the same time they make possible the formation of the civic, extended, or common self. They allow a way of being.

ALLOTMENT VERSUS THE COMIC GOOD

Clearly, choices regarding alienation can cut both ways, enabling or disabling particular ways of being. To explore the latter case, especially the ways in which the common self might lose its standing, its presence, its dignity, consider the story of the Dawes Severalty Act, enacted by the United States Congress in 1887. This was exactly a century after the Northwest Ordinance expressed the nation's original high ideals in regard to its native population, that "the utmost good faith shall always be observed toward the Indians," and that "their lands and property shall never be taken from them without their consent." A century of westward expansion followed and, decade after decade, appropriation of land and mineral wealth by settlers moving west drew the nation away from that founding expression of "good faith." By the 1870s, the majority of Indians were confined to western reservations.

In the view of many eastern "philanthropists," including the Severalty Act's prime sponsor, the Republican senator Henry L. Dawes of Massachusetts, life on the reservations made the Indians indolent, uninterested in their own advancement, and unfit for citizenship. Dawes and his fellow reformers thought that the underlying cause was the tradition whereby land was held in common by tribal patents. If only that system could be altered, all else would change. With common ownership, Dawes wrote, "there is no enterprise to make your home any better than that of your neighbors. There is no selfishness, which is at the bottom of civilization." And what does it mean to be civilized? For Dawes it meant to "wear civilized clothes . . . cultivate the ground, live in houses, ride in Studebaker [Conestoga] wagons, send children to school, drink whiskey [and] own property."

To solve the "Indian problem," the Dawes Act began the process of breaking up tribal holdings and giving individual Indians deeds to private plots of land. Land would no longer be owned "in the entirety" by a tribe but "in severalty" by individuals. Thus did the founders' vision of a nation of small freehold farms settle, a century later, over the Indian lands, a civilizing enclosure of a once native commons. (The language of the Dawes Act was, by the way, lifted from the enclosure movement in England, where common land was similarly subject to "allotment" and "severalty.")

In reconfiguring tribal land, the Dawes Act did more than cut the whole into parts; it also made the land itself alienable, turned it into a salable commodity. It should be noted that this alienation differs in several ways from the kind that Webster supported. First, the thing that alienation here erases is not the power of aristocratic families but a tradition of tribal collectivism whose hierarchies were hardly those of feudal Europe. Second is the matter of power. At the founding of the Republic, fee simple landholding was instituted by the citizens themselves; not so with the allotment of Indian lands. As an act of Congress, Dawes operated more like parliamentary enclosure in England: it was imposed from above, the people who actually used the land being given no voice in the matter.

As for the details of allotment under this law, there were initial constraints on the Indians themselves buying and selling land, but in fact not all the land in question went to Indians. One might have assumed that the way to break up common land, if it had to be done, would be to take the total acreage of a reservation, divide it by the number of inhabitants, and give each one an equal share. If there were 100 residents and 160,000 acres, each would get 1,600 acres. The grid of severalty cut more finely than that, however.

The Dawes Act sought to make farmers of the Indians and brought with it a supposed ideal size of farm: each Indian was allotted, at most, a quarter section of land (160 acres). All the remaining land was put up for sale. Using my hypothetical case, after each of the 100 residents got 160 acres, the remaining 144,000 acres would be opened up to homesteaders, or sold to settlers, to the railroads, to cattle ranchers, or (later) to the oil and gas industry. (The proceeds of these sales were to be invested in a trust fund to be used for the "education and civilization" of the Indians; it's a nice touch, as if some sect of True Believers were to seize and sell your home, then claim to demonstrate their goodwill by using the proceeds to send your children to True Believer school.)

Finally, the Dawes Act linked severalty to citizenship. A few years before the act was passed, the Supreme Court had ruled that Native Americans could be denied the right to vote because they were not U.S. citizens, a decision that those in favor of assimilation sought to remedy by adding a citizenship provision to the bill. After the process of allotment had been completed, the act said, "every Indian . . . who has voluntarily taken up . . . his residence separate and apart from any tribe . . . , and has adopted the habits of civilized life, is hereby declared to be a citizen of the United States." The law embodied a hidden syllogism: all U.S. citizens have private, alienable holdings; Indians accepting allotment will have such holdings; therefore such Indians, living "separate and apart," will be citizens. In this way does one kind of self become a citizen, enfranchised and visible to the law, while others drop out of sight. As if to underscore that point, the Dawes Act actually says that when it comes to hiring "Indian police," those who have accepted allotment "shall be preferred." Those who accept allotment are not just recognized by the law; they *are* the law.

The idea of allotment was not without contemporary critics. The majority of Indians opposed the plan (severalty "plucked the Indian like a bird," said one tribal leader). Whites who had lived and worked among the Indians opposed the plan, from U.S. government Indian agents, to ethnographers such as Lewis H. Morgan, to the former commissioner of Indian affairs, George W. Manypenny, who had negotiated several previous allotment treaties and come to regret them. "Had I known then, as I now know," he wrote in 1885, "what would result from those treaties, I would be compelled to admit that I had committed a high crime." There were even a number of U.S. senators who said clearly (in a minority report of the Committee on Indian Affairs) that "the main purpose of this bill is not to help the Indian," that the "real aim" was to "get at the Indian lands and open them up to settlement," and that it was a fantasy to suppose that a quarter section of land would make a farmer out of anyone ("there are hundreds of thousands of white men . . . who cannot be transformed into cultivators of the land by any such gift"). The bill, these senators wrote, "is formed solely upon a theory, and it has no practical basis to stand upon." If one wanted a basis for an Indian policy, they suggested looking to history, where one might find that "for centuries" the system of holding property in common "has kept bands and tribes together as families."

As for those who promoted allotment, it is hard from this distance not to see them as either naive or cynical. The act's supporters took one way of life—the possessive individualism supposedly embodied in freehold farmers—to be *the* way of life, and then set out to destroy an alternative way—tribal collectivism. They did so in the name of high ideals: self-improvement, self-reliance, education, citizenship, civilization, and Christianity. In the voice of one of the act's most forceful advocates, the Reverend Lyman Abbott, we hear the odd way in which high ideals can become grandiose and bullying. Abbott thought that unallotted land should not be left in Indian hands but simply taken from them by eminent domain. "Barbarism has no rights which civilization is bound to respect," he wrote. He was happy to see the railroads enabled in their westward push, the steam engine being "a Christianizing power [that] will do more to teach the people punctuality than schoolmaster or preacher can." He had no time for tribalism or tribal sovereignty: "I would . . . scatter the Indians among the white people."

The Dawes Act did not so much convert Indians to possessive individualism as allow the already converted, the settlers and the railroad companies, to increase their wealth and power at the expense of the destroyed collectives. Over a hundred reservations were broken up by allotment, and through the sale of "surplus" lands and other alienable holdings, the Indians eventually lost 86 million acres, over 60 percent of the land that they had held prior to 1887. Moreover, in the years that followed, the money held in trust for the tribes was horribly mishandled by the government. As late as 1999, a federal judge held both the secretary of the Interior and the secretary of the Treasury in contempt of court for the government's continued failure to account for the trusts, as much as $10 billion having failed to reach its beneficiaries during the last century.

But let's turn from the grain of this event to the assumptions that organized it. It is not just another example of alienation destroying identity, but of the legal, economic, and political practices by which the common self is made to disappear, lose its standing, and become invisible or inarticulate in the public sphere. It is clear in the Native American case that there was a way of being human that consisted of taking one's "self" to be a common thing, and that took land held in common to be not just that self's material representation but the place where it could exercise its rights of action and so have presence, standing, dignity.

As I said at the start of this section, our choices regarding alienation can cut both ways, enabling or disabling particular ways of being. This look at the Dawes Severalty Act has been an exploration of the latter case; as for a case in which inalienability protects a way of being, consider a common right that American law has long considered worth preserving as such: the public's "right of way" in roads and navigable waters. A foundational legal case, *Arnold v. Mundy*, reached the New Jersey Supreme Court in 1821. One of the contesting parties had bought land that included a waterway and held that the purchase necessarily included the right of way. The court ruled that this was not possible, that in some cases the public's right to travel is held by the state as an inalienable trust. No state, acting as a responsible trustee, can "divest . . . all the citizens of their common right."

A centuries-old understanding known as the "public trust doctrine" lies behind this case and can be found in several other areas of American life. In most states, it applies to the seashores, for example, such that private property cannot block public access to the intertidal zone. It is sometimes applied to "public natural resources" as, for example, in the constitution of the Commonwealth of Pennsylvania, which declares these to be "the common property of all the people, including generations yet to come," and names the Commonwealth "as trustee of these resources." A similar trusteeship exists in regard to public meeting places. As described in a 1939 Supreme Court decision, "traditional public forums" such as sidewalks, streets, and parks "have immemorially been held in trust for the use of the public, and time out of mind, have been used for purposes of assembly, communicating thoughts between citizens, and discussing public questions."

To return to the nineteenth-century case that addressed itself to roads and waterways, in saying that these are held in "an inalienable trust," the court indicated that not even the state legislature (which, after all, represents the public) can alienate this holding, inalienability here being the stint that preserves the commons, and preserves as well "mobility" as an essential part of public identity.

Why mobility? Because rights of way are the inalienables of a commercial culture, this being a clear case in which commerce and commons fit together without friction. And aptly so, for holding rights of way as common assets produces what economists call "returns to scale" and what Carol Rose, in her useful essay on this topic, calls comic consequences, comic "in the classical sense of a story with a happy outcome." Roads that carry commerce have a "more the merrier" attribute because trade will thrive where trade is thriving.

The public status of roads and waterways can be usefully analogized to the infrastructure of the Internet, for there, too, we find some "inherently public property," as Rose calls it, property that should rightly be preserved as inalienable commons. Conceiving of the Internet as dependent upon an underlying commons is what led, in fact, to the birth of the World Wide Web. Tim Berners-Lee, working at the European Organization for Nuclear Research

(CERN), developed the network protocols, the set of communication rules that made the Web possible; he then convinced his employers to release these to the public domain rather than exercise their legal right to monopoly privileges. By contrast, the University of Minnesota had, many years earlier, developed related network protocols (a system called Gopher); the university made them widely available but at the same time reserved the right to later charge licensing fees. The social worth of roads and waterways is of a kind that can be destroyed if any one owner exercises a right to exclude; in the case of Gopher, even the potential threat of a future commercial claim meant that software developers abandoned the system. Public goods need to be public goods.

To come back to Carol Rose's analysis of roads and waterways, in describing the rationale behind a common right that might trump not only private property but even the will of the legislature, Rose found herself turning to a tradition in British law that prevents private landowners from enclosing land used for customary festivities and recreation. An English case from 1665 upheld a community's customary right, held from "time out of memory," to dance on otherwise private ground, "at all times of the year . . . , for their recreation." Another case a century later preserved a right to play cricket on otherwise private ground; a later Scottish case preserved the right to play golf on the links at St. Andrews, not only for inhabitants but for all "who shall resort thither." A British case from 1875 allowed "the inhabitants of a parish to erect a Maypole in a certain piece of inclosed ground of a private owner in the parish, and to dance round and about the same." An 1883 case preserved the right to hold an annual horse race. A very early example recognized a common right to parade "in great jollity" a homemade dragon over otherwise private ground.

Public dances celebrating spring or midsummer's eve or the memory of an ancient battle all make good examples of *the comedy of the commons*, for they not only follow the more-the-merrier rule but belong as well to the kind of "Jocular Customs" (as one old book title puts it) whose enactment is social life itself. Community and common ground cannot be separated here; the latter is the stage where the former has its merriment, a reward that could be called "returns to scale" but is more simply named "the common good" or better yet "the comic good."

There is, it should be said, a limit to the comic side of the examples just reviewed. All embodied commons are dogged by the problem of carrying capacity: public roads can choke with traffic, too many feet can turn dancing grounds to mud. But I here recall the possibility of collapse not to undercut the comic so much as to widen the category to include cultural commons whose carrying capacity is endless. This is why those who have been the agents of the second enclosure seem such bad actors to those of us who would resist it; the higglers, hucksters, engrossers, forestallers, regraters, retailers, and speculators who brought us copyright term extension and all its ancillary legal strategies have brought severalty to the public domain. They have taken the comic good and plucked it like a bird.

And they have created a structure of ownership that makes it hard for the comic good to arise, and hard for its authors and actors to play their parts. Let us say, for argument's sake, that Tim Berners-Lee, all by himself, created the network protocols that made the World Wide Web possible; and let us acknowledge that the Web has produced immense wealth—all the income of all the successful Internet companies. Then let us ask: Who created this wealth? To whom does this value belong? Part of the point of Rose's description of comedic commons is that public property of this sort is most valuable when used by "indefinite and unlimited numbers of persons," which, I suppose, produces a foundational tautology: public goods are made good by the public. The best that can be said, then, is that Berners-Lee was a catalyst for the public value of the Web, but he did not create it; it was created by those many others who found it useful precisely because there were no exclusive rights in its infrastructure. The actions that created the Web amount to civic republicanism in modern dress. Just as in the eighteenth century, when gestures of self-negation preceded entry into the public sphere, so in this instance it is the intentional disowning of property that allows the public good to come to life. Berners-Lee is surely one author of this comedic commons, but he is not its owner, for if he were the owner he could not be the author!

"NOURISHED BY COUNTLESS INDIVIDUALS"

As noted in an earlier chapter, at one point in "Self-Reliance," Emerson's inspirational packet of individualist aphorisms, the body of Benjamin Franklin flashes by trussed in a rhetorical question: "Where is the master who could have instructed Franklin . . . ? Every great man is a unique."

Where the master? Well, as we've seen, there was Sir Isaac Newton for one, whose *Opticks* helped Franklin theorize about electricity; and Joseph Addison, whose essays in *The Spectator* helped Franklin learn to write; and there were six European authors whose books on fireplaces helped him design his famous woodstove; and there was John Checkley, from whom he stole the joke about how, if he achieved humility, he would be proud of it. It is not hard to make a long list, once you know a bit about the life, nor was Franklin himself reticent about his debts. The letters on electricity that made him famous in Europe carefully name his Philadelphia collaborators, each of whom contributed to the theory we now associate with Franklin.

Rather than speak of *self*-reliance, Franklin himself might have been more open to the kind of *other*-reliant image of the self offered by Johann Wolfgang von Goethe. Talking to a friend at about the same time that Emerson published "Self-Reliance," Goethe asks, "What am I?" and then answers:

> Everything that I have seen, heard, and observed I have collected and exploited. My works have been nourished by countless dif-

ferent individuals, by innocent and wise ones, people of intelligence and dunces. Childhood, maturity, and old age all have brought me their thoughts, . . . their perspectives on life. I have often reaped what others have sowed. My work is the work of a collective being that bears the name of Goethe.

How are we to imagine the creative self? Is it an individual and unique, or is it collective and common? Myself, I think it is always both of these, and that the question proposes a false distinction. In the United States, at least, the distinction persists, however, as does the presumption of an Emersonian answer with its tale of self-reliance, self-help, self-teaching, self-making, etc. These terms are part of the national myth, and as someone once said, a myth is a story you can't get out of, so I doubt any analysis of mine will alter it much. But note, at least, how wacky are such phrases as "self-reliance" and "self-help." *To rely, to help*: these are not reflexive verbs. When men and women yell "Help," they usually mean to indicate they have a problem they cannot solve on their own.

Sometimes it takes an outsider to hear how strange these locutions sound. In the 1830s, Frances Trollope—a British writer, the mother of the novelist—recounted a conversation she had had while traveling by stagecoach in upstate New York. "I nearly got myself into a scrape by venturing to remark upon a phrase used by [a] gentleman, and which had met me at every corner from the time I first entered the country." The passengers had been discussing art, one man finishing his praise of an American painter by saying "and what is more, madam, he is perfectly *self-taught*."

Trollope was puzzled to find the assertion to be praise rather than apology. After all, "study was necessary to the formation of taste, and to the development of genius," so how could a great artist be *self-taught*? But the question made no sense to her traveling companion. "There is no use in disputing a point that is already settled, madam," he said. "I then asked him, if he thought it was going to rain?"

My chapters on Franklin were, among other things, a gesture toward unsettling the point that Trollope found taken for granted in the 1820s. Much that Franklin accomplished *was* unique, of course, but we don't see him in the round if that is all we mark, nor can we hear his humor. Any human being can be made to look like a self-reliant unique if you adjust the lighting properly and drop a gray canvas behind the figure; but let history enter, and sufficient sunlight, and of a sudden will appear the horizonless, thousand-knotted net of human interdependence. The genius of a man like Franklin is as much *dividual* as it is individual.*

In this line, resistance to the second enclosure, to the aggressive conversion of cultural commons into private preserves, has little to do with the money involved and much to do with how we conceive of human flourishing. There are "collective beings," as Goethe calls them, who will thrive if there is a lively commons of art and ideas and who will disappear if there isn't. This was the point of describing Franklin's experiments with electricity in their full context. Creativity in science is almost always cumulative and collaborative; it proceeds collectively and thus thrives when barriers to collectivity are reduced. In Franklin's case, as we've seen, the actual experimentation was highly social; the theory came out of a four-man laboratory furnished with materials sent by friends in London. Franklin and his friends worked with an inherited tradition; they were the happy recipients of other men's inventions and ideas, from the Leyden jar to Boyle's laws, and they inhabited an emerging culture with an ethic of open communication. Remember that remark from one of Franklin's letters to London: "You are

*In modern times, only the anthropologists seem to have revived this useful old word, as in this observation by McKim Marriott: "Persons—single actors—are not thought in South Asia to be 'individual,' that is, indivisible, bounded units . . . Instead . . . , persons are generally thought . . . to be 'dividual' or divisible." Marilyn Strathern follows Marriott in a different context: "Far from being regarded as unique entities, Melanesian persons are as dividually as they are individually conceived. They contain a generalized sociality within."

at Liberty to communicate this Paper to whom you please." They wrote letters, printed pamphlets, and borrowed freely from what they read in the proto-scientific journals appearing in Germany, France, England, and America.

All this should be obvious. Franklin had a singular genius, to be sure, but what really made him unusual was not his individuality but his sociability, his talent for entertaining so much of the culture that surrounded him. He was a great cultural sponge, not a backwoods nature child.

Strange, then, how his image began to alter in the century after his death. There is a 1767 painting by David Martin that shows Franklin in an aptly sociable light: he is reading and off to the left is a bust of Sir Isaac Newton. He is a citizen of the Republic of Letters. Compare that to the way Benjamin West painted the famous kite experiment fifty years later. In the left background, Franklin's collaborators have been converted into slightly balding cherubs toying with a Leyden jar, and to the right behind the great man appears another group of toddlers helping to fly the kite. The Currier and Ives 1876 version of the kite story has a similar distortion, showing Franklin with what seems—judging from his height—to be a preadolescent boy (a half-truth: Franklin's son was with him the day he flew the kite, but William Franklin was then a grown man, not a boy).

Why did the passage of time turn Franklin's collaborators into children and baby angels? Because we are now in the early nineteenth century, the age of Emersonian individualism, and for Emerson "the nonchalance of boys" is the only "healthy attitude of human nature." Under the sign of American Romanticism, it takes a child in nature to perceive original truths. In nature a man "is always a child. In the woods, is perpetual youth . . . In the woods, we return to reason and faith." What artists from Benjamin West to Currier and Ives do is to strip Franklin of his community and re-present him as the American boy-man, an untutored savant who

David Martin's 1767 painting of Franklin with a bust of Isaac Newton and Benjamin West's 1816 image with Franklin alone but for the helpful cherubs.

writes no letters to London and reads no journals from Paris. All of which, of course, distorts the eighteenth-century sense that, as I said earlier, the breeding ground of truth lies in the conversation of the ingenious, not in the ambitions of "partial" individuals.

It is sometimes hard to remember how great was this conceptual shift, this discarding of personhood conceived as necessarily knit to the wider world and its replacement by the kind of American individualism whose essence lies in always being free to decline external demands. This latter self, the one whose identity arises not from attachments but from refusals, is the one that Emerson praised. In "Self-Reliance," he contrasts cautious city boys with their eager country cousins:

> A sturdy lad from New Hampshire or Vermont, who in turn tries all the professions, who teams it, farms it, peddles, keeps a school, preaches, edits a newspaper, goes to Congress, buys a township, and so forth, in successive years, and always, like a cat, falls on

his feet, is worth a hundred of these city dolls . . . He has not one chance, but a hundred chances.

This lad can master any trade because no trade masters him. He identifies with no one line of work because his identity lies in the constant quitting, the unending declarations of personal fungibility. The self here is to be found in its withdrawal from all constraint. "I shun father and mother and wife and brother, when my genius calls me."

Such assertions would have sounded very odd to eighteenth-century ears. To Emerson's forebears, individual liberty meant licentiousness, the freedom of beasts rather than that of human beings. *Human* liberty, on the other hand, carried with it an obligation to serve the public sphere. "It is a true rule that particular estates cannot subsist in the ruin of the public," wrote John Winthrop in his famous 1630 "City upon a Hill" sermon. "We must delight in each other, make other's conditions our own . . . , labour and suffer together, always having before our eyes . . . our community as members of the same body."

In the American colonies, the refrain continued well into the next century, as witnessed by this representative sample of eighteenth-century remarks:

'Tis the Business of the Legislature, in providing for the publick Good, to prescribe to all the Members of the Community, Limits and Restrictions of their Enjoyments and Conduct. (*New-York Mercury* [1753])

Brethren, we were born not merely for ourselves, but the Public Good! (Gilbert Tennent [1756])

A *people* is traveling fast to destruction, when *individuals* consider *their* interests as distinct from *those of the public*. (John Dickinson [1768])

The point is repeated so often in the eighteenth century, in fact, as to betray some anxiety, a suspicion that democratic self-governance did not, by itself, guarantee civil liberty's communitarian ends. Alexis de Tocqueville said as much after his visit to the United States in the 1830s:

> Not only does democracy make every man forget his ancestors, but it hides his descendants and separates his contemporaries from him; it throws him back forever upon himself alone and threatens in the end to confine him entirely within the solitude of his own heart.

Such solitude is of course a deficit in Tocqueville's view; Emerson managed to redescribe it as a benefit but in so doing he had to erase Tocqueville's assumption—shared by the nation's founders—that "Individualism . . . saps the virtues of public life . . . ; in the long run it attacks and destroys all others and is at length absorbed in downright selfishness."

All these opinions find their roots in more ancient valuations of individualism. As Hannah Arendt has shown, in early Greece and Rome only those who lived an active, public life were thought to have entered their full humanity. Private life was where the demands of necessity were met, especially biological necessity. In private we are born and die, get fed and clothed, and are nursed from sickness into health. Public life arises from this ground—the life of art, philosophy, and politics, all those activities proper to social beings and impossible for the solitary.

Mark then the language of this tradition. Belonging simultaneously to the private and the public, we each must distinguish between what is our own (*idios*) and what we hold in common (*koinon*). The first of these terms gives rise to the word "idiot," for it was the Greek assumption that any life spent wholly on one's own is by nature idiotic. If the public world is that in which we become fully human, then along with the positive, need-meeting senses of privacy come its negative or privative senses. Privacy can indicate loss—of public presence, public office, companionship, friendship, and dignity. An obsolete English verb, "to prive," means "to deprive" but also "to strip of office or dignity, to depose"; its Latin root means "to bereave, to be left alone, single, individual." Men and women who lose their spouses are prived; prisoners in solitary confinement are prived; Richard Nixon forced from office was prived. Full privacy is a thing to be avoided, belonging more to slaves and barbarians than to the civilized. This model sets liberty and privacy in opposition, for liberty means self-governance and self-governance is a common pursuit.

I began this chapter with Noah Webster and suggested that "the soul of a republic" might be a layered thing, combining fee-simple ownership of private land with a public set of civic inalienables. Access to knowledge—"the information of the people" in Webster's words—should belong to the public by right, not be entailed to private families or corporations. Land that has been freed from entail does not, of course, enter the public domain; it moves from hand to hand in the private realm "as time and accident may direct." The intangibles of expressive life, on the other hand, eventually must enter the public domain, at least so long as access to knowledge is one of the non-negotiable use rights that engenders "the public" and its actors.

Such, I should now confess, is *my* working out of the conclusion that seems to follow from the assumptions behind Webster's defense of the Constitution. It is not, ironically enough, the conclusion that Webster himself arrived at in his maturity. In Webster we find a lived equivalent to the transformations suffered by Franklin's image over time. Half a century and his own death separate the two Franklin paintings I reproduced: in the 1760s he is himself, as it were, a sociable civic republican; decades later he is the prived man, a solitary unique. As for Noah Webster, he did not need to wait for death, nor for outside help, to effect a similar alteration; he did it himself.

Among those who came of age during the Revolution (he was seventeen when the war broke out), it was Webster above all others who defended the idea that authors and their descendants have a natural, perpetual, and private right to their work. In an 1826 letter to his cousin, the Massachusetts senator Daniel Webster, he explains his reasoning: he begins with a labor theory ("If any thing can justly give a man an exclusive right . . . to a thing . . . , it must be the fact, that he *made* it"); he shrugs off the important distinction between tangible and intangible properties with a rhetorical question ("What . . . can make a difference between the produce of *muscular strength* and the produce of the *intellect?*"); he offers a novel reformulation of the metaphor by which an author's work is likened to a landed estate ("the copy-right is the *author's soil*"); and he ends with the sort of claim that had, fifty years earlier, been adjudicated and denied in Britain (to wit, that "an author has, by common law, or natural justice, the sole and *permanent* right" to his work, "and that his heirs . . . shall enjoy the right, unclogged with conditions"). (To his credit, cousin Daniel knew the British case law on copyright and, in a cordial reply, denied the "natural justice" claim ("property . . . must be the creature of law") and confessed that in regard to author's rights, he "frankly" objected to making them "perpetual").

Laying aside the logic and legal standing of Noah Webster's case, not to mention its divergence from the postulates of his 1787 pamphlet, what makes his position truly paradoxical is that it contradicts his own practice as an author. Both his early spelling book (1783) and his great *American Dictionary* (1828) are plausibly what we would now call derivative works. He didn't start from scratch to make his speller; he built it on the foundations of existing books by Thomas Dilworth and Robert Lowth. For the dictionary, he drew on more than two dozen existing works, everything from something as obscure as *The Mariner's Dictionary; or, American Seaman's Vocabulary of Technical Terms, and Sea Phrases* to a work as well-known as Samuel Johnson's 1755 *Dictionary*. By one count, Webster lifted fully a third of his definitions from Johnson (many verbatim), along with two thirds of the quotations he used as examples. Had he been obliged to work under the "perpetual natural right" view of ownership he himself favored, Webster could not have made the books he made, at least not without tracking down and haggling with the heirs of dozens of earlier authors.

My interest here, however, has less to do with Webster's inconsistencies than with this chapter's organizing inquiry into how our practices in regard to ownership enable or disable particular identities. In this case, we have, on the side of Webster and perpetual copyright, the empowering of private authorial selves whose legal personae and right to exclude survive well beyond their own generation. Or we have, on the other side, the subordination of these to a public domain whose inalienable use rights ease the way for citizens to know themselves as public beings, and to act as such. What everlasting exclusive rights do is bring "severalty" to the public domain, converting that commonwealth into a multitude of private estates. More than that, with perpetual ownership we have entail in the land of civic and artistic expression. I like to think, then, that if confronted with his older self, a young Webster, imbued with the spirit of the Revolution, might have offered the following counsel:

> Make laws, irrevocable laws in every state, destroying and barring cultural entailments; leave cultural properties to devolve upon the public such that no family or corporation can acquire power over a series of generations. Nothing is more dangerous to liberty than the power of entailed art and ideas. The very soul of a republic is the common citizen's inalienable access to knowledge.

8

THE COMMON SELF NOW

The argument: In looking at modern creative practice, it appears that the old
republican idea of a civic or public self necessarily endures.

.

Near the end of March, 1845, I borrowed an axe and went down to the woods by
Walden Pond . . . It is difficult to begin without borrowing.

—THOREAU

I don't believe in the individual Writer so much as in Writing . . .
All of writing is a huge lake. There are great rivers that feed the lake,
like Tolstoy and Dostoyevsky . . . All that matters is feeding the lake.
I don't matter. The lake matters.

—JEAN RHYS

I ended the last chapter by turning Noah Webster against himself, but maybe that was wrong. Maybe it would be better to take Webster in the 1820s as a prophetic figure, one who discovered in himself a model of creative personhood that was soon to become the favored form of American individualism. After all, there has never been a single model of creativity. Franklin may have declined to patent inventions, but Thomas Edison never did. Both were great inventors, and times change. Personhood in South Asia may very well be *dividual*, but *individuals* rule in a world of mass media, industrial agriculture, international capital markets, and the right to privacy. We're not in the eighteenth century anymore, and all this theorizing about collective selves and civic virtue may be a form of Romantic nostalgia, quaint but neither true nor useful in the present moment.

I obviously don't believe that to be the case, but I do nonetheless feel some obligation to bring my argument forward and see how well it serves to illuminate contemporary practice. To that end, this chapter offers three short studies, one of a scientist (the molecular biologist John Sulston), one of an artist (Bob Dylan), and one of a political and spiritual leader (Dr. Martin Luther King, Jr.). Behind these accounts lie several questions whose answers my argument has been meant to suggest. What is the best way to describe the creative self? How should we conceive of the relationship between creative persons and the context that informs their work? Do the rules that govern cultural property help or hinder that work? When creators mix their labor with contemporary material, or with an inherited tradition, what portion of the new creation may they claim as their own, and for how long?

Contemporary responses to such queries are best sought in the grain of actual practice, and to that end it will help to turn to specific cases.

"LIKE A TERMITE MOUND"

The story of the mapping of the human genome offers a striking way to interrogate the differences between common and proprietary scientific inquiry. Between the time that biologists developed a way to read the sequence of a gene's amino acids (around 1975) and the time that a more-or-less complete map of the genome was published (2001), two different sequencing projects arose, one public and one private. The former of these, the Human Genome Project, was underwritten by government funds and private philanthropy. On the commercial side, the major player was Celera Genomics Corporation, supported typically by drug companies who bought exclusive licenses to Celera's eventual patents and data. As these efforts got under way, the question naturally arose whether knowledge about the genome should be treated as a common asset, part of the public domain, or whether it would be better to treat it as a proprietary good belonging to those who developed it. After all, time, money, expertise, and hard work are needed to create such knowledge; why shouldn't these be rewarded with profits? And wouldn't the promise of reward provide an incentive that might speed the work, and target it toward useful ends? Why especially call on taxpayers to pay for something when the money could as easily be raised by venture capitalists?

A full version of the commons response to such questions can be found in John Sulston's book *The Common Thread*. From 1993 to 2000, Sulston was director of the Sanger Centre in England, where he led the British arm of the international team working on the Human Genome Project. In 2002 he shared the Nobel Prize in Physiology or Medicine.

Sulston's account of the genome project suggests a number of related reasons why genomic knowledge should not be taken private. First of all, the genome is a part of nature, of the given world, and—as pointed out in the chapter on cultural enclosure— knowledge about nature is *discovered*, not *invented*. In the history of intellectual property, and in patent law particularly, there is a long tradition whereby the things we discover about the natural world cannot be owned. You can't own the fact that lightning is electricity, even if you were the first to figure that out. An invention like the lightning rod, however, a device derived from the natural fact—that you may own. "I am one of those who feel that the earth is a common good," Sulston writes. Enclosures should apply to what we add to that commons but not to the commons itself:

> It seems to me that your fencing off of a gene should be confined strictly to an application that you are working on—to an inventive step. I, or someone else, may want to work on an alternative application, and so need to have access to the gene as well. I can't

go away and invent a human gene. So all the discovered part of genes . . . needs to be kept pre-competitive and free of property rights.

Discussing Franklin's reluctance to take out patents, I pointed out that, by his own account, the value he placed on *not* identifying with his own insights led to a valued way of being, one where quiet and sweet temper arise from associating with truths that lie outside the self. In both Franklin's case and here, the point doesn't necessarily apply to what Sulston calls "an inventive step"; an "I" can own what an "I" has added. But the old norm of refusing patents on the facts of nature points to a need to keep the categories clear; no "I" created human genes, and thus to fence one off is an astounding act of self-aggrandizement.* There may always be a first "I" who describes the gene, but the description itself is a "thought without a thinker"; once the apparatus of discovery is in place, someone else would have done the job if "I" had not. (Such was Madison's explanation of the limited term of patent, by the way: "[The] monopoly . . . ought to be temporary . . . in the case of inventions, because they grow so much out of preceding ones that . . . the discovery might be expected in a short time from other hands.")

Beyond these normative issues lie practical concerns about the nature of the human genome sequencing project itself. DNA is not a simple substance. There are about six feet of it in every cell in the human body; if you made a scaled-up model with a strand of DNA only as thick as sewing thread, the result would stretch over 150 miles. The human genome contains *three billion* paired nucleotides and somewhere around *thirty thousand* distinct genes.

---

*On the other hand, artificial genes are now being created, and here, too, we find self-aggrandizement. When J. Craig Venter's research institute built the first synthetic chromosome, he "watermarked" it to contain a code that spelled out his own name.

To develop knowledge about something as staggeringly complex as that requires a similarly complex structure of inquiry, one that can subdivide the labor, facilitate an emergent group intelligence, and integrate the results. The resources needed to sequence but one bit of the genome—chromosome 22—offers a snapshot of such complex science: the Sanger Centre in England collaborated with labs in Missouri, Japan, and Oklahoma to do most of the sequencing, and five other institutions—in the United States, Canada, and Sweden—were needed to complete the mapping phase.

During the 1990s, as I've said, Celera Genomics Corporation, a research company headed by J. Craig Venter, was the private counterpoint to the public genome project. Celera regularly announced that the data they developed would be made "available" to others, but this availability always came with restrictions. Researchers using Celera data were not allowed to annotate it, for example, even though unannotated genome sequences are of greatly diminished use. Celera also insisted that academic users sign a "non-redistribution clause," which effectively meant that "no public sequencing lab could even look at the data without laying itself open to a potential lawsuit." Data released with use and redistribution restrictions are balkanized data or, to put it more simply, they are not actually released.

The work of science, Sulston writes, is

> like a termite mound, each of us industriously constructing little bits of the castle, adding extra chambers, repairing damage, knowing that later generations may build on our work or demolish it and build something different. But the enterprise succeeds only if our handiwork is in the open for all to see and make of it what they will.

There needs be a community of scientists and the community needs to have open channels of communication so that new information can be spread and integrated rapidly ("You are at Liberty

to communicate this Paper . . ."), and it has long been the understanding in science that common property regimes offer the best
way to meet those needs.

There is another thing to be said about the complexity of the
genome, and it leads to yet another reason to treat it as a commons.
Commercial science is by definition directed toward commercial
ends, and these tend to be tightly focused. A map of the genes for
brown eyes is less likely to pay off than a map of the genes for breast
cancer. Commercial research zeros in on sites that are most likely
to prove useful and leaves the "junk" unexplored. And there is a
lot of seeming junk in the human genome; there are long stretches
of code that appear inert, expressing nothing. They seem to be fos-
sils, as it were, brought along from some now-dead-ended path in
evolution.

Fine, but at the moment the point of sequencing the entire
genome is that we don't necessarily have any idea what will be useful and what will be useless. (Some of what once seemed barren
later turned out, for example, to constitute control sequences that
turn genes on and off.) Once the decision has been made that the
human genome is worth mapping, the best way to make sure that
the whole thing gets done is to treat the project as pure rather than
applied science. Pure science *explores*, rather than *exploits*, the
genome; it demands open-ended rather than goal-driven inquiry.
"This is sometimes called 'ignorance-driven' or, more grandly,
'Baconian science,'" Sulston remarks; it is the kind of science
that seeks to accumulate observations so as to arrive at the whole
picture, without knowing anything in advance about what that
picture will be like.

Some examples will flesh out this distinction between the
open-ended and the goal-driven. Absent a full understanding of
how the genome works, it is the habit of commercial science to
stake out broad claims, then sit back and wait, hoping to strike a
rich vein. This is what happened with a gene called CCR5, which
encodes a receptor on the surface of cells. Nobody knew what the

receptor did when CCR5 was first sequenced, but a private concern, Human Genome Sciences, nonetheless applied for a patent on it. Only later did a group of publicly funded researchers in the United States figure out that a defect in this gene produced resistance to HIV infection. Pharmaceutical companies that wanted to follow up on this promising discovery then had to buy licenses from Human Genome Sciences in order to begin their research. Sulston asks the rhetorical questions: "But who made the inventive step? The company that made a lucky match to a randomly selected [gene]? Or the publicly funded researchers who identified that in people resistant to HIV the gene was defective?"* The custom of giving rights to the former amounts to what I earlier called a "third enclosure," the colonizing of wilderness.

At the end of his 2002 Nobel lecture, Sulston repeated the point that a search for "profitable applications" can't be the only engine driving research. Having a set of short-term goals is not a good way to explore the natural world, for one thing, and for another, "many of the most important potential applications—for example the neglected diseases such as tuberculosis and malaria, found mainly in the poorer parts of the world—cannot be researched through funding for profit: there is no market to repay the investment." (Needs such as these are part of what led to the founding of the nonprofit Science Commons.)

With something as complicated and poorly understood as the human genome, if one wants the whole picture, and if parts of that picture have no obvious market value, then goal-driven science is an inferior discipline. It will leave much of the territory unexplored and what it does explore will get divided into fiefdoms, each with a "partial view," as the old pamphleteers would say.

*Note again that the choice here is not between commons and commerce; we can easily have both. CCR5 should have been in the public domain, whereupon plenty of commerce, perhaps *more*, would have followed upon the description of its sequence and the growing understanding of its functions.

A simple way to summarize all that I've said so far might be to assert that knowledge about the genome should be a cultural commons because it is *sacred*. What pertains to this category is usually thought of as a matter of definition or belief, and consequently there is not really much "argument" to be made here. Nonetheless, a few things can be said in regard to nominating the genome in this way. To begin with, it probably isn't very helpful to say that the genome is one of the essences of life, and that life is sacred. Molecular biologists, at least, are interested especially in unsettling the boundary between the organic and the inorganic. Ever since Friedrich Wöhler synthesized urea in 1828, the idea that there is something special and different about organic molecules has been eroded.

I find it more useful to follow a line of thought that the political philosopher Michael Sandel developed in his Tanner Lectures entitled "What Money Can't Buy." In the course of discussing limits to commodification, Sandel distinguished between arguments from coercion and arguments from corruption. An argument from coercion posits that some things should not be sold because certain markets force the poor into an unacceptable situation (a market in blood, for example, or in sexual services).

An argument from corruption, on the other hand, is an argument about categories. All corruption arguments, Sandel writes, call into question "an assumption that informs much market-oriented thinking," that is, "that all goods are commensurable," that they can be "translated without loss into a single measure." One of his examples has been mine as well: voting. If our conception of the ideal democracy includes the idea that each citizen is capable and obliged to deliberate about political ends, then we will resist situations in which citizens are allowed or encouraged to sell their votes. We do so because commercialization corrupts the ideal; it inappropriately moves voting from one category to another, from politics to commerce.

Moreover, categories such as democracy or citizenship have much to do with our sense of the good. We are not sorting peas and beans here, but social practices—issues, in this case, of civic engagement and self-rule. By resisting the sale of votes, we assert "the good" of a certain kind of citizen. In the case of knowledge about the genome, we assert "the good" of all the things I have said so far, the list I've been making of reasons for preserving the genome as a commons. To say that the genome should be a commons because it is sacred is a shorthand way of affirming the values articulated in that list. I mean something almost secular when I say that the genome is sacred; I don't mean to bring forward all the apparatus of religion (though I also don't mean not to). I mean something analogous to saying "in a democracy, the vote is sacred, sacred because if you have a market in votes, you no longer have a true democracy." If knowledge about the genome is commodified, you no longer have patent law's time-honored distinction between discovery and invention; you eat away at the infrastructure out of which markets grow; you risk undoing the elaborated discourse of the scientific community, and thus either slowing down the inquiry or simply failing to accomplish it; and you abandon the kind of open-ended research that can yield results never imagined.

Two core values, two "goods," may be rendered from that list: one is the old resistance to giving anyone a monopoly power when it comes to the givens of this world, the laws and facts of nature; the other is a model of scientific inquiry—open-ended, communal, intergenerational, and in need of an easy flow of ideas and data.

With these in mind, it may be time to revisit my earlier question about whether or not the work and expertise that goes into creating knowledge about the genome shouldn't be rewarded. Of course they should. And in fact they are, under both the private property and the common asset models. Those in the public sector who labored with the genome were well rewarded—with salaries, with prestige (the kind that leads to larger salaries, in fact), and with prizes. No one who worked on the public side ended up poor. The "reward" question is a red herring, at least as long as we still honor the quest for knowledge as a common pursuit. In fact, with something as basic and pervasive as the human genome, asking that we choose between a private or common property regime sets up a false or premature dichotomy. Just as public roads and waterways (or public domain Internet protocols) provide a common infrastructure out of which markets may grow, so publicly available knowledge about the genome allows for a variety of uses, many of them commercial. If you want a lively commerce arising from our understanding of the genome, treat it as a commons.

Both the public and private human genome mapping projects announced their results on the same day in the summer of 2001, Celera's being published in *Science* and the public project's appearing in *Nature*. To an outside observer, it seemed as if the public/private race had ended in a tie. But it hadn't. Once the private results were published, Sulston writes, it "was immediately obvious . . . that Celera had made no attempt at all . . . to assemble their own sequence data alone . . . They had . . . incorporated the public data into their data set." In addition, they based their analysis of the genome on the public data, not on what was in fact their own piecemeal set. In short, they had made a raid on the public domain and taken what they could of it private.

The ethics of such transfers are not what concern me here, however; I have laid out this story in some detail in support of a simple assertion: today, as in Franklin's time, a knowledge commons is the better, perhaps the necessary, environment for scientists dedicated to open-ended research on complex problems. Practical arguments can be offered in support, as when we speak of the fit between complexity and the distributed intelligence of an open community; but there are matters of belief at work here as well ("the earth is a common good"; "ignorance-driven," Baconian science matters), and with these the best we can sometimes say is that to resist the enclosure of knowledge is to protect a valued way of being human. Common property regimes allow common selves (e.g., scientists like Sulston) to flourish.

"I AM THOUGHT"

With similar questions in mind—about the creative self and about its relationship to the surrounding culture—let us turn from science to art and consider the case of Bob Dylan. In his autobiographical *Chronicles*, Dylan writes candidly about his debts to artists who came before him. About the time he arrived in New York City, for example, Columbia Records had purchased all of Robert Johnson's blues recordings and was about to reissue them. John Hammond gave Dylan an early acetate copy of the record.

> Over the next few weeks I listened to it repeatedly, cut after cut, one song after another, sitting staring at the record player . . . The songs were layered with a startling economy of lines . . .
>
> I copied Johnson's words down on scraps of paper so I could more closely examine the lyrics and patterns.

Something similar had happened in Minneapolis a few years earlier, when Dylan first heard Woody Guthrie recordings.

> That day I listened all afternoon to Guthrie as if in a trance and I felt like I had discovered some essence of self-command, that I was in the internal pocket of the system feeling more like myself than ever before. A voice in my head said, "So this is the game." I could sing all these songs, every single one of them and they were all that I wanted to sing. It was like I had been in the dark and someone had turned on the main switch of a lightning conductor.

Dylan also describes large debts to the old English ballads as collected by Francis James Child.

> I could rattle off all these songs without comment as if all the wise and poetic words were mine and mine alone. The songs had beautiful melodies and were filled with everyday leading players like barbers and servants, mistresses and soldiers, sailors, farmhands and factory girls.

The young Dylan had a great absorptive ability. Another folk singer of the time, Eric von Schmidt, recalled that the one time the nineteen-year-old Dylan came to his apartment, "he wasn't much interested in playing; he wanted to listen . . . It was something the way he was soaking up material in those days—like a sponge and a half." Liam Clancy of the Clancy Brothers had the same impression:

> Do you know what Dylan was when he came to the Village? He was a teenager, and the only thing I can compare him with was blotting paper. He soaked everything up. He had this immense curiosity; he was totally blank, and was ready to suck up everything that came within his range.

But of course he didn't simply soak things up; he then mixed them, added and subtracted, and wrung himself out. Witness the first time Dylan recorded songs for Leeds Music, his earliest publisher. The day he went to the Leeds offices, he writes,

> I didn't have many songs, but I was making up some compositions on the spot, rearranging verses to old blues ballads, adding an original line here or there, anything that came into my mind—slapping a title on it . . . I would make things up on the spot all based on folk music structure.

About the Merle Travis song "Sixteen Tons," Dylan writes: "You could write twenty or more songs off that one melody by slightly altering it."

By his own account, Dylan is "not a melodist," which explains in part the largeness of his debts to borrowed tunes. A musicologist at the Library of Congress, Todd Harvey, has tracked down the sources behind the first seventy songs Dylan ever recorded. "Almost every song . . . had a clear predecessor," Harvey writes; his documentation shows that about two-thirds of Dylan's melodies from that period were lifted directly from the Anglo- and African-American traditional repertory. Toward the end of a 2004 conversation with the *Los Angeles Times*, Dylan described how he goes about songwriting.

> What happens is, I'll take a song I know and simply start playing it in my head. That's the way I meditate . . .
>
> I'll be playing Bob Nolan's "Tumbling Tumbleweeds," for instance, in my head constantly—while I'm driving a car or talking to a person or sitting around or whatever . . . At a certain point, some of the words will change and I'll start writing a song.
>
> . . . That's the folk music tradition. You use what's been handed down. "The Times They Are A-Changin'" is probably from an old Scottish folk song.

In fact, that song's melody derives from a nineteenth-century hymn, "Deliverance Will Come," perhaps written in the 1830s by one John B. Matthias or in the 1870s by a certain W. McDonald, or else simply indigenous to southwest Virginia, origin unknown. Dylan probably heard the hymn on an early recording by Uncle Dave Macon or by the Carter Family. The "original" hymn included the lines

Palms of Victory, crowns of Glory
Palms of Victory I shall wear.

These lines are of interest because in fact Dylan first used the "Deliverance" melody for his own song "Paths of Victory," which simply places new words over the old:

> *Trails of troubles, Roads of battles,*
> *Paths of victory, We shall walk.*

Dylan clearly liked the tune, because variants of it can be found in "When the Ship Comes In," "One Too Many Mornings," and of course, "The Times They Are A-Changin'."

Perhaps the most striking example of Dylan's early receptivity concerns a time that his girlfriend took him to hear an evening of Bertolt Brecht/Kurt Weill songs. The song that knocked him out was "a show-stopping ballad" called "Pirate Jenny": "I found myself taking the song apart, trying to find out what made it tick, why it was so effective." In his memoir, Dylan eventually offers a partial list of his own early songs—"Mr. Tambourine Man," "The Lonesome Death of Hattie Carroll," "A Hard Rain's A-Gonna Fall," and others—and then says:

> If I hadn't . . . heard the ballad "Pirate Jenny," it might not have dawned on me . . . that songs like these could be written. In about 1964 and '65, I probably used about five or six of Robert Johnson's blues song forms, too, unconsciously, but more on the lyrical im-agery side of things. If I hadn't heard the Robert Johnson record when I did, there probably would have been hundreds of lines of mine that would have been shut down—that I wouldn't have felt free enough or upraised enough to write.

It is in this context that Dylan writes of reading Arthur Rimbaud's line *Je est un autre*, "I is someone else." "When I read those words the bells went off. It made perfect sense. I wished someone would have mentioned that to me earlier." Rimbaud's sentence comes from his so-called seer letters, written to friends

in the spring of 1871, in one of which
declared:

> Right now I'm debauching myself as
> want to be a poet, and I'm working to
> a matter of getting to the unknown by t
> *senses* . . . The suffering is tremendous,
> to be born a poet, and I know that's wh
> fault. It is wrong to say: *I think*. One should say: *I am thought* . . .
>
> I is someone else. Too bad for the wood that discovers it's a
> violin . . . !

And too bad for the ego's pretensions to ownership and mastery.
No solitary imagination gives birth to song, any more than spruce
alone gives birth to violin music. That being the case, Rimbaud
set out to attack the Romantics—"idiotic generations," "one-eyed
intellects," "old imbeciles"—who "discovered only the false meaning of the Ego." The seer letters are rambling and enigmatic, but it
would seem that Rimbaud's distinction between false and true ego
hinges on the doubleness that can be preserved if the "I" refrains
from appropriating its own creations. Rimbaud thus refuses the
normal syntax by which subjects swiftly possess their objects. "I
think my thoughts" becomes "I am thought," and Descartes's old
"I think therefore I am" gets flipped: "I am thought, therefore 'I'
am not," or at least "'I' is someone else."

And who, or what, is that someone else? The letters at one point
speak of "universal intelligence," so plausibly Rimbaud's "not-I" is
a version of the inherited tradition of art, a bow to all those who
came before. (Dylan's certainly is; he cites Rimbaud in the midst
of acknowledging the debts I've been describing.) More often, however, Rimbaud's "not-I" is simply the unknown—*l'inconnu*—and
the poet is the "thief of fire" of ancient myth whose task is to cross
the line and return with something "strange, unfathomable, repulsive, delicious."

saw, the artist as thief. "Immature poets imitate;
ets steal," wrote T. S. Eliot. "All artists borrow; great art-
al," said Picasso, perhaps swiping the idea from Eliot. But
at least one distinction is in order, for not all thieves are the
same. If Rimbaud's thief of fire refers to a figure like Prometheus,
then we are in a story about an ancient conflict between gods
and humans in which theft arises because the immortals are so
strangely stingy; nothing can be brought to the humans but by
cunning and deceit.

The distinction that Eliot and Picasso make, however, is not
directed toward matters so primordial. Their way of speaking is
better illuminated by the old Hindu story of the baby Krishna,
who, when asked by his mother if he has stolen butter from the
pantry, answers with a question of his own: "How could I steal?
Doesn't everything in the house belong to us?" The context here is
not cosmic discord but earthly relations. If a child feeds from the
forbidden cookie jar, that may be "stealing" to the mother, but let
us at least note that it is human artifice that produces the thief. The
mother who forbids entry to the pantry not only draws a line the
child is not supposed to cross; in doing so she helps create the child
as a separate being, an "I" who must either respect the syntax of self
and other or break the rules. From the mother's point of view, "I is
a cookie" would be impudent speech (though if said with enough
charm, and Krishna is charming above all, the mother might smile
and loosen her attachment to the rules).

The point is that in matters human the assertion of thievery
begs the question of how to imagine the self. What is the best way
to speak of Picasso when he derives a work from Velázquez, or of
Muddy Waters when he gets a song from Son House? Promethean
fire may be a stolen good, but how shall we speak of Shakespeare's
description of Cleopatra, copied nearly verbatim from Plutarch's
life of Mark Antony (and also later nicked by T. S. Eliot for *The
Waste Land*)? Or of my use of this last sentence, for that matter,
lifted (syntax, diction, and all) from an essay by Jonathan Lethem?

We can call these things theft if we wish, but notice at least that, as with that mother putting butter off-limits, it is our own sorting of the world that brings thieving into being, and that in insisting on that sorting we affirm a particular image of the artistic self. It is a self, for one thing, distinct from the "others" whose material it uses, and that distinctness creates, I think, what Rimbaud calls "the false meaning of the Ego." Emerson makes Franklin a unique by presenting him as independent of what were in fact his informing sources. Seen that way, the language of theft is part of a rhetorical tool kit for the creation of genius, and it has in it not a little self-importance. When Eliot and Picasso speak of the "mature" and the "great," who, after all, might they be thinking of?

In none of this do I mean to diminish Bob Dylan's accomplishment. Not many young musicians are so attentive and hardworking. How studious he was, taking songs apart to see how they were made, as if he were a farm kid learning mechanics by tearing down a tractor and putting it back together. And he had a remarkable talent, a gift waiting to be informed and enlarged, just as another young person might have a talent for mathematics, chess, or dance. But to speak of talent only pushes the question of "self" further back, for where does talent come from, and what is the right relationship between it and the ego, the thing that so swiftly makes a "me" out of the sea of the given world?

Remember that in Dylan's account of his first exposure to Woody Guthrie recordings, he said they left him "feeling more like myself than ever before." How strange! What "self" is it that stirs to life when meeting someone else's art? The self that trades in common stock, I'd say, in things like air, light, fire, and song, in things that nature made "incapable of confinement, or exclusive appropriation." Let us not speak of thieves and ownership, then, but of hosts and generosity. Benjamin Franklin, knowledge-hungry and omnivorous, became who he was because he had such a welcoming intelligence. Young poets need to be fed; mature poets spread out banquets. The commons of culture is a huge lake; young artists are sponges at its shores. Some become great rivers as well, and feed the lake. "All that matters is feeding the lake." I doesn't matter.

INTELLECTUAL PROPERTIES MANAGEMENT, INC.

I argued in the last chapter that practices in regard to cultural property can enable or disable certain kinds of collective being. This chapter has filled out that argument with modern examples, first from science and then from art. The latter makes for a more complicated case, I realize, because Bob Dylan is a commercial artist who owns his work and depends on royalties for much of his livelihood. To describe him only in that way does not, however, do justice to his origins. I focused on the young Dylan because that is where we can see how both an inherited folk tradition and lively communities in Minneapolis and New York enabled him to become more and more *like himself*, as it were. Dylan could easily have been an appropriating sponge in those early years in part because the anxiety and litigation regarding "piracy" had not reached today's fevered pitch.

Could a young songwriter arise in the same way today? Maybe, but consider some of the changes the intervening years have brought. In the 1960s, a songwriter could, for example, depend on what's known as the de minimis exception to a charge of copyright infringement. *De minimis non curat lex* is the old formula, "the law is not interested in trivial matters," and courts have traditionally dismissed cases in which the alleged infringer's use was clearly insignificant. At least they did so until recently. A copyright infringement suit from 2004 concerned a three-note, four-second-long guitar riff that had been "sampled" from the plaintiff's recording. The defendants had copied two seconds of this riff and altered it, lowering the pitch and looping it for sixteen beats. The first court to hear the case dismissed it on de minimis grounds, saying that the sampling did not "rise to the level of a legally cognizable appropriation." The appeals court disagreed. Noting that digital sampling was a relatively new phenomenon and that a 1971 law extending copyright to sound recordings had changed the rules of the game, the judges decided that a "literal reading" of the statute forced them to rule that even a two-second sample constituted infringement. The judges themselves seemed uncomfortable with their decision, suggesting that "if this is not what Congress intended," the plaintiffs should "go back to Congress" and get the law changed.

The musicians in this case had not bothered to play their own version of the riff in question; they copied the original. The judges presumed that direct copying like that "is never accidental," a point that led them to make what seems like an important distinction: "It is not like the case of a composer who has a melody in his head, perhaps not even realizing that the reason he hears this melody is that it is the work of another which he had heard before." The implication is that *unintended* replication might be given more lenient treatment under the law. As they surely knew, however, in recent years no composer can be sure of that, either. In 1976 the former Beatle George Harrison found himself in court under a claim that his song "My Sweet Lord" illegally appropriated the tune of the Chiffons' 1962 hit, "He's So Fine." In the subsequent court proceedings it became apparent that while Harrison and his collaborators knew the Chiffons' song, none of them (in the judge's words) "were conscious of the fact that they were utilizing the 'He's So Fine' theme." So what happened? "I conclude," the judge wrote, that as Harrison tried out various tunes,

> there came to the surface of his mind a particular combination that pleased him . . . ; in other words, that this combination of sounds would work. Why? Because his subconscious knew it already had worked in a song his conscious mind did not remember . . . Did Harrison deliberately use the music of "He's So

Fine"? I do not believe he did so deliberately. Nevertheless . . . , this is, under the law, infringement of copyright, and is no less so even though subconsciously accomplished.

The infringement charge was thus upheld, and Harrison was ordered to surrender the majority of royalties from "My Sweet Lord."

Now let's return not so much to Bob Dylan as to the creative ecology that surrounded him in the early 1960s. Remember his remark about the Merle Travis song "Sixteen Tons": "You could write twenty or more songs off that one melody by slightly altering it." That may well have been the case in 1962 when Dylan's first album appeared; today you'd better *radically* alter the melody, leaving no three-note passage untouched, or else make sure you have in hand twenty or more licenses from the Merle Travis estate.

Or remember that Dylan himself doesn't seem to know that the tune for "The Times They Are A-Changin'" derives from "Deliverance Will Come," nor that "Deliverance" was possibly written by one W. McDonald in the 1870s. If it was, and if Mr. McDonald enjoyed the exclusive rights that today's composers enjoy, it is entirely possible that his heirs could appear and, like the owners of "He's So Fine," get a "subconscious infringement" ruling and claim Dylan's royalties.*

Or remember that Todd Harvey's study of early Dylan recordings concluded that "almost every song . . . had a clear predecessor." As long as those predecessors lay in the public domain, Dylan was free to use them. One of these was "Deliverance Will Come," of course, which could *not* have been owned by anyone precisely

---

*To clarify: Assume McDonald registered a copyright around 1875 and then lived until 1900. Current copyright gives an author exclusive rights for a term of "life plus seventy years," so McDonald's copyright would not lapse until 1970. Thus, by today's rules, any songwriter who unconsciously borrowed his tune during the 1960s could be sued for infringement.

because the copyright term was much shorter fifty years ago, and thus creative work more swiftly entered the public domain, that happy land where no songwriter need think about a de minimis defense nor worry that his subconscious mind will be called to the witness stand.

In short, the litigious age of industrial entertainment still lay in the future when Dylan started out. The second enclosure had not yet settled over the cultural commons and it was thus a lot easier for him to become himself, a collective being with both great powers of absorption and great gifts to bestow. Yes, he is a commercial artist, but his story amounts to another case in which commerce more easily arises when there is a foundational commons to build upon.

This contrast between the present and the 1960s, and between conflicting models of personhood, can only be sharpened by looking at one final case, the sorry story of what has happened to the legacy of Martin Luther King, Jr., to his image, his archives, and the famous "I Have a Dream" speech that he delivered on the Mall in Washington, D.C., during a 1963 march for voting rights. Dr. King's estate (largely controlled by his son, Dexter Scott King) now treats all these things as private intellectual property and exploits them for their commercial value. In the early 1990s, Dexter King established two for-profit corporations in the state of Georgia: Intellectual Properties Management, Inc., and Estate of Martin Luther King, Jr., Inc., the former being the agent for properties belonging to the latter. As of 2009, Dexter King was chief executive officer, chief financial officer, and secretary of both corporations. (He was also chairman of the nonprofit Martin Luther King Jr. Center for Nonviolent Social Change.)

Under Dexter King's management, the estate has registered "I Have a Dream" as a trademark and has successfully blocked attempts to secure similar marks (such as "We Have a Dream"), noting in its defense that the estate uses "I Have a Dream" for

"T-shirts, posters, pens, key chains, letter openers, books and other printed materials." They have vigilantly guarded their ownership of Dr. King's literal image: when Alpha Phi Alpha, the black fraternity to which Dr. King belonged as a student, tried to erect a monument to Dr. King in Washington's Tidal Basin, the estate blocked the proposal by demanding a fee for the use of the civil rights leader's likeness. After Barack Obama was elected to the presidency, the estate threatened to sue vendors selling T-shirts, buttons, and posters that juxtaposed images of Obama with images of Dr. King, claiming that millions of dollars in licensing fees were at stake. As for the archives, the estate has received a $10 million tax exemption (it is a for-profit corporation, after all) and $52 million in cash from the federal government and the city of Atlanta in exchange for portions of Dr. King's private papers.

Most egregious of all may be the way the estate has exploited the copyright it holds for the "Dream" speech.* When the 1987 documentary *Eyes on the Prize* used images of Dr. King without first obtaining permission, the estate threatened to sue and turned down an initial $100,000 offer for rights. In 1993, when *USA Today* printed the text of the speech, the estate successfully sued for infringement. The same thing happened in 1997 when CBS television tried to use its own footage of the speech in a documentary. The author Richard Lischer told *The Washington Post* that when he was writing *The Preacher King*,

> I called the commercial agency that handles [the estate], I was told, "If you think you're going to quote from that speech, it's going to cost you." I always thought "I Have a Dream" is the 20th-century parallel to the Gettysburg Address . . . I was shocked.

*It was Dr. King himself who registered the copyright soon after he gave his speech. All proceeds from this and his other holdings King donated to the civil rights movement, to his church, and to Morehouse College, his alma mater.

There are cases in which an estate uses its control of inherited cultural property to protect the reputation and dignity of an author, but that seems not to be the issue here, because Dr. King's heirs have readily licensed his work and image for use in trivial and demeaning contexts. Cingular Wireless paid for the right to juxtapose Dr. King's image with Kermit the Frog singing about "dreamers like me" (the point being, a spokesman explained, that the wireless market had become "a ghetto of competing rate plans"). In the most striking example, the communications company Alcatel used the "Dream" speech in a thirty-second commercial that begins with a close-up of Dr. King at the Lincoln Memorial on that famous day, delivering his charge with a commanding cadence:

I have a dream
that one day
this nation will rise up
and live out the true meaning of its freedoms . . .

At this point, the camera draws back to show a digitally altered scene: the civil rights crowd has been erased; Dr. King stands alone on an empty platform, speaking to a silent and empty field. The voice of the advertiser then begins a macabre call-and-response:

AD: Before you can inspire . . .
KING: We hold these truths to be self-evident . . .
AD: Before you can touch . . .
KING: That all men are created equal.
AD: You must first connect. And the company that connects more of the world is Alcatel [the screen goes black to show the company name and logo], a leader in communication networks.

Cut back to Dr. King saying, "I have a dream today," more animated now, shaking his head back and forth; before him finally appears the roaring crowd, stretching out to the horizon.*

None of the commercial ventures I have listed are the least bit illegal, of course; the statutes that govern intellectual property dovetail very well with Dexter King's entrepreneurship. As one of his defenders has said, "I don't see how it's any different from the Disney corporation saying, 'We own Mickey Mouse, and if you want Mickey Mouse on your pages you have to pay a fee.'" Indeed, though from my perspective it is precisely the erasure of the distinction between Dr. King and Mickey, the remarkable divergence of what Dr. King's heirs have made of him and what he once made of himself, that needs to be interrogated.

To feel the sharpness of that split, it helps to know a bit about Dr. King's practice as a preacher and the foundations upon which he built his most famous oration. In the early 1950s, as a student at Crozer Theological Seminary in Pennsylvania, Dr. King had taken a class in homiletics, the art of preaching, in which students learned standard structures for sermons. The "ladder sermon," for example, presents an idea in its simplest form and then slowly expands it until the full meaning is clear. The "jewel sermon" addresses a key text again and again from many different points of view. King and his classmates developed yet another form and gave it a name: the "rabbit in the bushes" sermon experiments with a series of phrases or ideas until the preacher finds one to which the congregation particularly responds, at which point he "keep[s] addressing the same idea, just as a hunter might shoot repeatedly into the bushes to see if a rabbit is there." In this model, the "response" part of "call-and-response" is not a passive reflex but has, rather, a shaping and informing function. Whatever theme

---

*Note, by the way, that 38 percent of the words that Dexter King sold to Alcatel were written by Thomas Jefferson.

becomes the center of the sermon is therefore produced collaboratively; preacher and audience are its co-creators.

All this is reported by Drew D. Hansen in *The Dream*, his book
about Dr. King's speech, and it is Hansen's position that the last
seven minutes of Dr. King's speech at the March on Washington
"are best heard in this light, as a gifted preacher testing phrases and
ideas to see what will draw a response from the crowd." Whether
or not this best describes what Dr. King did on that day, it surely
describes what he had been doing in the years leading up to it.
Dr. King had been developing the image of America as "a dream
yet unfulfilled" since at least 1960, and by 1963 it was one of his
set pieces. He came to Washington having learned from previous
audiences what rabbits are hidden in an American crowd, and how
to flush them out.

Dr. King also knew a great deal of political and biblical rhetoric by heart, and the speech is full of other people's language and
other people's ideas. Gandhi's call for "soul force" appears, as do
half a dozen direct lifts from the Bible, including a long verbatim
quotation from Isaiah. All the major themes of the speech have
roots in the tradition of African-American resistance and preaching, from the opening image of a promissory note turned "bad
check" (an analogy previously used by James Baldwin, Malcolm
X, and others) to the closing refrain, "Let freedom ring" (used exactly the same way by Archibald Carey in a 1952 address to the
Republican National Convention).

One of Dr. King's biblical references is worth expanding upon:
early in the speech, he declares that, with faith, "we will be able to
hew out of the mountain of despair a stone of hope." The image
echoes a line from the Book of Daniel in which the story is told of
how Daniel, alone among the wise men of Babylon, proved himself
able to interpret King Nebuchadnezzar's dream. Dr. King once
told his graduate adviser at Boston University that he believed that
dreams emanated from the mind of God; we mortals merely relay
them to others. Such is certainly how dreams are understood in

the Book of Daniel and, moreover, the dream that Daniel expli-
cates turns out to reveal that the Kingdom of God will triumph
over the earthly kingdoms erected by human beings.

In his reading of "the American dream," Dr. King is therefore
working in what's known as the typological interpretive tradition,
one in which events in the Bible are "types," or foretellings, of
things that are to come in actual fact. "I have dreamed a dream,"
says Nebuchadnezzar; the founding fathers "dreamed this dream,"
says Dr. King, who thus presents himself as one who has come
before us, like Daniel, to make sense of something that the rulers
themselves don't understand. It is as if, like Nebuchadnezzar, neither the nation's founders nor its current political elite know how
to read their own dream, and a voice from the kingdom's "captive"
population must step forward to tell them.

Or, rather, the captive has to come before the rulers not as
an individual who has figured something out on his own but as
a messenger of powers greater than himself. Daniel only knew
Nebuchadnezzar's dream because the Lord had revealed it to him
while he slept. As for Dr. King, early in his career he developed the
habit of retreating into solitude to call upon God for help when
preparing public presentations, a pattern he did not break for the
"Dream" speech: well before arriving in Washington, he had separated himself from his advisers so as to be alone and "counsel with
the Lord."

To whom, then, does this great speech belong? By law it belongs
to the King estate, of course, but the more we know about the nature of the thing owned, the more the law seems a procrustean device, distorting rather than responding to the world as it is. Martin
Luther King made his oration from a mix of congregational con-
firmation, inherited material, and inspiration credited to God. The
speech is deservedly famous as a high point of American oratory,
and Dr. King famous as its maker, but the wit of his creation lies,
first of all, in the social work of seeking the "rabbit in the bushes"—
amplifying not his own ideas merely but those to which audiences

assented—and, second, in his ability to absorb the surrounding spiritual and political traditions and reshape them to fit the historical moment. The genius behind "I Have a Dream" is the genius of a talented host, of a collective or public being.

To reiterate one last time the thesis motivating this and the previous chapter: our practices around cultural property allow us to be certain kinds of selves; with them we enable or disable ways of being human. There are practices that constitute us as commercial beings with "partial views," and others that constitute us as public citizens. What Dexter Scott King has done with the "intellectual property" he manages is to move his father from one category to another. He has prived his father, converting a public voice into a chattel. He has managed, in the few decades since Dr. King's death, to reenact in miniature the history by which the founders' civic republicanism slowly mutated into its current commercial form. If Dr. King knew himself by the social movement that contained him, by his collectivity and its encumbrances, the son knows himself (and his father's estate) by the freedoms of the marketplace, by the unencumbered play of fungibles. "In the kingdom of ends everything has either a *price* or a *dignity* . . . Whatever is above all price, and therefore *admits of no equivalent*, has a dignity." There used to be a religious and political being, Dr. Martin Luther King, Jr., the public man; that man has become harder and harder to locate. Soon he will be among the disappeared, a son's erasure of his father's dignity being a form of patricide.

9

ENDURING COMMONS

The argument: The public domain has turned out to be an
unregulated, common-pool resource, subject to all sorts
of cunning appropriations. There are ways to protect it,
however, and thus preserve it as a durable cultural commons.

·

One Law for the Lion & Ox is Oppression.
—WILLIAM BLAKE

With these previous two chapters on the collective self, the main
work of this book is done. Simply put, my project has been to
enlarge the set of stories that might usefully guide our thinking
about the ownership of art and ideas. The major players in the
entertainment and knowledge economies have a compelling tale
to tell, of course, one that (in its boldest form) typically begins
with two assertions: that creators have a natural, unending right
to their work and that the property secured by this right does not
differ in kind from property in land or houses. The conclusion follows swiftly: to invade or take this property without permission is
a crime. After all, theft is theft.

To be sure, there is a less bold form of this tale, one to which
I myself ascribe in its properly limited form. It begins by asserting
that art and ideas, unlike land or houses, belong by nature to a cultural commons, open to all. It then allows for certain chosen exceptions: in the interest of the public good, government sometimes
graces artists and thinkers with monopoly power over their work

and lets them thereby enclose parts of that commons. A more modest and technical conclusion follows: creators to whom we grant such privileges receive as well the right to sue for damages should someone infringe their copyright. After all, a statutory tort is a statutory tort.

That rendering of the tale lacks the gut-level appeal of the natural-rights/theft version, I realize (and it yields no stirring slogans), but it is a more accurate description of how creative ownership has been conceived for the last three hundred years. It leads, moreover, directly into the other narratives that this book has charted, while by contrast, the story based on natural rights closes them off. It sometimes seems, in fact, as if the real point of the bolder vision of creative ownership is simply to preclude debate through a sort of conceptual enclosure. Once we accept that houses and ideas may be lumped together as the same kind of property, and that their owners have *natural* property rights—the kind that supposedly exist prior to all human law—then there is little left to argue about. We are in the realm of first principles and belief, not of public deliberation over contending values.

To speak of privileges and of the public good, on the other hand, leads directly into deliberation and debate. Where property is understood to be a creature of society, society must necessarily argue the ends to which it will be dedicated. Citizens will have to name and defend the "good" that enclosure is meant to serve, and explain how it is to be achieved. Admittedly, one such good might be to maximize the wealth of ingenious men and women (or the corporations that employ them). That, however, has never been a stated goal in the tradition inaugurated by the revolutionaries whose opinions this book set out to recover.* The founders' thoughts on

---

*Nor is it today, whenever the issue reaches the Supreme Court. Justice Sandra Day O'Connor, writing in 1991: "The primary goal of copyright is not to reward authors, but 'to promote the Progress of Science and the useful Arts.'" Chief Justice William Rehnquist, writing in 1994: "We have often recognized the monopoly privileges that Congress has authorized . . . are limited in nature and must ultimately serve the public good."

these matters focused not on private wealth but on other, more collectively valued ends. For John Adams before the Revolution or for James Madison after his term as president, the goal was democratic self-governance. For Benjamin Franklin as a young inventor or for Thomas Jefferson in his retirement, the goal was "the Progress of Science." And for all of these, there was the value of civic virtue, the honor accorded to citizens who seek to enlarge the commonweal. After all, democracy is democracy, creative communities are creative communities, and collective persons are collective persons.

It was with such ends in mind, I believe, that the founders hoped to establish a Republic of Letters, an animating soul for their political republic. What has become apparent, especially in the last fifty years, is that they did not, however, leave us with any good way to beat the bounds of that estate. As my chapter on cultural enclosure set out to show, the public domain has turned out to be highly vulnerable to private capture. How might that vulnerability be reduced? How might an unguarded public domain be converted into a rule-governed and thus durable cultural commons?

In this chapter, I respond to these questions from three points of departure, focusing first on individual commoners, then on communities, and finally on what I call "carrier commons," the mediating institutions that allow for conversation across the internal divides of a complex society such as ours.

COPYDUTY

At a turning point in Coleridge's *Rime of the Ancient Mariner*, the suffering seaman finds himself amazed by the sight of water snakes below the ship:

> *They moved in tracks of shining white,*
> *And when they reared, the elfish light*
> *Fell off in hoary flakes . . .*

O happy living things! no tongue
Their beauty might declare:
A spring of love gushed from my heart,
And I blessed them unaware . . .

The mariner does not decide to bless these creatures; his blessing *arises*. We do not always decide how we respond to the world. We can pick what movie to see this weekend, but some things claim us before all choosing. We are each born into a situation—a particular body (its race, sex, health . . .), a set of ancestors, a community, a nation—and born into the stories told of each of these. Many things precede us, or arise in us choicelessly, like the mariner's blessing.

The freely choosing self is a small part of the whole; larger is the "encumbered self," as Michael Sandel calls it, asking that we remember how often we are "obliged to fulfill ends we have not chosen." Even freedom of conscience, Sandel writes, is not a freedom to make choices. The voice of conscience doesn't present alternative paths; it tells us what to do. "Where freedom of conscience is at stake, the relevant right is to perform a duty, not to make a choice." The waiter in a restaurant will sometimes say, after you pick your entrée, "Good choice"; this is not an appropriate remark to make about someone's beliefs or sense of obligation. We respect (or scorn) someone's beliefs because of the person they become for having them, not for the intelligence displayed in their acquisition. We don't say to a man like Nelson Mandela, drawn into the struggle against apartheid, "Good choice."

It doesn't sound all that attractive, to be encumbered, and yet these things that constrain us (nature, family, convictions) are not things we can easily dispose of, either, and in fact accepting the limitations they bring can lay the foundation for freedoms unavailable without them. Remember the more-the-merrier principle by which roads and waterways, or ancient maypole dancing grounds, must be treated as common assets. No one born to those commons can block the road or fence the festive ground; that choice is removed by a prior duty to the public good. These are restrictions in service of a collectivity that, in the fullness of time, holds the promise of conviviality, merriment, even comedy.

Sandel is a political philosopher, and he places the idea of an encumbered self in the tradition of civic republicanism where "liberty depends on self-government, and self-government depends on the members of a political community's identifying with the role of citizen and acknowledging the obligations that citizenship entails." For democracy to thrive, citizens need to be literate, well-informed, schooled in the contending pluralism of public debate, and so forth. There are duties as well; if judicial power is to be dispersed in the population, then, for example, citizens must serve on juries when called to do so.

Is the *cultural* citizen similarly encumbered? If so it would seem, at least initially, to be a matter of awareness. If "I am a collective being" or if "I is someone else," then there is a limit to what "I" can own, even of "my" creations. Encumbrances constrain control over one's own work, constrain it because no work is wholly "mine" to begin with. The duty of the citizen in the cultural commons is to find the right relationship between the private ego (the one that responds to need and earns a living) and the public ego (the one that receives from the given world and hopes to spread a banquet in return).

To see what such cultural citizenship might mean in concrete terms, how one might act on the duties of an encumbered and comic self, consider an often-told story from the early software community. Programmers at MIT had written code such that when their shared printer jammed or had some other problem, it automatically sent a notice out so that someone could go fix it. When the group later bought a new printer with proprietary software, one of the programmers, Richard Stallman, asked the vendor to send him the machine's source code so that he could add this useful feature. The vendor of course refused, much to Stallman's irritation.

The code almost certainly contained "community property," code written by others and previously shared: what gave someone the right to enclose it and deprive the programming community of its customary right to common? Moments such as this triggered the free software movement.

The issue for Stallman and his peers was not the money especially; the "free" in free software means open access to the source code, not that there can be no commerce in well-made programs. "Free software is a matter of liberty, not price," says the philosophy page of the free software website; it goes on to list four kinds of freedom that the users of software should have:

- The freedom to run the program, for any purpose.
- The freedom to study how the program works, and adapt it to your needs . . .
- The freedom to redistribute copies so you can help your neighbor.
- The freedom to improve the program, and release your improvements to the public, so that the whole community benefits . . .

But how does one keep creative work free in these senses? The solution in this case was to devise a kind of guarded public domain through a cunning combination of copyright and contract law. The creator takes a copyright in the work, then turns around and releases it to the public under a "general public license," or GPL. The GPL lets you use or modify someone else's work so long as, when you are done, you pass along to others all the rights you received, and make sure that they, too, can get at the source code. You may use the work so long as you don't take it private; the work enters the public domain as an alienable good with inalienable freedoms. It is a stinted commons with a limit on enclosures rather than a limit on access. It formalizes the ancient right to resist encroachment.

Innovations like this package of copyright and public license have come to be called "copyleft," an unfortunate term because it falsely implies that measures of this sort have a place on the political spectrum. The "right" in copyright refers to a privilege secured by law and its correlative is "duty," not "left." The GPL imposes a copy-*duty* on its users; they have duties to the commons, the duties of encumbered and comic selves.

The word "common" is said by some to derive from the Latin *com-* (together) and *munis* (under obligation), or perhaps *munia* (duties) from *munus* (office, duty). In the second chapter, I described a commons as "a kind of property in which more than one person has rights," but here we see the corollary: so that others may have these rights, each of us has a duty to resist enclosure. With copyduty we are "together under obligation," which is to say, we are in the commons as originally conceived.

To come back to the general public license, the freedoms of this property regime are directed toward "your neighbor," "the public," "the whole community," a communitarian focus connected to the context out of which it emerged. In the 1970s and early '80s, programmers at places like MIT worked collaboratively, swapping innovations and building reputations rather than fortunes. Computer programs were often collective works, their authors collective beings with a perhaps unconscious sense that, as such, certain actions should be out of bounds. The GPL makes explicit these otherwise unstated norms, and gives them legal backbone.

It does not, as noted, prohibit commerce so long as the foundational freedoms are preserved. As such, in allowing for a mixture of the common and the commercial, the free software philosophy recognizes the plurality of human selfhood. Human ends and contexts are exceedingly various, and if either custom or law mandated them to be governed by some unitary rule, the consequence would surely be oppression, as Blake suggests in this chapter's epigraph. A free software purist who demanded that everything lie in the commons would be as much of a tyrant as a market purist who demanded that all things be commodified.

This need to respect human complexity, and the oppressive consequences of failing to do so, is the subject of one of the reflections to be found in Blaise Pascal's *Pensées*. Loosely translated, it says something like this:

> It is in the nature of tyranny for one realm of life to desire power outside its own sphere, and over the whole world even. There are different kinds of persons—the strong, the handsome, the smart, the devout—and each of these hopes to shine in his or her own sphere, though not by that in another.
>
> Sometimes two spheres meet, and the wise and the rich fight for mastery—foolishly, for their mastery is of different kinds. They misunderstand each other, and each makes the mistake of aiming at universal dominion. Nothing can win this, not even money, for it is powerless in the kingdom of the wise.
>
> The following statements, therefore, are false and tyrannical: "Because I am handsome, so I should command respect." "I am rich, therefore you should love me." "I am strong, therefore you must believe what I believe." "I am entertaining, therefore elect me to office." "My industry is key to our economy, therefore let me teach your children."
>
> Tyranny is the wish to obtain by one means what can only be had by another. We owe different duties to different qualities.

That is actually my slight remix of a passage from the *Pensées*, one I first found in Michael Walzer's *Spheres of Justice*, a book based on the idea that there are discrete areas of social life (family, church, market, school, labor, the legislature, the military, art, entertainment, the media, the environment, and more), that each of these has distinct norms and values, and that if we can manage to protect each from becoming dominated by one of the others, we might live with a kind of equality commensurate with the complexity of actual social life.

While the story of the origins of the GPL makes a good illustration of how individuals can move to preserve the integrity of their common holdings, Walzer's reading of Pascal allows us to widen the frame and speak of how communities might do the same. In regard to social complexity, Walzer's point is that a basic form of inequality, if not tyranny, arises whenever one sphere of social life begins to command the others. In an aristocracy, family of birth is paramount, and claims about breeding are used to legitimize control over land, education, the clergy, and so on. In a theocracy, those who say they know the word of God can reach out and control family life, the military, the markets, and so on. Technocracies, meritocracies, plutocracies—all these carry seeds of dominion as well, for in each a range of goods beyond their proper sphere lies at the bidding of one particular group, those who have technical expertise, say, or higher learning, or access to capital.

The concern here is not with relative domination *within* any one sphere. There will always be politicians skillful enough to command more power than their peers; there will be investors who manage risk more skillfully than others; there will be scholars who rise to authority in their disciplines. Such internal hierarchies are one thing; it is quite another when politicians can manipulate the stock exchange, or when the calls of capital can run the universities, or when some version of meritocracy can bar common citizens from the voting booth or the jury pool.

In the modern age, the worst form of tyranny has arisen when state power commands every other sphere. Nothing on that initial list (family, church, market, school, etc.) lies untouched in a totalitarian state. Less grim, surely, but no less common is plutocracy in its modern form, in which capital commands goods well beyond its markets. For Walzer, it should be said, capitalism is not by itself unjust; the creation of surplus value is a function proper to one sphere. The question is "whether this surplus value is convertible, whether it purchases special privileges, in the law courts, or in the educational system, or in the spheres of office and politics." These it surely does, such that "in the United States today it is the tyranny of money that most clearly invites resistance."

When it comes to the cultural commons, the monied spheres that threaten domination are a handful of influential fiefdoms within the larger kingdom of capital, especially those dedicated to entertainment and biotechnology. At issue are not the values proper to each of these but rather their reach. Perhaps it makes sense within the entertainment industry to have every creation be owned in perpetuity and then to negotiate permissions and fees around each use. But that is not a norm appropriate to science, nor to the creative arts, nor to the circulation of knowledge among self-governing citizens, and to extend it into those spheres is an insult to their integrity, an act of simple tyranny in Pascal's sense.

The death of the singer and congressman Sonny Bono (who crashed into a tree while skiing) happened to coincide with the entertainment industry's last big copyright bill in the U.S. Congress. Known colloquially as the Mickey Mouse Protection Act, this legislation was in fact named by Congress after the fallen entertainer. The Sonny Bono Copyright Term Extension Act: it seems an accident built on an accident, this memorializing juxtaposition, but the confluence of forces it represents is indicative. Entertainment has sufficient command of political power that laws appropriate to its world become the laws of the land and, heralded always by FBI warnings, they penetrate every other sphere.

Most egregious may be the way that Hollywood has exported its rules for intellectual property to the college campuses. I began this book with the industry's propaganda campaign meant to encourage educators to teach the "theft is theft" story of cultural ownership. A 2006 letter sent by the University of Southern California's "deputy chief information officer" to all incoming freshmen gives a striking example of obedient follow-through. Warning students against sharing files on the Internet, the letter gave a flatly false description of copyright infringement (failing to explain educational and fair use exceptions, for example), it threatened "legal sanctions" and loss of privileges, and it contained the revolutionary assertion that the university's "purpose is to promote and foster the creation and lawful use of intellectual property." In Southern California at least, entertainment's dominion over education has neared completion.

Happily, there are contrary examples. In 2007 the U.S. Congress considered an entertainment industry proposal that would have forced colleges and universities to place file-sharing filters on their computer networks in the hope of detecting unauthorized downloading. As worthy as that goal may be, it is not one well fitted to the actual uses of academic computing. As MIT's chief "information services" officer, Jerrold Grochow, explained in a letter to Congress, no "deterrent technology" yet exists that can block illegal file-sharing while still allowing the flow of information needed for teaching and research. "Filesharing occurs on an on-going basis in the scientific research process," Grochow explained, and sharing "large datasets with colleagues across campus and across the country" has become "a cornerstone of academic research." MIT both educates its students in regard to unauthorized downloading and maintains strict "Rules of Use" agreements, but beyond that, filtering the entire network "is simply not an acceptable option in the research context."

> Even if deterrent mechanisms are developed that do not disrupt legitimate data sharing, the proposed software deterrents we have reviewed are not able to scan our network traffic at the bit rate at which a research-intensive university network such as ours operates (rates as high as 10 gigabits per second).

Network filters would, in short, amount to an encroachment upon the university's necessary knowledge commons; that being the case, a line must be drawn and Congress should certainly not help the industry erase it.

In early modern times, they used to speak of "property as propriety," a phrase that has gone out of style but might usefully be revived in a context like this. In a proprietarian model, one's property brings with it responsibility to one's community. As the legal scholar Carol Rose writes, "What is 'proper' or appropriate, on this vision of property, is that which is needed to keep good order in the commonwealth or body politic." Especially where we make property out of the creations of the human mind and imagination, we may rightly interrogate the propriety of the ends for which the privileges of ownership have been secured. If the proper mission of a university is to preserve, create, and disseminate knowledge, and if that mission conflicts with values from other spheres, then propriety demands resistance. College information officers should not so happily accept the sheriff's badges sent them from Hollywood. They should rather annually walk the boundaries of the campus, repairing the stints and tearing down encroachments. What Walzer calls "complex equality" depends on acknowledging that distinct spheres of social life exist, and that their values differ; the plurality of these is worth preserving, it being among other things a stay against tyranny.

FREEDOM OF LISTENING

I have now spoken of durable commons from two points of view, that of individual commoners (developing rules to express their sense of duty, à la Sandel) and that of particular communities (resisting the encroachment of other spheres, à la Walzer). Software licenses requiring downstream sharing, a university refusing to let the entertainment industry filter its network—each of these brings to the surface exactly the kind of usage rules or stints that have always served to keep a commons, cultural or otherwise, durable and robust.

I want now to speak of the more complicated problem of how to preserve the integrity of the common spaces that lie *between* distinct communities in any complex society. I once found myself speaking of institutional resistance to a representative of the music industry, and his response to my distinction between education and entertainment was to ask, "Yes, but who is encroaching on whose sphere?" From his point of view, student downloading of copyrighted songs was an assault on his territory, not the other way around. That seems right, and makes more pointed the question of how distinct spheres of value, or people with differing senses of duty, are to meet and speak to one another. What happens to the old idea of public virtue if the alternative to tyranny turns out to be a series of walled gardens? Is there a way to preserve the integrity of a stinted commons and still have a conversation about the common good?

Both art and politics have ways to answer these questions, and I want to turn to another anecdote from the life of Benjamin Franklin in order to approach one of these.

In 1739 a Methodist minister named George Whitefield arrived in Philadelphia to preach evangelical Protestantism. At first the local clergy shared their pulpits with the visitor, but soon they turned against him and forced Whitefield to deliver his message in the streets and fields. Franklin tells us that although he did not usually agree with Whitefield, he enjoyed his oratory and was sometimes moved despite himself. Agreeing or not, Franklin objected to the way that the established churches denied a roof to Whitefield and thus he and a group of friends raised a fund and built a large lecture hall, a hundred feet long and seventy feet wide,

expressly for the Use of any Preacher of any religious Persuasion who might desire to say something to the People of Philadelphia,

the Design in building not being to accommodate any particular Sect, but the Inhabitants in general, so that even if the Mufti
of Constantinople were to send a Missionary to preach Maho-
metanism to us, he would find a Pulpit at his Service.

This lecture hall later became the initial building of the Philadelphia
Academy and the Academy in turn eventually became the University of Pennsylvania.

In terms of spheres of value, this space seems at first to belong
to religion, but oddly so, for all are invited, not just one (that would
have made it a church). More properly it might be said to belong
to religious difference or—when it eventually becomes part of a
university—to difference as it arises in and among the branches of
knowledge. In either case, the building might be thought of as dedicated to a search for the good and the true, with the background
assumption that beliefs about these are various and in contention.

What the rival ministers of Philadelphia did when they forbade
Whitefield the use of their pulpits was to suppress a contending
voice, one that called their sense of the truth into question. They
were arguably right to do so: not every sphere of social life is obliged
to admit other values, especially those in flat disagreement with its
own. Anglicans do not have any obligation to invite a Methodist
to occupy their pulpit; I see no reason to fault the ministers whose
antagonism to Whitefield led them to draw the line.

At the same time, to create a space where real difference can
be spoken and explored seems a useful contribution. A distinction
is in order, then, between the kind of antagonism that closes the
door and silences opponents, and this other thing that welcomes
conflict, entertains it, enjoys it even. One line of political thought
now calls this latter category not "antagonism" but "agonism," an
agon in ancient Greek drama being a verbal contest between two
characters on the stage, both of whom appeal to the audience, neither having any necessary claim to the truth.

More broadly, Greek democracy would seem to have borrowed from drama in this case, for democracy flourishes whenever antagonism can be converted into agonism. As the psychoanalyst Adam Phillips has explained in a useful essay, antagonism pits enemies against one another, each side trying to destroy or silence its opponents; agonism, on the other hand, is a conflict among equals, and while some will be more persuasive, none are silenced, all are in play. Seen in this way, the space that Franklin and his friends built belongs not so much to religion as to democracy, where democracy is an experiment in agonistic pluralism.

For democracy to flourish after the American Revolution meant discarding both the tools by which oppositional voices were silenced and the consequent aristocratic norm of pretended consensus. In the Colonies as in England, remember, it was illegal to publish parliamentary debates, newspapers were printed only "by authority," and dissenters could be jailed, exiled, or executed. All that changed in the decades after 1776. The shift in tone and practice is nicely caught in Washington Irving's tale of Rip Van Winkle. Old Van Winkle goes hunting in the mountains, plays at ninepins with some odd-looking fellows dressed in "the antique Dutch fashion," drinks their liquor, and falls asleep for twenty years. When he returns to town, the sign at the inn sporting the "ruby face of King George" has been replaced with one showing General Washington holding "a sword . . . instead of a sceptre." Van Winkle has slept through the Revolution: "The very character of the people seemed changed. There was a busy, bustling, disputatious tone about it, instead of the accustomed phlegm and drowsy tranquility." The old man fell asleep under monarchy and woke up in democracy, in a world of agonistic pluralism where public life includes the pleasures of discord. The old aristocratic orders are gone and political parties have sprung up; as he comes into town, people ask Van Winkle if he's a Federal or a Democrat.

Franklin reports that, in appointing trustees to manage the lecture hall, care was taken "to avoid giving a Predominancy to any Sect, so that one of each was appointed, viz. one Church of England-man, one Presbyterian, one Baptist, one Moravian, &c." The hall was clearly meant to accommodate freedom of speech; as long as that speech is sectarian, however, and where at the same time no one sect can dominate, it would be better to say that it was dedicated to *freedom of listening.* Individual speakers present singular views; individual listeners entertain plurality. Listeners get the synoptic view, or rather the *synauditory* hearing. Over time they get to hear the multiplicity of Christian sects and, if the Mufti of Constantinople and others were to come, the multiplicity of the non-Christian world as well. The hall was thus built to serve the eighteenth-century ideal of replacing the partial self with a plural or public self, one who is a host to many voices, even those otherwise at odds with the singular being you thought you were when you first walked in the door.

If we take free listening to be the true end of free speech, then freedom itself takes on a different aspect. The freedom to listen we have in our collectivity, not in our individuality. It is a common freedom, not an individual or private one. Remember from an earlier chapter Hannah Arendt's reading of the Greek distinction between what is our own (*idios*) and what we hold in common (*koinon*), and the consequent implication that any life spent wholly on one's own is by nature idiotic. Franklin shares that assumption: intelligence arises in the common world, where many voices can be heard; it belongs to collectivity, not privacy, and is available especially to those who can master the difficult art of plural listening.

A modern example of that difficult art, one at once dramatic and political, can be found in Anna Deavere Smith's 1992 theater performance, *Fires in the Mirror.* Smith took it as her task to dramatize the story of the 1991 riot in Crown Heights, Brooklyn, among African-Americans and Lubavitch Jews following an automobile accident in which a Jewish driver killed a seven-year-old

black boy and a young Jewish scholar was murdered in retalia-
tion. Soon after these events, Smith sought out dozens of citizens
in Crown Heights, asking each to talk about what had happened.
In the resulting solo performance, Smith brought twenty-six of
her respondents to life, letting them speak through her, taking on
their gestures, postures, accents, and opinions, giving them body
and presence. In a sense she made herself into the collective being
that was the neighborhood of Crown Heights, complete with all its
partial views, misunderstandings, and unresolved conflicts. The
result was not some cheerful "image of all of us holding hands,"
she once told an interviewer, but rather an embodiment of serious
difference. "Crown Heights is no melting pot."

And yet Smith herself, as dramatist and actor, performed for
her audience the kind of self-abnegation necessary if something
larger than difference is to arise. She transformed lethal antagonism into artful agonism. Smith has said that she was never drawn
to the dramatic technique in which actors are supposed to find
some commonality between themselves and their characters. She
assumes she's *not* like her characters; to play them she simply listens, and lends her voice. "Put on your headphones, repeat what
he said. That's all. That's it." Except that isn't it, not entirely, for in
giving space to twenty-six truly distinct voices the actor's "I" must
become Rimbaud's "someone else." "Many of the characters have
chiseled away at the gate that's between them and Anna," Smith
has said, speaking in the third person where we'd normally expect
the first person, as if to distinguish the dramatic plural self from
the singular Anna who buys the groceries and takes them home
at night.

To return then to the hall that Franklin and friends built, mark
again how the trustees of that institution were divided such that
none of the many sects had control. Anna Deavere Smith's drama
and that listening space—that *auditorium*—are artistic and political versions of what lies between potentially contending spheres of
social life, the point being that the very fact of betweenness means

that in neither case can there be any one center of power. The dramatist may repeat the voices she has heard, her representation of them may have consequences, but her own agency is restricted to giving them a hearing. In the case of Franklin's auditorium, no one sect by itself can set policy or approve or disapprove of programs. The trustees' task is to keep the door open and preserve audibility.

In this regard, their trusteeship is a model in miniature for what later came to be called the "divided sovereignty" of American governance.* With divided sovereignty, no leader has the kind of full command we associate with monarchs, dictators, and tyrants. In a democracy that honors listening, leaders do not so much decide policy as enable conversation, helping the public remain audible and visible to itself. A leader's obligations are to transparency and to keeping the noise low enough that no speaker gets drowned out.

It will be useful to pause here and elaborate on a distinction made only briefly above. The focus of this chapter is the problem of how to structure enduring cultural commons. The first answer harks back to the agricultural commons of old: consider the stints that protect any commons from internal misuse and external encroachments. Any number of creative communities offer illustration as, for example, those that develop free software or those that annotate the human genome. What I'm calling "Franklin's auditorium" is not precisely one of these communities, however; it belongs to a different category, one arising from allowed plurality. Where there are sects and factions, or where there are multiple spheres of social life, in-between spaces necessarily appear, gaps

---

*The phrase referred originally to *federal* government, one in which no national power can command the states; it has come to describe as well the divisions of power built into the national government itself such that no branch rules unchecked. I use it here to indicate a precondition of complex equality and also, by putting an emphasis on "divided," to point to the between spaces where no one governs such that plural listening becomes possible.

where difference must be acknowledged and then, if possible, enjoyed. In such spaces, we find the commons of "common carriers."

This phrase has a particular meaning in the law (referring for example to railroads obliged to carry any passenger or to telephone companies obliged to let all paying customers use their lines), but I mean to use it here to denote any institution, medium, or space that carries or allows for public conversation. Franklin's auditorium was a common carrier in this sense, as are the telephone or postal systems, Internet service providers, newspapers, broadcast media, public roads and waterways, or the "traditional public forums" mentioned some chapters ago, the sidewalks and parks that "have immemorially been held in trust for the use of the public and, time out of mind, have been used for purposes of assembly, communicating thoughts between citizens, and discussing public questions."

Not all such "carriers" need be public or common, of course; there are plenty of private auditoriums, courier services, and so forth. But some are expressly public, and these are what interest me. Franklin's lecture hall was built for "the Inhabitants in general," and Anna Deavere Smith created her art, or so it seems to me, not just to reflect on the Crown Heights riots but to demonstrate how listening functions if one tries to quit all faction and stand attentive in the gaps between.

My point, then, has been to distinguish between commons that pertain to specific communities and "carrier commons" (to flip the usual term), those that enable the interstitial conversations of complex or plural society. And it is in thinking about the durability of this latter category that I began to address the idea of divided sovereignty, the idea being that when it comes to carrier commons a prohibition on unitary sovereignty can serve as a protective stint.

The suggestion that sovereignty need not be unitary took hold in the early American Republic in part because the founders were exceedingly wary of power itself. Oliver Noble, writing in

1775 from Rhode Island, gives a typical expression: "Men in high stations . . . increase their ambition, and study rather to be more powerful than wiser or better . . . Voracious like the grave, they can never have enough, *i.e.* of power and wealth." The love of power being insatiable, it being "whetted, not cloyed, by possession," as another writer put it, the idea of dividing it against itself had considerable appeal.

In regard to freedom of listening, divided sovereignty is meant to provide a structural restraint such that those in power might find it harder to suppress contending voices. If the freedom of listening can be had only in our collectivity, it follows that in the public sphere no single power should be able to control the range of particular voices. In terms of the "spheres of social life," then, the public sphere is unique. It is the in-between sphere that allows the others to converse among themselves. It is the space of the carrier commons, and when it comes to these, ideally, no one should have a veto power over what can and cannot travel.

Liberty therefore has a marked meaning in the public sphere, one that early modern political thinkers recovered from antiquity. In London in the late sixteenth century, the ancient Roman political theorists and philosophers—Cicero, Livy, Tacitus, and more—appeared for the first time in English translation, and these in turn widely influenced civic republican thought regarding liberty. The *Digest* of Roman laws summarized a key distinction: "all men and women are either free or slaves." This opposition, *libertas* versus *servitus*, had a wider meaning in Roman usage than the one we bring to it if we think only of slavery as it later appeared in America. In Rome, slavery or servitude meant living under *any* condition of domination or dependence. In Quentin Skinner's summary: "To enjoy liberty . . . it is not sufficient to be free from coercion or the threat of it; it is necessary to be free from the *possibility* of being threatened or coerced."

If the monarch's word is final in all things, then subjects are slaves no matter how benevolent their ruler, no matter if his or her power is rarely exercised, and no matter if most laws originate in Parliament. Of servitude in this sense, Cicero declared that "the most miserable feature of this condition is that, even if the master happens not to be oppressive, he can be so should he wish." To be ruled by laws rather than men thus means that even monarchs must be subject to the constraints of law and, wrote Cicero, in this case "the highest law is the well-being of the people," *salus populi suprema lex esto.*

By the 1640s, when Charles I and the British Parliament began the confrontation that would lead to civil war, it had become a commonplace of English thought that the liberty of citizens should be defined as freedom from any and all superior power. Significant then was Charles I's claim to possess what was called a "Negative Voice" when it came to laws enacted by Parliament. Essentially a veto power, Negative Voice came to be understood by the Crown's opponents in classical terms: if the king had such prerogatives, all citizens were slaves.

I have paused to recall this historical opposition between liberty and the monarch's Negative Voice because I believe it to be one of the things that lay behind the founders' wariness in regard to giving anyone monopoly power over the common stock of knowledge, ideas, and expression. As we have seen, when it came to the circulation of knowledge, men like Madison, Adams, and Jefferson were always concerned with questions of power and subordination. Remember that essay of Madison's in which, after laying out reasons for limiting copyright and patent, he declared that "perpetual monopolies of every sort are forbidden . . . by the genius of free Governments." And remember Adams's attack on the Stamp Act: it was a long complaint about feudal law, which he read as a system "of iniquity" devised simply to gratify "the desire for dominion," that "encroaching, grasping, restless, and ungovernable power." And remember that liberty for Adams was above all the liberty to learn and that America was its home, Puritans in England having been "vexed and tortured . . . for no other crime than . . . their freedom of inquiry and examination."

Supreme Court Justice Stephen Breyer nicely brought this line of thought into the present when he once underscored a connection between the idea of a limited monarchy and the Constitutional language intended to limit monopoly privilege. Dissenting from the Court's affirmation of the Sonny Bono Copyright Term Extension Act, and noting that it is "well established" that copyright "must serve public, not private, ends," Breyer paused to point out that Samuel Johnson's *Dictionary*—the one the founders would have known—illustrated its definition of "limited" with the phrase "a *limited* monarch," meaning a monarch "restrain[ed]" and "circumscribe[d]," "not [left] at large."

To juxtapose monarchy and monopoly seems exactly right in this context, for it brings a foundational idea about liberty to bear in the present: in the sense that the framers inherited from Roman law, where an unlimited monarch has the last word in legislative matters, or where content owners have the last word in speech, no citizen is truly free. If democratic practice (not to mention creativity) depends on plural speech and plural listening, then we should rightly be reluctant to give any modern form of Negative Voice a presence in the public sphere.

But of course we have.

APHASIA

Copyright's monopoly privileges are meant to encourage creative work, and this they surely do. That said, once a state-sanctioned right to exclude has been granted, it can encourage many other things as well, including attempts to control public discussion and debate. Here are a few examples I came across while writing this book:

- The estate of the lyricist Lorenz Hart refused to allow a biographer who mentioned Hart's homosexuality to use any of the songwriter's lyrics.

- A niece of James McNeill Whistler refused his first biographer permission to print the painter's letters.
- The Church of Scientology has regularly tried to silence critics with claims that they infringe on the Church's copyrights; they have sued *The Washington Post* for quoting Church documents; in 1995 they managed to get federal marshals to seize the home computer of a former Scientologist on the grounds that it contained copyrighted material.
- John Lennon's heirs sued to force the removal of a fifteen-second sample of his song "Imagine" from a film critical of Darwin's theory of evolution.
- In the late 1960s, the widow of E. E. Cummings refused to allow the poet's antiwar poems to appear in an anthology opposing the Vietnam War.
- A woman who published interviews offering "the Pro-Choice view" of abortion denied a later author's request to use excerpts from her book to frame his own discussion of the debate; when the latter author, a Catholic priest and professor of theology at Notre Dame, used excerpts without permission, the pro-choice author sued for infringement.
- The Picasso estate refused to let the filmmaker James Ivory use any images of the painter's work in his film version of Françoise Gilot's *Life with Picasso*.
- The author of a book on children's art and modern artists could not obtain permission to use a photograph of Picasso watching his daughter draw because the owner of the image disagreed with the book's thesis.
- The estate of the poet Countee Cullen refused to let Poet Laureate Robert Pinsky use one of Cullen's poems in his documentary "Favorite Poem Project" after learning that the young man who recited the poem spoke also about his own homosexuality.
- The conservative talk show host Michael Savage has used copyright infringement suits in his attempts to constrain critics who post samples of his show on their websites.

- The author of a history of Depression-era American photography who wanted to reproduce images from a 1932 book about chain gangs found herself blocked by the Georgia Bureau of Prisons, which denied permission, preferring to have the material suppressed.
- NBC refused to license a video clip of President George W. Bush for use in Robert Greenwald's 2003 documentary, *Uncovered: The Whole Truth About the Iraq War.*
- For Greenwald's 2004 *Outfoxed: Rupert Murdoch's War on Journalism*, CBS refused to let Greenwald use a clip of Richard Clarke's appearance on *60 Minutes* (despite an offer to pay a licensing fee), and WGBH in Boston wouldn't let him use excerpts from *Frontline* for fear of looking too "political."
- Samuel Beckett's estate refuses to allow theater companies to perform his plays in versions it deems unorthodox.
- Robert Frost's publisher refuses all requests to set his poems to music.
- In the 1980s, when the Soviet refugee artist Mihail Chemiakin, frustrated by Americans' ignorance of Russian iconography, painted an image of Mickey Mouse handing a can of Campbell's soup to a Russian aristocrat, the Walt Disney Company threatened an infringement suit, got the Mickey image covered with brown paper at Chemiakin's gallery, and forced cancellation of planned reprints.
- In 1975, taking advantage of certain restrictions on imports of copyrighted material, Disney managed to impede the importation of *How to Read Donald Duck*, a Marxist reading of their cartoons printed in London. Fifteen years later, Disney denied the author of an article about the incident permission to reprint quotations from their letters sent during the course of negotiations with the Center for Constitutional Rights and the Treasury Department.
- In 2008, Harvard University refused to let the authors of a book about digital information print a screen shot of the

university's own Web posting of Harvard President Lawrence Summers's remarks on women in science (apparently to protect Summers from embarrassment).

Denials such as these have been even more common in recent years as a consequence of the 1998 Digital Millennium Copyright Act. This law offers Internet websites such as Google or YouTube a safe harbor from litigation if they respond quickly to copyright infringement complaints by taking down the allegedly offending posts. The websites themselves are not in a position to evaluate the claims they receive (litigation over the fair uses of someone else's material are famously complicated), so sites receiving complaints invariably respond by removing the material rather than risking their safe harbor. It is true that the alleged infringer can then demand that the content be restored, but filing a counter-take-down notice is complicated and time-consuming. Consequently, the DMCA has turned out to offer a handy new way to hamper someone else's speech. Some examples of DMCA interventions include:

- During the 2008 presidential campaign, as noted at the start of this book, news organizations, including both Fox and CBS, demanded that John McCain commercials be removed from YouTube because they infringed the organizations' copyrights.
- When the activist group the Yes Men posted a parodic critique of Dow Chemical's response to the toxic chemical spill in Bhopal, the company used the DMCA to sever the Yes Men's link to their Internet service provider.
- Similarly, when e-mail messages were leaked from Diebold, Inc., the maker of electronic voting machines, the company used the DMCA to get them removed from the Internet.*

*The e-mails in question described software flaws, sham tests, and machines running on uncertified code. "For a demonstration I suggest you fake it," read one; "Program them both so they look the same, and then just do the upload . . . That is what we did in the last . . . demo."

Among the many sites posting these documents was one run by students at Swarthmore College who were planning a symposium on voting security. After Diebold's DMCA request, the college removed the students' posting.

It is true, of course, that there are complexities to many of these cases. Some involve questions of privacy or personal reputation and some a concern for the ongoing integrity of an artist's creation. But in the United States, where free expression is itself celebrated, none of these things is supposed to be central to copyright.*

It is also true that some of the cases I have listed were eventually resolved in favor of speech. John Lennon's heirs lost in court, as did the author of the pro-choice book; the Yes Men eventually got their Internet service back; after the 2004 election was over, the Swarthmore students prevailed against Diebold. But in most of the other cases, it was the constraint of speech that prevailed and, either way, in all of them it is the sequence of events that is troubling: it is easy to deny permission but time-consuming and costly to challenge the denial.

Consider a case that I touched on in the opening chapter but omitted from this list because it is worth looking at in some detail. The estate of James Joyce has been notoriously litigious ever since it was inherited by the novelist's grandson, Stephen James Joyce. Hostile particularly to scholars, Stephen Joyce forced a biographer of Joyce's wife, Nora, to delete part of her book; he blocked public readings of *Ulysses* (including one sponsored by the government of Ireland) and sued to halt publication of a scholarly edition of that novel; he halted release of a multimedia version of *Ulysses* by demanding a $1.5 million fee; and he forced the Stanford scholar Carol Shloss to remove 40 percent of the citations in her book

---

*In U.S. law, for example, privacy belongs more to the living than to the dead. As the legal scholar Melville Nimmer has written, in general "the right of privacy may not be asserted by heirs or an estate on behalf of a decedent."

about Joyce's daughter Lucia (whereupon reviewers criticized the work for lacking evidence). Surveying this history in a *New Yorker* essay, D. T. Max concluded that scholarly and creative response to James Joyce, which "was once an area of exploration and discovery," has now become merely "an embattled outpost of copyright law." Just as the heirs of Martin Luther King, Jr., have diminished the civil rights leader's public voice, so has Stephen Joyce managed to hobble a generation of interest and discussion of his grandfather's work.

I have been enumerating these examples of blocked or balky permissions not just to illustrate the idea that we've allowed a new form of Negative Voice to enter the public sphere, but also to connect that fact to the earlier idea that plural listening is one of the things that enables collective being. Aristotle defined a human being as both a "political animal" and an animal "capable of speech." These are linked definitions, of course, so long as politics is conducted through persuasion, and the link implies a reversal: those whose speech is blocked cannot be political and so cannot be fully human. To come back to Hannah Arendt's reading of this tradition, in the Greek view "everyone outside the *polis*—slaves and barbarians—was *aneu logou*, deprived . . . of a way of life in which speech . . . made sense and where the central concern of all citizens was to talk with each other." Supreme Court Justice Louis Brandeis once said the same thing in the American context:

> Those who won our independence believed that the final end of the State was to make men free to develop their faculties . . . They believed . . . that the greatest menace to freedom is an inert people; that public discussion is a political duty, and that this should be a fundamental principle of the American government.

As in the line of thought I have been tracing from the days of Charles I through the American Revolution, prohibitions on speech turn agents into subjects, free citizens into servants or worse. The

growing reach of private monopoly privilege divides and encloses
formerly open fields, allows the right to exclude to trump the right
to common, and leaves each woman and man less likely to mature
into the kind of plural self best suited for creativity, spiritual life,
and politics.

The result I think of as a kind of cultural aphasia. Actual aphasia (the consequence of a stroke or other brain injury) is a loss of
speech that, at its simplest level, manifests as an inability to call
words to mind. An aphasiac is not without thought; he or she
might be able to play chess but unable to say "king," "queen," and
"bishop." The cultural aphasiac would be someone like the Joyce
scholar not permitted to communicate 40 percent of the evidence
for her book. Such a scholar has no trouble thinking about her
case; she just can't produce the words that back it up. Swarthmore
students have no trouble finding evidence related to voting security; they just can't produce it in public until after the election has
passed. The Yes Men's critique of Dow Chemical was finally re-
posted, but it took them days to get their voices back.

In each case, the law makes it easy to block speech and difficult
to recover it. Years after Carol Shloss's book was published, the
Stanford Law School's Fair Use Project brought a suit against the
Joyce estate for having bullied Shloss out of her fair use right to
quote from the novelist's work and papers. The suit was successful and Shloss has posted her evidence on a website. One might
then say that speech prevailed over the estate's Negative Voice, that
the system worked. But note the sequence: the Joyce estate's monopoly comes first, the recovery of speech second. Copyright law
allows the "fair use" of other people's work, but fair use currently
operates more as a *defense* against a charge of infringement than
as a legal right, and a successful defense of a fair use claim is ex-
pensive, prohibitively so if no public interest law clinic steps in to
help. In point of fact, the court found that in the Joyce case the
estate had so misused its copyright powers that it owed the plaintiffs their attorney fees and costs. These amounted to $240,000. In

the Diebold case, they amounted to $125,000. If this is the kind of wealth needed to defend a fair use claim, few will take the risk. Thus even cases resolved in favor of expression are examples of cultural aphasia: speech comes after great struggle. We no longer live in the founders' auditorium.

GOVERNING THE COMMONS

There was a time, now long past, when most of the examples of blocked or aphasic speech just enumerated could not have happened, simply because the right to exclude was more strictly limited in time and scope. If the founders' copyright laws were still to govern cultural ownership, the work of most of the authors just mentioned would lie in the public domain and the dead hand of the past would be powerless to meddle with expression in the present. But, as we saw in the chapter on enclosure, the history of copyright has been a story of constant expansion in all regards.

Let me, then, return to the questions asked at the opening of this chapter. The public domain has, as I said, turned out to be vulnerable to private capture, each generation of content owners helping themselves to yet another slice. How might that be changed? How might the public domain be converted into a protected, durable, and rule-governened commons? Is there a way to give a cultural commons the kind of internal stints that ensured the longevity of traditional agricultural commons? When threatened by encroachments, how might those with use rights in that commons beat the bounds of their villages? What would be the cultural equivalent of an annual perambulation with cakes and beer, the inhabitants armed with axes and crowbars to act on the ancient rule that citizens may tear down enclosures when they arise?

I doubt we will be able to devise anything as convivial as that, but, nonetheless, over the past few decades (as I've begun to show) enough resistance has arisen, and enough innovations have appeared in regard to setting rules for longevity, that we can begin to chart some patterns and (to echo a phrase from Paul Goodman) hammer out some rules of thumb.

Consider, for example, how in the early 1960s a small group of folksingers addressed the puzzle of who "owns" the civil rights anthem "We Shall Overcome." The song's history is difficult to document, although Pete Seeger, whose account I follow here, supposes that its roots go back to a gospel song published in 1903 and written by a Philadelphia preacher, Rev. Charles Tindely. Called "I'll Overcome Some Day," Tindely's lyrics end with "If in my heart I do not yield, I'll overcome some day." (The version sung in the civil rights movement ends "Deep in my heart, I do believe, we shall overcome some day.") There is, in addition, a folk song, author unknown, called "I'll Be All Right." It has similar words but different music and a faster tempo. It ends: "Deep in my heart, I do believe, I'll be all right some day."

Which came first? No one knows.

We do know what happened next, however. In 1946 a woman named Lucille Simmons used to sing "I'll Be All Right" on the picket line during a tobacco workers' strike in Charleston, South Carolina, only she slowed the song down and changed "I" to "we": "We do believe . . ." From there the song migrated to the Highlander Folk School, a center for civil rights activists (Rosa Parks trained there before that famous day when she refused to move to the back of the bus). Seeger himself learned it at Highlander and subsequently published it as "We Will Overcome" in a 1947 collection, *People's Songs*. In 1960 another singer, Guy Carawan, taught the song to a group of civil rights activists, altering the pace once more by making the rhythm more pronounced. No one knows who changed "will" to "shall" ("It could have been me with my Harvard education," says Seeger).

Soon "We Shall Overcome" was *the* movement song. At that point, however, the problem arose of how to protect something that no one owns. As Seeger tells the story: "In the early '60s our publishers said to us, 'if you don't copyright this now, some Hollywood types will have a version out next year like "Come on Baby, We shall overcome tonight."'" As Seeger remarks in another context, "In a social system where everything has to be owned . . . , to leave something 'un-owned' means to simply abandon it and allow it to be mistreated. Look what's happened to the air and water."

Since the 1960s, when Seeger first asked these questions, what actually happened in regard to air and water is that an environmental movement arose to protect them (one that includes Seeger's own efforts to clean up the Hudson River). Such movements never arise fully formed, however; they get invented bit by bit until some inflection point comes when people see that the bits can fit together into something larger. As for the "cultural commons" bit contributed by Seeger in regard to "We Shall Overcome," he and three others who had been singing and changing the song for a decade "signed a 'Songwriter's contract.'" In so doing, they didn't take the song private, however: "All royalties and income . . . go to a non-profit fund . . . which annually gives grants to further African-American music in the South." Whenever Seeger himself publishes the song, the copyright notice typically says that "royalties derived from this composition are being contributed to the We Shall Overcome Fund . . . under the trusteeship of the writers."

This is of course an ad hoc, one-off arrangement, and it could obviously be abused (what are the terms of that trusteeship? how long does it last? who are the successor trustees?), but still, it rather neatly manages to recognize the comic encumberedness of Seeger and his friends: they have duties to a movement, and to creators going back at least to 1903, and if monopoly privileges are to be had, the granted copyrights should be wed to copyduties so that they might serve public rather than private ends. When an entire nation adopts a song for civil rights, it would seem we are in the comedy, not the tragedy, of the commons.

I tell this story because I take it to be the earliest example of what later became the more general claim-and-release rules of the

General Public License as described earlier. Under both the GPL and Seeger's trusteeship, cultural goods are assured of their commonality by speeding up copyright law's old Republican Two-Step: first private ownership, then public benefit. In these cases, the stints that help fend off enclosure are grounded in the law itself: first there is private ownership assured by copyright law and then there is a licensed release to the public assured by contract law.

Beginning with community-specific innovations among folksingers and computer programmers, this model later blossomed into a worldwide movement best exemplified by Creative Commons, a nonprofit organization founded in 2001 by Lawrence Lessig and others. Creative Commons offers a set of licenses that allow owners to publish their creations under a range of terms more liberal than those offered by standard copyright law. An amateur songwriter might, for example, release work under an attribution-noncommercial license that says, essentially, "Anyone is free to copy this song, remix or adapt it, so long as they name me as the author and don't use it to make money." Or a poet who cares about the integrity of her texts might release poems under an attribution-noncommercial-no-derivative-works license, which says the same thing but adds that users "may not alter, transform, or build upon this work." That is a more limited grant, of course, but still, if you want to make copies of the poem to teach in a high school class, you do not need to chase after its owner for permission. For educational purposes, the poem lies in the commons on terms set by its author.

Creative Commons licenses are a great invention. They now allow millions of works to circulate without the permissions-and-fees aphasia that automatically attends all other copyrighted material. They let creators act on their sense of copyduty; they make it easier to share and to build upon the work of others whose sense of themselves is not merely economic.

This is not to say that copyduty licenses don't come with their own limitations and problems. Most of them don't grant the full range of freedoms that are central to the free software movement (e.g., the freedom to change and improve on a work, then distribute it "so that the whole community benefits"). There is, moreover, a puzzle about what happens if someone tries to combine works released under differing and incompatible licenses (as, for example, a license that allows commercial use and another that doesn't).

This incompatibility problem cropped up, for example, in the world of genome science. A project called HapMap had as its goal the creation of a public database or map of haplotypes (the individual variations found in stretches of human DNA). Worried that their released data might be a target for "parasitic patenting," the project directors devised a GPL-like license; it required, among other things, that users "disclose data . . . only to other parties who have first confirmed . . . in writing that they too are licensees . . . and so are bound by equivalent terms and conditions."

As well-intentioned as such constraints may have been at the outset, it soon became apparent that they could as easily erode a commons as protect it; specifically, it was impossible to incorporate data obtained under a HapMap license into a more open database, at least not without making the latter conform to the former's more restrictive rules. In this case, that is, a license designed to prevent private capture merely gummed up the works, and after a few years, the project simply dropped it. HapMap results are now released to the public domain with no legal stint other than the still-viable tradition that no one can patent something once it has become public knowledge. In cases where data need to be shared and integrated, it turns out to be better not to guard them with licenses but to offer them from the outset as fully free cultural property.

That is an understanding, it turns out, that had been well known for some time elsewhere in scientific circles working on the human genome. In 1996 all the labs working on the publicly funded Human Genome Project sent their directors to Bermuda to talk about what they nicely called the "etiquette of sharing." At first they considered a claim-and-release license like the GPL, but soon they rejected that idea under the assumption that data about the genome are discovered natural facts and so can't be owned in the first place.

Instead of devising a license, what they did was to write a formal declaration of the rules that they believed ought to govern genomic research. The key element of these "Bermuda Principles" called for all genome sequences above a certain size to be released to the public via the Internet within twenty-four hours of their first description.

This simple rule made it impossible for any one research center to hoard results and gain itself a privileged position in the field; more important, it made it impossible for genomic data to be captured by private parties. It also enabled what soon became a worldwide system for coordinating gene annotations. To annotate a gene is to name its apparent biological function (as, for example, "this sequence is linked to lactose tolerance"). Unannotated genes are almost useless in research, whereas annotated genes can serve to predict what might be found elsewhere in the genome, help identify new drug targets, and more.

The task of annotation is as vast and complex as the genome itself; it not only requires many eyes looking at the problem but some way of integrating what all those eyes have seen. The World Wide Web has been an invaluable tool in this regard. Specifically, it has allowed for the Distributed Annotation System, an Internet protocol that manages the sharing and integration of annotated sequences. Under the Bermuda Principles, labs release their findings on a daily basis and on a daily basis the database is revised. Every morning around the world, all research centers have access to the same, freshly emended knowledge commons.

This is a commons guarded not by law but by norms, by an expressed agreement among those who use it. In this case, the norms have turned out to have social force. There was a time, for example, when the U.S. Department of Energy, under pressure from Congress to work with the private sector, considered offering one of the for-profit sequencing companies an exclusive right to use public data to seek out genetic drug targets, an arrangement that would have contravened the Bermuda Principles. As soon as news of this proposal became public, however, the department dropped it: their scientists had in fact signed on to the Bermuda model of, well, property as propriety.

Given that the scientists working on the genome are a fairly homogeneous group with a clearly defined mission, it may seem at first that the customary commons they have built is an anomalous creation. It isn't. Many other communities of practice have common holdings made durable and lively through normative rather than legal stints.

One of these may be found, oddly enough, in the legal community itself, where, as in some scientific circles, collective tasks get done and "collective beings" come to life through the agreed-upon *non*-ownership of creative labors. The fact is that in legal circles when judges issue opinions they often "plagiarize" from the briefs presented by the contending parties. To take but one example, in 1937 Supreme Court Justice Benjamin Cardozo lifted, without attribution, verbatim sections of the Roosevelt administration's brief in his decision upholding the Social Security system. Of course "plagiarism" is the wrong term here, for legal writing does not come from the kind of author to whom credit is due. Legal writing is mostly collaborative, for one thing, produced by writing communities. In addition, legal opinions are public documents, belonging to no one because they belong to all of us. Nobody has ever successfully claimed copyright infringement for the unauthorized use of someone else's legal argument. In fact, legal writers *want* to have their work appropriated. Peter Friedman, a lawyer whose analysis I'm drawing on here, has written: "I knew I had written the best brief I possibly could on a motion when the court's opinion announcing its decision was directly cut-and-pasted from my brief."

If lawyers were the kind of authors who claimed a property in their work, they would potentially deprive both the work and themselves of their public roles. As with eighteenth-century pamphleteers, or with the creators of the World Wide Web, self-erasure attends a lawyer's entry into the public sphere, not self-assertion. The law is collective; it belongs to all citizens, and consequently we ask that its practitioners present themselves as public persons with copyduties rather than copyrights. In this context, to sample someone else's brief is a favor, not a theft; it helps a lawyer be a lawyer. Common ownership makes that species of public life possible.

It should be added here that in all the communities I've touched on—science, law, software, and so forth—the norms preserving collectivity do not necessarily undercut individual autonomy. Software's General Public License in fact supports an independence that less sophisticated uses of copyright would remove. As one free software website explains, in the freedoms that the GPL protects, "it is the *user's* purpose that matters, not the *developer's* purpose." The company making your printer driver is constrained so that you, the freelance programmer, are not; the for-profit company seeking lucrative targets in the genome is constrained so that you, the scientist doing open-ended research, are not. In each case, the norms protecting the commons also protect individual agency. Nor, in any case, do they necessarily conflict with earning an income. Lawyers are not impoverished by appropriating judges. Software developers working with the GPL may take their creations to market if they wish. "Free software does not mean non-commercial." Whoever can figure out how to make money while leaving the source code open may do so; many have.

That said, however, whether done by law or custom, the point of stinting a cultural commons is to assure that the forces of enclosure never deprive the commoners of their use rights, the background fact being that the liberties of comic and encumbered selves are sometimes prior to those of the free market's purportedly self-reliant individuals.

I realize that this chapter has covered a lot of ground, from the Ancient Mariner to Benjamin Cardozo, and I assume it will therefore be helpful to round it out by summarizing how its several topics connect to the theme of durability.

I began the chapter with the image of a self, at once comic and encumbered, who lives with choices but also with callings. All of us sometimes find ourselves faced with external demands to which dignity itself requires that we attend. In regard to cultural property, this means—at least in a democratic, creative, and civil society—that ownership's expressive rights cannot necessarily be separated from its expressive duties. Dr. Franklin invented a stove, but not all by himself; Dr. King wrote the "Dream" speech, but not all by himself: some part of any creative work comes from a place where we are "together under obligation." Consequently, those who claim rights of ownership have related duties to stint their claims such that anyone coming later will (in Locke's words) find that "enough, and as good" has been "left in common." Simply put, if the commons are to be made durable, the commoners need to act on, to codify even, the duties that arise from being who they are.

The same is true of cultural communities. From John Adams's colonial Boston (with "education of all ranks," "knowledge diffused generally") to a modern research university (with file-sharing at "rates as high as 10 gigabits per second"), the durability of the commons depends on community members having a clear enough sense of their values and purposes that, when these are threatened (by the Stamp Act, by network filters), they will draw the line. As with individuals, spheres of social life have their comic encumbrances, things that they must or cannot do if they are to be themselves. In cultural matters especially, then, there is no property without propriety, and where longevity is at issue, there will be the propriety especially of resistance to enclosure.

These images of people and communities insisting on their integrity led my argument into the problem of how we are to speak to one another across integrity's necessary divides. Complex, democratic societies seem to require institutions like Franklin's auditorium; more generally, they need carrier commons fitted to serve the cultural landscape in the same way that roads and waterways serve the physical.

And what assures the durability of carrier commons? First of all, it helps simply to define them as such, as commons. Remember that, in regard to roads and waterways, no state acting as a responsible trustee can "divest . . . all the citizens of their common right"; and remember the doctrine under which "traditional public forums" are "held in trust for the use of the public." Some similar set of rules needs to govern those public media that bring to life "freedom of listening" and thus offer the possibility of a pluralism that is contending but not oppressive, agonistic but not tyrannical. As long as we believe that republican identity depends on the inalienable freedoms of speech and listening (as the First Amendment implies), then let us simply acknowledge some foundational truths regarding expression: not "theft is theft" or "property is property," but "the public sphere is public" and "the carrier commons are common."

In this instance, because these carriers occupy the in-between spaces of public life, to be common means that control cannot belong to any single sphere; it must be diffused among us. Where liberty means freedom even "from the *possibility* of being . . . coerced," no surviving echo of monarchy's Negative Voice should be given standing in the public square. More specifically, when it comes to the control of cultural expression, the constitutional call for limited monopoly has to be read in light of the founders' wariness about unchecked power. Placing a clear and reasonable boundary on the term of monopoly privileges enlists the simple passage of time to help with the necessary task of dividing sovereignty. Yes, there is a clause in the Constitution that allows the Congress to bestow copyrights and patents; even as it does that, however, it hedges those grants by asking that they survive only for "limited times." That simple phrase names the temporal stint by which, if we can reaffirm it, an otherwise vulnerable public domain might more easily survive as an enduring cultural commons.

AFTERWORD

The final chapter of this book outlines some of the steps already taken to make the public domain a durable cultural commons. After the book first appeared, a number of readers indicated that they wished I had taken time to propose future interventions as well. What comes next? If the commons of the mind is under threat of enclosure, what else should we do to reclaim and protect it? This afterword offers two suggestions.

I: BRING BACK COPYRIGHT FORMALITIES

Noah Webster's first "American" dictionary bore the following notice on the back of the title page:

> DISTRICT OF CONNECTICUT, SS.
> Be it remembered, That on the fourteenth day of April, in the fifty-second year of the Independence of the United States of America, Noah Webster, of the said District, hath deposited in this office the title of a Book, the right whereof he claims as Author, in the words following, to wit:
> "An American dictionary of the English language . . . By Noah Webster, LL.D. In two volumes."

In conformity to the act of Congress of the United States, entitled, "An act for the encouragement of learning, by securing the copies of Maps, Charts and Books, to the authors and proprietors of such copies, during the times therein mentioned."

CHAS. A. INGERSOLL, Clerk of the District of Connecticut.

April 14th, 1828.

Webster was here complying with one of the "formalities" of traditional copyright, these being the steps authors were required to take in order to secure their privileges—to wit, registering the title with a federal district court, depositing a copy with the secretary of state (later with the Library of Congress), and publishing a notice, not only in the book itself but "in one or more of the newspapers printed in the United States, for the space of four weeks." In addition, once the initial copyright term expired, authors were required to register a second time if they wanted a renewal. These demands have varied over time (the call for newspaper notice was modified in 1831 and dropped in 1909, for example), but until about thirty years ago copyrights were affirmed and made secure through formalities such as these. Said conversely, for most of U.S. history, a failure to comply with the formalities could void a copyright (or prevent it from arising in the first place), whereupon the work passed into the public domain.

Formalities are a useful part of any copyright regime. They help create efficient markets, for one thing. For users seeking licenses, they indicate who owns what and for how long. For owners whose work may be infringed they give clear title and a way to pursue damages. As with real property, so with intellectual property: public records reduce transaction costs and facilitate trade.

Formalities also make it less likely that works will become orphaned, orphan works being those that are still under copyright but whose owners cannot be found. Orphan works are a problem for owners and users alike. A striking example on the owners' side can be found on the website of the Harry Fox Agency, the primary licensing agent for U.S. music publishers. On a page asking for help locating rights holders, the agency lists music publishers it has lost track of, an inventory running from Aardvark-TV to Zo's Muzik. All these multitudes—the list runs to 4,816 companies!—are urged to call home: Harry Fox "may be holding royalties" for them.

On the users' side, orphans are problematic because work for which rights holders can't be found usually can't be used, at least not without the threat of damages should the owner later appear. When Carnegie Mellon University tried to digitize a collection of out-of-print books, one of every five turned out to be orphaned. When Cornell University tried to post a collection of agricultural monographs online, half were orphans. The United States Holocaust Memorial Museum owns millions of pages of archival documents that it can neither publish nor digitize. These cases not only represent a loss of potential markets but, more broadly, indicate the degree to which orphan works impede the very Constitutional purpose of copyright, "the progress of science."

Formalities are a boon to the market side of the copyright bargain, then, but they benefit the commons side as well. Public records indicate when ownership expires, for one thing, but they do more than that. Formalities help enlarge the commons as soon as new work comes into being. A registration requirement, after all, asks creators to make a simple judgment: Does this work have commercial value worthy of capture? In many cases, the answer is no, whereupon the work doesn't get registered and immediately enters the public domain. According to one study, of the approximately 15,000 maps, charts, and books published during the decade 1790–1800, only 779 were registered. Everything else—sermons, political pamphlets, newspapers, and so forth—passed to the public immediately.

Data for later periods in U.S. history are harder to come by, but it appears that of all works published in the nineteenth century, only about half were registered. No matter the exact figure, the point is simply that by asking authors to assess the value of their work early on, a registration formality makes it more likely that everyone gets unimpeded access to work that, while judged to have little commercial value, may nonetheless have significant cultural value (for history, science, politics, religion, and so forth).

Focusing on the benefits of an initial registration requirement tells only one part of this story, of course. Whenever copyright offers a second term, the renewal formality has even stronger commons-enhancing effects. After all, the commercial value of most creative work is exhausted fairly early. A study done of copyrights registered in 1934 found, for example, that half of them were worthless after ten years, 90 percent after forty-three years, and 99 percent after sixty-five years. It should consequently come as no surprise that many rights holders did not renew after the initial twenty-eight-year term. The numbers vary year to year and by genre (music rights being renewed more often than books, for example), but roughly speaking, when owners were given a right to renew, only 15 percent chose to do so. As with initial registration, a renewal formality serves as a filter, releasing commercially dead work to the public without depriving authors of a longer term if they wish to have it. Put another way, formalities effectively shorten the term of the copyright grant; for most of the twentieth century, 85 percent of copyrights lasted only twenty-eight years.

Given the clear value of formalities, why have we dispensed with them? The answer has to do with international trade. There has always been significant variation from one nation to another when it comes to the steps that authors must take to secure a copyright. A novelist lucky enough to have her work appear in a dozen foreign tongues might have to seek out a dozen foreign rights experts and file for protection under a dozen different procedures. So as to mitigate these burdens, the primary international accord governing copyright, the Berne Convention, declares that "the enjoyment and the exercise of [copyrights] shall not be subject to any formality." It should be added that the difficulties of multi-jurisdictional authorship are not the only source of Berne's antipathy toward formalities: the agreement originated in continental Europe, where copyright has often been viewed as arising more from natural rights than from positive law. Where natural law is the point of departure, formalities are entirely out of place: no author should need to ask the state for rights that nature itself has bestowed.

The Berne Convention was first put into force in 1886. The United States did not consent to its terms until 1989, however, in large part because U.S. law historically had a statutory or utilitarian basis and therefore did indeed find it proper to insist upon formalities. Beginning in 1976, however, the formalities began to drop away and now have almost entirely disappeared. While it is true that an author may still register a copyright and, by doing so, be better positioned in the event of litigation, registration is voluntary, not required. Nor do we anymore have a renewal requirement, having abandoned the practice of dividing the full term of copyright into several shorter terms.

Gone, then, are the market efficiencies that formalities once brought to users and owners alike, and gone are the benefits they brought to the commons. Registration and renewal long helped divide the commercial from the noncommercial and moved the latter into the public domain. We now lack any mandated way to prompt that useful sorting. Default copyright presently encloses everything as soon as it is "fixed in any tangible medium," even works that authors themselves do not care to own or to protect.

What is to be done? Is there any way to bring back formalities, the traditional stints that so usefully focused the market and enriched the commons for almost two hundred years?

Yes, there is, and at two different levels—nationally and internationally. First of all, it isn't actually the case that the Berne Convention forbids all formalities: it does so only in regard to authors publishing in foreign lands. Authors publishing "in the country of origin" may be "governed by domestic law." Each of Berne's signatory nations is entirely free to ask its own citizens to comply with formalities. Christopher Sprigman, professor of law at the University of Virginia, has suggested a way for the United States to do this so as to capture the benefits of the old formalities without forcing those who fail to comply with them to lose their copyrights.

Sprigman's "new-style formalities" have two parts. To begin with, registration would continue to be optional, but authors who declined to register their work would not enjoy the full allowance of exclusive rights. Their work would instead be subject to a "default license" under which anyone who made use of the work would be liable for no more than a modest royalty defined by statute. If you published my work without my permission I could come after you for payment, but the payment would be nominal and no other kind of damages would be available to me.

The suggestion is that this payment should not only be nominal but actually lower than what the market is likely to bear. For authors with commercially valuable work, that is not such a good deal, of course, but that is exactly the point of the default license: it is there to encourage those who care about marketing their work to go ahead and register it and thereby receive the full range of exclusive rights. Unregistered work, for all intents and purposes, enters the public domain in that anyone may make use of it knowing that there is very little risk involved.

Sprigman would also have us revive the renewal requirement. The current term of copyright runs an undivided lifetime plus seventy years for individual authors and ninety-five years for corporate owners. Under new-style formalities, these terms could be divided into two or more shorter spans with the full term always available to those who renew.

How long should the shorter spans be? Happily, this is a question that research can probably answer. The value of most copyrights depreciates rather quickly, as indicated above in the study of works registered in 1934. If that study were our guide, we might suggest three terms for copyright and ask for renewal twice, once after ten years (at which point 50 percent of work is commercially dead and, if not renewed, would enter the public domain) and again after forty-three years (moving another 40 percent into the public domain). Perhaps a third renewal at sixty-five years would be useful (at that point only 1 percent of the original cohort has any value), but for now we can set aside the problem of how best to time the intervals. For now the point is to fit the law to the actual facts of commerce so as to better balance private incentive and public access, the contending goods that copyright is meant to serve. Periodic renewals do nothing to dilute the incentive (the full term is always available), but they do a great deal to improve access. To say this in terms of the founders' concern for free speech, renewal requirements help square copyright's monopoly privileges with the First Amendment.

Changing domestic law to bring back formalities is not the only way to improve on the current state of affairs, nor is it the best. After all, Berne allows each nation to impose formalities on its own but not on foreign authors, and any nation doing so would thus give foreign authors a competitive advantage. It would be much better, then, to revise Berne itself to allow for formalities and to subject all authors to similar rules. There are complexities to such a change, to be sure. There would need to be some sort of reciprocity such that authors who have met their own nation's formalities would automatically have complied with all others; and there would need to be international baselines so that formalities could be harmonized in cases where they otherwise differed from one nation to the next. In Sprigman's view, at least, these would be "relatively small changes to Berne" and, if done properly, would let each nation benefit from formalities without bringing back the costs and pitfalls of earlier multi-jurisdictional publishing.

To bring formalities back to copyright would nicely beat the bounds of the cultural commons. I doubt it was apparent in the late 1970s that abandoning formalities would amount to a taking from the commons, but that is what it has turned out to be. To restate but one piece of what has already been said: in the old days, with a renewal requirement, 85 percent of all work passed into the public domain after twenty-eight years; now, without it, that sizable portion remains enclosed (uselessly so) for another generation or more.

As noted in the third chapter's discussion of enclosure, the last time that Congress added years to the term of copyright, a group of economists, both liberal and conservative (including five Nobel laureates) filed a brief with the Supreme Court arguing that the extension made no economic sense. (Milton Friedman supposedly asked that the brief contain the phrase "no brainer.") It is patently clear to almost everyone that the term of copyright is now senselessly long. At the same time, it is almost certainly politically impossible to retreat from it; the few who benefit are too well connected and the many who do not are too thinly spread. To my mind, the greatest appeal of new-style formalities, then, is that they would leave the nominal term untouched (and accord it to all who care) while greatly reducing the effective term. Sprigman calculates that during the twentieth century, when the vast majority of rights holders did not avail themselves of the renewal option, the effective term of copyright was only thirty-two years.* That's just four years longer than the nominal term the founders offered in 1790. Simply put, by reducing the de facto reach of monopoly privileges, formalities enrich the cultural commons. If they also remind us that copyrights are creatures of positive law, not of natural right, and thus push back against conceptual enclosure as well, so much the better.

*He derives this average by adding the 15 percent who renewed (and thus took the full fifty-six years) to the 85 percent who took only the first twenty-eight years: (0.15 * 56) + (0.85 * 28) = 32.2.

II: CLAIM FAIR USE RIGHTS

In 2008 the poet and critic Rosanna Warren published a book of essays on lyric poetry, *Fables of the Self*. As is customary, her publisher, W. W. Norton, asked her to pay the permission fees for poems and translations cited in her text. Norton's guidelines require permission to be sought whenever an author quotes more than two lines of a poet's work. At a 2009 meeting of the Modern Language Association, Warren reported that the result was an "astronomical" bill:

> I had to pay for the translations of the passages in many of the ancient poems I wanted to use . . . I had to pay of course for the 20th century poets like Auden and H.D., and for our contemporaries . . . In many cases I had to pay a double fee.

For three lines from Ezra Pound's *Cantos*, Warren paid a total of $240, half to the American publisher and half to the British publisher.

> And I was not willing to give up those lines, any more than a biologist would be willing to give up the cell tissue of the organism in which she had discovered a peculiar formation.

At a first pass, Warren's permission fees exceeded $20,000 (this for a book that would be lucky to earn its author and publisher a tenth of that sum). After pleading her case with sympathetic rights holders, Warren managed to reduce the bill to $17,000. Two private foundations then chipped in $7,000, and Warren paid the remaining $10,000 out of her own pocket.

The case is not unique. In trying to understand what had happened to her, Warren spoke with several prominent scholars and editors and found a number of cases in which "they had canceled contracts for works already undertaken, or had refused to undertake projects of anthologies or criticism because of the costs." My own account of the prohibitive fees charged by the estates of James Joyce and Martin Luther King, Jr., speak to the same problem.

The argument here is not that permissions should never be paid. In most cases where there is money to be made, authors and their publishers should get their cut. Rosanna Warren is the daughter of Robert Penn Warren; I'm sure she would agree that if Columbia Pictures wants to make a movie of *All the King's Men*, the Warren estate deserves a piece of the action. Permissions are rightly in order most of the time; clearly, however, there are instances in which the fees get so out of line as to upset the balance between incentive and access that any copyright regime must preserve if it is to serve "the progress of science" or "the encouragement of learning."

The fair use doctrine is one element of our system that is supposed to help maintain that balance. Fair use is the right to use copyrighted material without permission or payment under some circumstances. Properly understood and employed, it enables creators in all disciplines to overcome the kind of impediments that Warren and others have faced.

A few words about the history and content of this doctrine are in order if we are to understand how practitioners might better claim the rights it offers. The U.S. Constitution contains two potentially conflicting provisions in regard to the circulation of knowledge. The First Amendment guarantees that "Congress shall make no law . . . abridging the freedom of speech, or of the press," while at the same time one clause in Article I allows that same Congress to give authors control of their own expression: "The Congress shall have power . . . to promote the progress of science and useful arts, by securing for limited times to authors . . . the exclusive right to their . . . writings." As Supreme Court Justice Stephen Breyer wrote in a 2003 opinion, "when working in tandem, these provisions mutually reinforce each other," the Copyright Clause "serving as an 'engine of free expression,'" and the amendment "assuring that government throws up no obstacle to its dissemination."

This useful complementarity will suffer, however, whenever the "Copyright Clause bounds" expand in such a way as to "set Clause and Amendment at cross-purposes, thereby depriving the public of the speech-related benefits that the Founders . . . have promised."

As outlined in the third chapter, the history of copyright in the United States has been the constant expansion, in both scope and duration, of the bounds of the Copyright Clause. The original American term of copyright was fourteen years, once renewable; the grant applied only to "copies of maps, charts, and books," and "copies" essentially meant literal, verbatim reproductions. No one needed permission to make what are now called derivative works—translations, sequels, abridgments, and so forth. At present, copyright subsists in any work "fixed in any tangible medium of expression, now known or later developed," and these works include not only the obvious—novels, songs, motion pictures—but *any* "fixed" thing, whether formally registered with the Copyright Office or not. The term can now easily run well beyond a century.

Fair use is one of the few doctrines to have arisen to try to preserve the balance of free expression in the face of this great expansion. The doctrine found its first formulation in *Folsom v. Marsh* (1841), a case that pitted the publisher of an eleven-volume *Writings of George Washington* against the publisher of a later two-volume *Life of General Washington*. The editor of the shorter work had taken more than a third of his content from the longer one, whose publisher sued for infringement and won. Supreme Court Justice Joseph Story wrote the opinion in the case; in it he muses at length on "what may be called the metaphysics of the law," admitting what was in fact true at the time, that "a fair . . . abridgment of an original work is not a piracy," but then posing the otherwise-begged question: "What constitutes a fair . . . abridgment?" Story's response gave birth to the language of fair use:

> We must often, in deciding questions of this sort, look to the na-
> ture and objects of the selections made, the quantity and value of

the materials used, and the degree in which the use may prejudice the sale, or diminish the profits, or supersede the objects, of
the original work.

Story's list of factors that the law might "look to"—the nature
of the selection, the value of the materials, etc.—became the point
of reference by which questions of fair use were settled until 1976,
whereupon one of our periodic revisions of the Copyright Act entered a formal list of fair use factors into law. Since that time, as if
in answer to Justice Breyer's worry that "Clause and Amendment"
might be set "at cross-purposes," the Supreme Court has regularly
pointed to fair use as being one of copyright's "traditional First
Amendment safeguards."

Section 107 of the copyright act spells out the details of how
that safeguard is to be applied, saying that, notwithstanding the
rights granted to copyright owners,

> The fair use of a copyrighted work, including such use by repro-
> duction in copies or phonorecords . . . for purposes such as criti-
> cism, comment, news reporting, teaching (including multiple
> copies for classroom use), scholarship, or research, is not an in-
> fringement of copyright.

> In determining whether the use made of a work in any particular
> case is a fair use the factors to be considered shall include—
> (1) the purpose and character of the use, including whether
>   such use is of a commercial nature or is for nonprofit edu-
>   cational purposes;
> (2) the nature of the copyrighted work;
> (3) the amount and substantiality of the portion used in re-
>   lation to the copyrighted work as a whole; and
> (4) the effect of the use upon the potential market for or value
>   of the copyrighted work.

Thus laid out, the fair use doctrine creates what has been called a "situational public domain," exempting a range of expressive uses from the monopoly powers elsewhere granted to rights holders.

Be that as it may, the statute's implied promise of a wide range of free expression has turned out to be difficult to realize in actual practice. For one thing, the language of the four factors is deliberately vague. Several concerns lie behind this lack of clarity. One is the fear that if the factors were stated more concretely they would likely block uses we might later realize ought to be considered fair. In addition, we live in an age of rapid technological change and it makes sense to leave the rules loose enough to be adapted to emerging situations.

As sensible as these motives may be, however, the ambiguity of the factors has left many users confused as to what exactly they are entitled to. Take Factor 3, "the amount and substantiality of the portion used." The impression might arise that the wording here means that it is illegal to copy an entire work, that one may take only a portion of the whole (ten percent, say, or six seconds of a film, or two lines of a poem). Such is not the case; copying an entire work is sometimes fair. In 1984 the Supreme Court ruled that copying a complete TV show for later home viewing is fair use. Publishers themselves have agreed that an entire article or speech may often be used in a classroom setting. The statute, in fact, contains *no* rule as to the "fair" amount. It is silent, for example, as to how many words may be taken from a book. In 1986 a U.S. Court of Appeals found that reproducing seven thousand words from an out-of-print book for purposes of commentary was fair use.

Or take Factor 1 and the question of "whether [the] use is of a commercial nature": the impression might arise that fair use does not apply to commercial work, but that also is not the case. Often at issue in regard to the question of purpose is a distinction between "transformative" and "derivative" uses. Nowadays, most derivative uses (translations, for example) are not considered fair—the user must seek permission—but transformative uses are. Transformative use builds on the original to forge something new, or serves some purpose other than that of the original, as, for example, to enable educational or political discourse. Thus the documentary filmmaker or the parodist who uses copyrighted material for cultural critique can usually claim fair use, no matter the commercial success of the new work.

Finally, take the way that the word "purpose" in Factor 1 seems to refer back to the first paragraph of the statute (the preamble), which contains a list of seemingly exempt purposes: "criticism, comment, news reporting, teaching (including multiple copies for classroom use), scholarship, or research." Sadly, each of these is only *potentially* non-infringing; any particular use needs to be scrutinized in light of the four factors, for they—not the preamble—are the meat of the law.

The need for such scrutiny introduces the flip side of the statute's vagueness: to know for sure about any specific use, one does well to have a properly focused lawsuit that yielded a clear judgment. These are hard to come by, as an inquiry into the status of educational uses will show. In what sense does the preamble's mention of "multiple copies for classroom use" indicate an allowed use? There have been two instances of litigation around student course packs, and in each the creators of the course packs were found to be infringing. These judgments have been taken to prove that course packs cannot be exempt under the fair use doctrine, but they prove nothing of the kind. In the cases that went to trial, the creators of the course packs were for-profit copy shops, and the fact of their commercial purposes weighed heavily in the decision. What does this mean for "nonprofit educational purposes"? We don't know. Suppose that a media studies professor made a course pack of contemporary advertisements, each one annotated as to its strategies and followed by study questions; and suppose that this course pack was produced by the college copy shop and sold to students at cost. Would this be an educational fair use? The statute seems to imply that it would, but in fact we can't be sure; there is no applicable case law.

In sum, the first problem faced by anyone hoping to benefit from the fair use doctrine is that the available information is at once too general and too specific. On the one hand, the enumerated factors are so fuzzy as to offer a conscientious user little guidance and, on the other, where clarity has arisen it has come from court cases so particular as to be of little use in making general judgments.

Over the years, users and owners have tried to add clarity to fair use by developing guidelines, rules of thumb by which both sides of potential litigation might know beforehand what is allowed and what is not. These too, however, have proven to be at least as problematic as they are helpful.

Perhaps the best known attempt in this line appears as the "Agreement on Guidelines for Classroom Copying in Not-for-Profit Educational Institutions" in the notes that accompany the fair use statute (giving the history of the work that led to its passage). As the 1976 revision of the copyright law was being developed, Congress asked content owners and users to meet and negotiate these guidelines. The owners were represented in part by the Association of American Publishers; the users, by the American Association of University Professors. The results of their meetings are now preserved in the legislative history and it is there that we find language such as this:

I. Single Copying for Teachers
>A single copy may be made of any of the following by or for a teacher at his or her individual request for his or her scholarly research or use in teaching or preparation to teach a class:
>>A. A chapter from a book;
>>B. An article from a periodical or newspaper;

C. A short story, short essay or short poem, whether or
not from a collective work;

D. A chart, graph, diagram, drawing, cartoon or picture
from a book, periodical, or newspaper;

II. Multiple Copies for Classroom Use

Multiple copies (not to exceed in any event more than one copy
per pupil in a course) may be made by or for the teacher giving
the course for classroom use or discussion; provided that:

A. The copying meets the tests of brevity and spontaneity
as defined below; and,

B. Meets the cumulative effect test as defined below; and

C. Each copy includes a notice of copyright.

The definitions of such terms as "brevity" and "spontaneity" follow. Brevity for prose works means, among other things, "(a) Either a complete article, story or essay of less than 2,500 words, or (b) an excerpt from any prose work of not more than 1,000 words or 10% of the work, whichever is less, but in any event a minimum of 500 words." Spontaneity means that "the inspiration and decision to use the work and the moment of its use for maximum teaching effectiveness are so close in time that it would be unreasonable to expect a timely reply to a request for permission."

All this seems quite clear, but the very clarity obscures three serious flaws.

First, the notes call the guidelines an "agreement," but they were not that at all. They were produced by the content owners over the objections of the users. The notes themselves say as much:

Representatives of the American Association of University Professors and of the Association of American Law Schools have written to the Committee strongly criticizing the guidelines, particularly with respect to multiple copying, as being too restrictive with respect to classroom situations at the university and graduate level.

The notes fail to reproduce these dissenting letters.

Second, the guidelines have no standing as law. Simply put, the legislative history of a law is not the law. Neither side in a court case may base a claim on it. In fact, in one of the course pack cases, when content owners appealed to a prohibition on anthologies that appears in the guidelines, the court refused to allow the claim, saying simply that any anthology would have to be judged by the four factors found in the law, not by any guideline found in the notes. (It should be added, then, that the guidelines' definitions have no clear standing in law either; the statute never mentions "brevity" or "spontaneity," and it is fully conceivable that classroom use may be fair even though it is neither brief nor spontaneous.)

Finally, it is not entirely clear whether the guidelines indicate minimums or maximums. This should not be the case—the notes say directly that they "state the minimum and not the maximum standards of educational fair use"—but confusion has arisen nonetheless, primarily from an agreement on guidelines that was reached in the 1980s between New York University and the publishing industry. At the time the publishers had brought suit against several for-profit copy shops making course packs. Both settled without trial, whereupon the publishers filed suit against NYU and several of its faculty.

As did the copy shops, NYU chose to settle rather than go to court, and the settlement that they agreed upon incorporated the classroom guidelines from the legislative history. That is to say, when threatened with litigation, a major research university adopted fair use guidelines that have no basis in the law, and that were formulated by content owners despite the stated objections of professional organizations in higher education. Even worse, NYU agreed to drop the proviso in the notes that called the guidelines "the minimum and not the maximum." Faculty at NYU are now asked to follow the guidelines strictly, not as a minimal safe harbor but as a ceiling on fair use. Any uses beyond the stated limits require advance approval of the university counsel.

Similar protocols are now common nationwide. After reaching the agreement with NYU, the publishing industry sent out hundreds of letters to colleges and universities suggesting that they too adopt the guidelines or risk facing litigation. By one estimate, four out of five universities have adopted policies similar to those found at NYU.

In short, it has been the strategy of content owners not to negotiate guidelines but to develop them on their own; to litigate and win clearly commercial cases that are close to but not the same as "nonprofit educational" fair use; and to then threaten educators with similar action in a manner such that the educators have signed on to a shrunken version of fair use, one that the very same educators refused to endorse when the law was being written. In the academy at present, fair use has therefore become a little-used set of rights, weakened by confusion and fear, and this despite the statute's clear privileging of teaching, research, and scholarship.

Given that the law is vague, the owners litigious, and current guidelines extralegal and restrictive, what is to be done? How can fair use be reclaimed as an effective part of the social bargain that copyright law is meant to embody?

Some years ago Peter Jaszi, a law professor at American University, and his colleague Patricia Aufderheide of American University's Center for Social Media came up with a novel answer. Why not help various creative communities, one by one, reclaim the fullness of their fair use rights by developing "statements of best practices" that are expressive of their norms? In this approach, users look not so much to the statute and the case law as to what their own disciplines can articulate as fair and reasonable.

The first and most successful example of this model is the "Documentary Filmmakers' Statement of Best Practices in Fair Use." Published in 2005, the statement was authored by five professional filmmakers' associations and based on research conducted by Jaszi and Aufderheide. The statement outlines a short list of typical situations faced by documentarians (as when, for example, in the process of filming something else, the filmmaker captures copyrighted material—a poster on a wall, incidental music playing on a radio or TV screen, etc.); the statement then articulates principles by which a filmmaker might reasonably decide whether the use is fair or not.

The documentarians' statement produced immediate and remarkable results as soon as it was published. Filmmakers have seen:

- the saving of millions of dollars in unnecessary licensing costs ($400,000 in one film alone, *Wanderlust*);
- the release of films that could never have been seen publicly, or possibly even finished (*Hip-Hop: Beyond Beats and Rhymes, This Film Is Not Yet Rated, The Trials of Darryl Hunt*);
- the adoption of the statement into the business practices of many public television stations and cable companies;
- and the acceptance of the statement by all four major U.S. insurance companies for errors-and-omissions insurance of fair use claims.

There have also been several significant follow-on projects, one of which will bring us back to my opening story about Rosanna Warren's book of essays.

In 2009, Katharine Coles, poet laureate of the state of Utah and then director of the Harriet Monroe Poetry Institute in Chicago, initiated a project to develop a fair use code for the poetry community. Coles and her colleagues* convened seven small group meetings, each with ten to twenty poets: one in Boston, two each at the

---

*Jennifer Urban of the University of California–Berkeley School of Law joined Coles, Jaszi, and Aufderheide as co-facilitators. Three lawyers with expertise in copyright were enlisted to make sure that the proposed practices were in accord with current legal understanding; I myself served as "cultural and literary" adviser.

Harriet Monroe Poetry Institute offices in Chicago, at the 2009 Modern Language Association convention in Philadelphia, and at the 2010 Associated Writing Programs convention in Denver.

At these meetings, participants discussed a series of hypothetical examples designed to raise questions about the scope and limits of fair use. May a poet, under fair use, adapt a poem to offer a direct critique of its author? May a poet use quotations from someone else's work as the content of poetry-generating software? Do you need permission to use poems as epigraphs for the chapters of a book? In response to these and other questions, the conveners found that while poets, like all writers, "certainly wish to appropriately control their own work, and to make money where money is to be made," those who were gathered at these meetings "also expressed a strong wish to affirm the importance of their ability to make reasonable unlicensed uses of copyrighted material and their support for such uses by others of their own works."

The final declaration of practices "in fair use for poetry" isolate seven situations in which questions of fairness typically arise for these artists: in parody and satire; in new works "remixed" from other material; in criticism, comment, and illustration; in epigraphs; in poetry online; and in literary performance. Not surprisingly, the practice outlined in the "criticism" category speaks directly to the issue that faced Rosanna Warren when she sought permissions for her book of essays:

DESCRIPTION: Poetic quotations are frequently employed by writers and artists in other disciplines. Perhaps the most non-controversial example is that in which a scholar, critic, or reviewer quotes from a poem in order to make a point about the poet in question or about his or her work. Because poetry arises out of and speaks to the particular circumstances (social, cultural, economic) of its writing, members of the poetry community were . . . united in their opinion that scholars and creators in other fields should be entitled to use apt selections of poetry for purposes other than criticism. Thus, they were supportive of quotation both for textual "illustration" and in the practice of visual artists who take inspiration from poetic works.

PRINCIPLE: Under fair use, a critic discussing a published poem or body of poetry may quote freely as justified by the critical purpose; likewise, a commentator may quote to exemplify or illuminate a cultural/historical phenomenon, and a visual artist may incorporate relevant quotations into his or her work.

LIMITATIONS:

- This principle does not apply to reproductions in textbooks and anthologies where quotations appear without an independent critical apparatus.
- Quoted passages should be reproduced as accurately as possible to reflect, and not so minimally or selectively as to mislead about, creative choices embedded in the poem.
- Critics, commentators, and artists should provide conventional attribution for their chosen quotations.
- They should also have an articulable rationale for the relevance of their chosen quotations to their own work.
- Likewise, the extent of quotation should be appropriate to the purpose of the use.
- Uses that are solely "decorative" or "entertaining" should be avoided.
- Permissible quotations used for exemplary purposes generally should be briefer than those used for critical purposes.
- Visual artists generally should not incorporate entire poems in a merely decorative fashion without the copyright holder's permission.

A best practices approach to fair use manages the neat trick of converting the doctrine's ambiguities into virtues. The law sometimes offers us "per se rules," ones that must be applied regardless of circumstances; the fair use statute, on the other hand, offers a "rule of reason." When trying to decide whether an unlicensed use of copyrighted material is fair or not, users (and lawyers and judges) must take into account the particulars of the situation at hand. That is to say, the looseness of the statute makes it portable, able to be applied to different communities, to different times, and to emerging technologies. The facilitators of the poetry code, the scores of poets whose discussions produced the statement itself, the lawyers who vetted it: all agree that the principle articulated in regard to criticism is a reasonable response to the permission problems that arise when an essayist addresses herself to contemporary poetry. Had it been in place when Warren published her book, it would have saved her thousands of dollars. More pointedly, had it been in place years ago, we might have those many books that authors and publishers have simply abandoned under the assumption of impossible permissions barriers.

I indicated at the outset of this afterword that I would sketch some prospective interventions in regard to protecting the cultural commons, rather than describe what is already being done. Looking forward, then, a fair use movement will need to do at least two things. First of all, many practice communities have yet to do the work of thinking through their norms and stating them clearly. Scholars and teachers in higher education ought, for example, to generate a statement fitted to their profession (after all, the encouragement of learning has been a named goal of copyright regimes for three hundred years, and education is expressly singled out for protection in the statute itself).

Second, best practices need actually to be practiced. No set of standards has any force until practitioners know about it, own it, trust it, and use it. Practitioners in this context are not only the users of proprietary work but also the many gatekeepers with whom users must work. People who run copy shops, librarians, university counsels, permission departments at publishing houses, editors of academic journals, internet service providers, insurance companies in film and video—all of these need to be introduced to the practice statements and, where appropriate, urged to publicly assent to the norms that they expresses. Only then will clarity and agency replace the confusion and caution that are now so often the rule. Only then will the exclusive rights of owners be balanced by the common rights of users. Only then will fair use truly be what the Supreme Court claims it is, a safeguard of the First Amendment.

SELECTED SOURCES

Formalities

My primary guide to the formalities question has been Christopher Jon Sprigman's essay "Reform(aliz)ing Copyright" (*Stanford Law Review*, November 2004). Jane C. Ginsburg offers a more skeptical view and a good history in "The US Experience with Copyright Formalities: A Love/Hate Relationship" (*Columbia Journal of Law & the Arts*, 2010). Both of these essays are available online through the Social Science Research Network (SSRN). For the examples of orphan works, see "Economic Scene: Copyrights That No One Knows About Don't Help Anyone," *The New York Times*, May 31, 2007; the American Library Association's letter of March 25, 2005 (on the Copyright Office website: www .copyright.gov/orphan/comments/OW0658-LCA.pdf); and Marybeth Peters, "The Importance of Orphan Works Legislation," September 25, 2008 (also on the Copyright Office website: www.copyright.gov/orphan).

Fair Use

For a complete analysis and history of the best practices approach, see *Reclaiming Fair Use* by Patricia Aufderheide and Peter Jaszi (University of Chicago Press, 2011). Justice Breyer's remarks on the tension between copyright and the First Amendment are from his dissent in *Eldred v. Ashcroft* (2003); the assertion that fair use is a First Amendment safeguard comes from Justice Ruth Bader Ginsburg's majority opinion in the same case. My discussion of the problem with fair use guidelines is derived mostly from Kenneth Crews's essay "The Law of Fair Use and the Illusion of Fair-Use Guidelines," published in 2001 in the *Ohio State Law Journal*. The two copy-shop cases are *Basic Books v. Kinko's Graphics* (1991) and *Princeton University Press v. Michigan Document Services* (1994). The case allowing the copying of a complete TV show is *Sony v. Universal* (1984). *Maxtone-Graham v. Burtchaell* (1986) is the case that declared a seven-thousand-word use to be fair.

NOTES

BIBLIOGRAPHY

ACKNOWLEDGMENTS

INDEX

NOTES

1: DEFENDING THE CULTURAL COMMONS

3   *Most people act*: Geoffrey Stephen Kirk et al., *The Presocratic Philosophers*, 2nd ed. (New York: Cambridge University Press, 1983), p. 187. My thanks to Stanley Lombardo for pointing me to this text.

"THEFT IS THEFT"

3   *AIDS drugs*: http://keionline.org/content/view/37/1, accessed 19 September 2009.

3   *McCain commercial*: Saul Hansell, "McCain Fights for the Right to Remix on YouTube," *New York Times* online, http://bits.blogs.nytimes.com/2008/10/14; Zahavah Levine, "YouTube Response to Senator McCain," www.youtube.com/press_room_entry?entry=5LeSYzJyggM.

4   *Joyce . . . permission*: David Pierce, ed., *Irish Writing in the Twentieth Century: A Reader* (Cork, Ireland: Cork University Press, 2000); see also "Declaration of David Pierce," document 36 in *Shloss v. Sweeney* (Case 5:2006-cv-03718, United States Court, Northern District of California); www.scribd.com/doc/2614976/Shlossv-Sweeney-et-al-Document-No-36, accessed 18 September 2009.

4   *"intellectual property"*: In "Theories of Intellectual Property," William Fisher writes: "The term 'intellectual property' refers to a loose cluster of legal doctrines that regulate the uses of different sorts of ideas and insignia. The law of copyright protects various 'original forms of expression,' including novels, movies, musical compositions, and computer software programs. Patent law protects inventions and some kinds of discoveries. Trademark law protects words and symbols that identify for consumers the goods and services manufactured or supplied by particular persons or firms. Trade-secret law protects commercially valuable information (soft-drink formulas, confidential marketing strategies, etc.) that companies

attempt to conceal from their competitors. The 'right of publicity' protects celebrities' interests in their images and identities."

Fisher's essay demostrates that it is almost impossible to find any theoretical unity in this "cluster." This book is concerned primarily with copyright and, to a lesser degree, with patent.

4   *"keep his Lucubrations"*: James Graham, *The Petition of Gavin Hamilton & John Balfour, and others, Booksellers in Edinburgh, Andrew Stalker and Others, Booksellers in Glasgow, Defenders, against Andrew Millar and others, Booksellers in London, Pursuers* (15 January 1747), p. 6. Copy held in the Advocates' Library, Edinburgh: Elchies Papers XV: A–B, case no. 45. My thanks to Ronan Deazley for providing a photocopy of this document. The text is also cited in Deazley, *Origin*, p. 123.

6   *"the Authors and Proprietors"*: The Statute of Anne, more correctly titled "Copyright Act 1709 8 Anne c. 19," was enacted in 1709 and entered into force on April 10, 1710; http://copyrighthistory.com/anne.html, accessed 18 September 2009.

6   *public relations campaigns*: I'm indebted to Tarleton Gillespie's work for my analysis of these campaigns; also useful is Kelly Gates's essay "Will Work for Copyrights."

6   *hundreds of thousands of children*: Kathleen Sharp, "Laying Down the Copyright Law—to Children," *The Boston Globe*, 25 April 2004; Gillespie, p. 38.

7   *"the implications"*: Gillespie, p. 6.

7   *"write and perform"*: Motion Picture Association of America/Los Angeles Area Boy Scouts, p. 1.

7   *"publication party"*: Gillespie, p. 22.

7   *"Living in a Fishbowl"*: Ibid., p. 39.

8   *"students to reach"*: Ibid., p. 42.

8   *"If you haven't paid"*: Ibid., p. 50.

8   *"Intellectual Property is no different"*: Motion Picture Association of America/Los Angeles Area Boy Scouts, p. 1.

8   *"As the creator"*: Gillespie, p. 30.

8   *"Never copy"*: Ibid., p. 30.

9   *"Students who have learned"*: Ibid., p. 34.

9   *"What really is the difference"*: Ibid., p. 17; for "theft is theft," see also Fisher, *Promises to Keep*, p. 134.

10   *"we need to educate kids"*: *The New York Times Magazine*, 6 February 2005.

11   *altered canola*: The farmer was Percy Schmeiser and the seed company Monsanto. See www.organicconsumers.org/monsanto/canolawar.cfm; and www.percyschmeiser.com, both accessed 5 March 2009.

11   *Indian Parliament to outlaw*: Suketu Mehta, "A Big Stretch," *The New York Times*, 7 May 2007.

12   *1991 fall of the Soviet Union*: I have expanded on this point in two essays; see "Being Good Ancestors," *Kenyon Review*, vol. 30, no. 1 (Winter 2008), pp. 1–14, and "The Children of John Adams: A Historical View of the Fight over Arts Funding," *Art Matters: How the Culture Wars Changed America*, edited by Marianne Weems, Brian Wallis, and Philip Yenawine, (New York: New York University Press, 1999), pp. 253–75.

12n *"Sealed Crustless Sandwich"*: Boyle, *The Public Domain*, pp. xi, 249–50.

"COMMON TO ALL"

13   *Sweetwater Alliance*: www.waterissweet.org, accessed 16 October 2009.

13   *Blue Planet Project*: www.blueplanetproject.net, accessed 16 October 2009.

13   *"as we . . . regulate"*: Benkler, "Overcoming Agoraphobia," p. 287.

14   *Native Seeds/SEARCH*: www.nativeseeds.org, accessed 16 October 2009.

14   *"I am one of those"*: Sulston and Ferry, p. 266.

14   *"the common ownership"*: Ibid., p. 200.

14   *"the global consequences"*: Sulston, "Autobiography."

14   *Science Commons*: www.sciencecommons.org, accessed 16 October 2009.

15   *"Human intelligence"*: Langland, p. 131 (B-text, VII, lines 53–54).

15   *"The field of knowledge"*: Jefferson, *The Jefferson Cyclopedia*, p. 791.

16   *Native Land Act of 1865*: Thompson, p. 166.

16   *Forest Acts*: Linebaugh, pp. 151–52.

16   *"A thief who stole"*: Hesse, p. 28.

16   *The WTO flew a group*: Michael Slackman, "The (Not So) Eagerly Modern Saudi," *The New York Times*, 6 May 2007.

16   *"100 Orders"*: www.cpa-iraq.org/regulations, accessed 14 March 2009.

16   *Order 83*: Pdf available at www.cpa-iraq.org/regulations/#Orders, accessed 16 October 2009.

17   *Order 81*: Ibid. The citations come from §51 (A)(1 & 7), and §66(B).

17   *the many ironies*: Jeremy Smith, "Iraq: Order 81," *The Ecologist*, vol. 35, no. 1 (1 February 2005); www.mindfully.org/GE/2005/Order-81-Iraq1feb05 .htm, accessed 13 March 2009.

18   propaganda: The modern word derives from this postclassical Latin term (as in the seventeeth-century title *Congregatio de propaganda fide*, "Congregation for propagating the faith"); see the *Oxford English Dictionary*, s.v. "propaganda."

18   *Loki . . . Idunn*: Jean I. Young, *The Prose Edda of Snorri Sturlson* (Berkeley: University of California Press, 1966), pp. 97–99.

19   *Norse legend tells of a spring*: Bruce Lincoln, *Death, War, and Sacrifice* (Chicago: University of Chicago Press, 1991), pp. 54–55.

19   *"Sing in me, Muse"*: Homer, *The Odyssey*, translated by Robert Fitzgerald (Garden City, N.Y.: Doubleday, 1961), line 1.

20   *"I have transmitted"*: Alford, "Don't Stop Thinking," p. 29.

20   *"If my poems"*: Ibid., p. 34.

20   *"an equation for me has no meaning"*: Robert Kanigel, *The Man Who Knew Infinity: A Life of the Genius Ramanujan* (New York: Charles Scribner's Sons, 1991), p. 78.

20   *goddess of learning*: Ibid., p. 36.

20   *"Knowledge is a gift of God"*: Hesse, p. 28.

21   *"Such a belief was stated"*: Stephen Rose, "The Mechanisms of the Music Trade in Central Germany, 1600–40," *Journal of the Royal Musical Association*, vol. 130, no. 1 (2005), p. 30.

21   *"I have heaped riches"*: Ibid.

21   *"Freely have I received"*: Ibid., p. 31.

21   *"To the highest God"*: Ibid.

21   *"the common . . . melodies"*: Ibid., p. 32.

21   *"that* storge *may be applied"*: Czeslaw Milosz, ed., *A Book of Luminous Things: An International Anthology of Poetry* (New York: Harcourt, Brace, and Co., 1996), p. 177.

22   *"The greatest lesson"*: Eugenio Montale, *The Second Life of Art: Selected Essays of Eugenio Montale*, edited and translated by Jonathan Galassi (New York: Ecco Press, 1982), p. 154.

2: WHAT IS A COMMONS?

23   *The rights of man*: Percy Bysshe Shelley, *Essays and Letters*, edited by Ernest Rhys (Boston: Scott, 1887), p. 382.

A RIGHT OF ACTION

23   *"God . . . has given the earth"*: Locke, *Second Treatise*, p. 18 (§25).

23   *"the common mother of all"*: Ibid., p. 19 (§28).

23   *"wild common"*: Ibid., p. 29 (§48).

23   *"America"*: Ibid., p. 23 (§36).

23   *"wild woods"*: Ibid., p. 24 (§37).

23   *"the children of Adam, or Noah"*: Ibid., p. 22 (§36).

23   *"In the beginning all the world was America"*: Ibid., p. 29 (§49).

23   *first condition*: Ibid., chapter 5.

24   *"The realist in all of us"*: Lessig, *The Future of Ideas*, p. 47.

24   *"that great and still remaining common"*: Locke, *Second Treatise*, p. 20 (§30).

24   a right of action: *Century Dictionary*, edited by William Dwight Whitney (New York: The Century Publishing Co., 1891), s.v. "property."

25   *"the right of ownership"*: Blackstone, vol. 2, p. 3.

25   *"dominion"*: Bailyn, pp. 55–56.

26   *"as a man"*: Madison, *Papers*, pp. 14–15.

26n   *"The hallmark"*: *College Savings Banks, Inc. v. Florida Prepaid Postsecondary Education, Inc.*, 119 S. Ct. 2219 (1999).

27   *"Generally a man"*: Linebaugh, p. 79 (see also p. 279).

ESTOVERS IN COMMON

27   pasturage: Blackstone, vol. 2, pp. 26–28.

28   *right to glean*: Neeson, pp. 313–14.

28n   *modern commons*: www.info-commons.org/blog/archives/000019.html; see also www.law.duke.edu/journals/icp, both accessed 24 July 2004.

28   *"shall have . . . her reasonable estovers"*: Magna Carta §7, as in Linebaugh, p. 284.

28   *"patrimony of the poor"*: Neeson, p. 55; see also Linebaugh, pp. 41–42.

28   *"Lands . . . are taken for tillage"*: Cornelius Tacitus, *Dialogus, Agricola, Germania* (Cambridge, Mass.: Harvard University Press, 1914), pp. 169–70.

28   *"Sometimes people owned"*: Malcolm Margolin, "Traditional California Indian Conservation," *News from Native California*, vol. 11, no. 2 (Winter 1997–1998), pp. 10–11.

29   system of English common land tenure: *Encyclopaedia Britannica*, 11th ed. (London: The Encyclopaedia Britannica Company, 1911), s.v. "manor"; Neeson, pp. 5 and 329; Crawford, pp. 11 and 47–48.

30   *"lands in fee simple"*: Webster, "Examination," p. 59 (emphasis deleted).

30   *"a Man holds"*: Thomas Hobbes, *The English Works of Thomas Hobbes of Malmesbury*, edited by Sir William Molesworth, 11 vols. (London: John Bohn, 1839–1845), vol. 6, p. 154.

31   serf's holdings: *Encyclopaedia Britannica*, op. cit.

31   *"the great law of subordination"*: Daniel Defoe, *The Great Law of Subordination Considered* (London: S. Harding, 1724).

BEATING THE BOUNDS

33   *"The rational herdsman"*: Hardin, "The Tragedy of the Commons," p. 1244.

33   *"Suppose two persons"*: W. F. Lloyd, *Two Lectures on the Checks to Population* (Oxford: Oxford University Press, 1833), p. 19 (see also pp. 30–31).

34 *the commons were . . .* stinted: Thompson, pp. 132, 142, and 147.

35 *"rights of common"*: Cox, p. 54; see also Neeson, pp. 59ff; Blackstone, vol. 2, pp. 26–28.

35 *"The weekly markets"*: Thompson, p. 195.

36 *"hucksters"*: Ibid.

36 *"exclaimed indignantly"*: Ibid., p. 198.

36 *"cannot then be said"*: Ibid.

37 *"beat the bounds"*: Bushaway, p. 83; Thompson, p. 111; Robert Chambers, ed., *The Book of Days: A Miscellany of Popular Antiquities*, 2 vols. (London: W. & R. Chambers, 1883), vol. 1, pp. 583–85.

37 *sowed grazing land*: Merricks, p. 124; Neeson, p. 100.

37 *installed rabbit warrens*: Loux, pp. 131 and 136.

37 *Ascension Day week*: Bushaway, pp. 83–84.

37 *"arable ground"*: The Great Charter of the Forest §12, as found in Linebaugh, p. 299.

37 *"is incommoded or diminished"*: Blackstone, vol. 2, p. 187.

37 *"If the Lord doth inclose"*: Thompson, p. 118n; for other cases, see Neeson, p. 107; Thompson, pp. 112–13.

38 *"at least where there is enough"*: Locke, *Second Treatise*, p. 19 (§27).

38 *"courts or legislatures"*: Gordon, "A Property Right in Self-Expression," p. 1608. The phrase "Lockean proviso" was coined by the philosopher Robert Nozick; see *Anarchy, State, and Utopia*, pp. 178ff.

38 *"lawless law's enclosure"*: From Clare's poem "The Mores," *The Penguin Book of English Pastoral Verse*, edited by John Barrell and John Bulls (New York: Penguin Books, 1982), p. 415.

38 *"Should a poor man"*: Neeson, pp. 26–27.

ALIENABLE PLOTS

39 *Beating the bounds now meant*: Neeson, pp. 65, 266, and 286; Merricks, pp. 124–25.

41 *Delamere Forest*: Thompson, p. 137.

42 *the vassal and the freeholder*: Pocock, pp. 386 and 436.

43 *"the older . . . culture"*: Thompson, p. 399 (see also pp. 36–38).

44n *"The Tragedy of the Unmanaged Commons"*: Hardin, "Extension of The Tragedy of the Commons."

3: THE ENCLOSURE OF CULTURE

"THE ENCOURAGEMENT OF LEARNING"

45   *"the second enclosure"*: Boyle, *The Public Domain*, pp. 42–53.

45   *"If you have an apple"*: The source for this quotation is unknown, though many websites repeat it (as, for example, www.wisdomquotes.com/002776 .html, accessed 19 October 2009).

46   *"The ancients may be considered"*: Henry Fielding, *The History of Tom Jones* (New York, Penguin Books, 1966), p. 552.

46   *"The Copies of ancient Authors"*: *Enquiry*, p. 6.

48   *windshield wiper*: www.me.utexas.edu/~me179/topics/patents/case3.html, accessed 19 October 2009.

48   *four traditional answers*: Fisher, "Theories of Intellectual Property."

50   *"a man of independent means"*: *Encyclopaedia Britannica*, 11th edition, s.v. "telescope," p. 560.

51   *"It was not the person"*: *The Gentlemen's Magazine* [London], vol. 60, no. 4, part ii (October 1790), pp. 890–91. For the full story of Dolland's case, I'm indebted to an essay by my father: W. L. Hyde, "The Telescope Doublet— Five Historical Mistakes," *Optical Society of America Research Newsletter*, 6 June 1966, pp. 1–3.

51   *Stationers' Company*: Mark Rose, *Authors and Owners*, p. 12.

51   *"the Author or Proprietors"*: Statute of Anne.

52   *"There seems to be in authors"*: James Boswell, *Life of Johnson, Together with Journal of a Tour to the Hebrides and Johnson's Diary of a Journey into North Wales*, edited by George Birkbeck Hill, 6 vols. (Oxford: Clarendon Press, 1934–64), vol. 2, p. 259.

53   *"It might be dangerous"*: Deazley, *Origin*, p. 172.

53   *"unavoidably raise the price"*: Lord Kames cited in Deazley, *Origin*, p. 187.

53   *"For the general good"*: Boswell, op. cit.

54   *"common benefit"*: Deazley, *Origin*, p. 100.

54   *name of the Statute of Anne*: *Considerations*, pp. 7–9.

54   *"Under the U.S. Constitution"*: *Eldred v. Ashcroft*, 537 U.S. 186 (2003), Justice Breyer's dissent, p. 6 (citing H. R. Rep. No. 100—609, p. 22 [1988], p. 17).

"FOREVER, MINUS A DAY"

55   *"hath been kept inclosed"*: *Company of Stationers v. Seymour* (1677), cited in *Vindication*, pp. 19–21.

55   *"the act of publication"*: Deazley, *Origin*, p. 144.

56   *"his conceptions have become"*: *Stowe v. Thomas*, 23 F. Cas. 201 (C.C.E.D. Pa. 1853), p. 206.

57   The Second Sex: Sarah Glazer, "Lost in Translation," *The New York Times*, 22 August 2004.

57   *"made the common tradesmen"*: Franklin, *Autobiography*, p. 57.

57   *"Nothing in this act"*: Copyright Act of 1790 (1 Statutes at Large, 124); http://en.wikisource.org/wiki/Copyright_Act_of_1790, accessed 22 October 2009.

57   *"fixed in any tangible"*: U.S. Title 17, Ch. 1, §106.

58   *poems of Emily Dickinson*: Elizabeth Rosa Horan, "Technically Outside the Law: Who Permits, Who Profits, and Why," *The Emily Dickinson Journal*, vol. 10, no. 1 (Spring 2001), pp. 34–54.

58n   *"to confer gratuitously"*: *Kendall v. Winsor*, 62 U.S. 21 How. 322 (1858), p. 62.

59   *"forever, minus a day"*: Robert S. Boynton, "Righting Copyright: Fair Use and Digital Environmentalism," *Bookforum*, February–March 2005; www.bookforum.com/archive/feb_05/boynton.html, accessed 18 February 2009.

59   *"the current copyright term"*: *Eldred v. Ashcroft*, op. cit., brief for George A. Akerlof et al. as Amici Curiae.

59n   *economists assumed*: Ibid., pp. 5–6 and 8.

60   *"When [Alessandro] Volta"*: Drahos, p. 209, citing a passage from *Lane Fox v. Kensington and Knightsbridge Electric Lighting Co.*

60   *penicillin*: Drahos and Braithwaite, pp. 152–54 and 157.

60   *hepatitis C virus*: Michael Crichton, "Patenting Life," *The New York Times*, 13 February 2007.

61   *"you get utility"*: Drahos and Braithwaite, p. 158.

61   *"Elevated uric acid"*: Michael Crichton, "This Essay Breaks the Law," *The New York Times*, 19 March 2006.

61   *Indian government estimated*: Suketu Mehta, "A Big Stretch," *The New York Times*, 7 May 2007.

61   *"utility patents"*: Drahos and Braithwaite, pp. 159–60.

61   *policy questions*: See Drahos, pp. 208–10; Drahos and Braithwaite, pp. 159–68; and Boyle, *The Public Domain*, pp. 68–71.

"THIS BOOK CANNOT BE READ ALOUD"

62   *"If our property"*: Barlow, "The Economy of Ideas."

63   *"What do record companies do?"*: Byrne.

65   *"generative Internet"*: Zittrain, chapter 8.

66   *"first sale doctrine"*: The statute in question is 17 U.S.C., Chapter 1, § 109: "Limitations on exclusive rights: Effect of transfer of particular copy or phonorecord."

67   *the following warnings*: The list is reproduced on the cover of Drahos and Braithwaite; see also www.lessig.org/content/standard/0,1902,22914,00.html, accessed 22 October 2009.

67   *restrictions on the Constitution*: http://lessig.org/blog/2004/06/this_is_the _constitution_on_dr.html#comments; www.boingboing.net/2004/06/24/ drmed-constitution-m.html, both accessed 26 April 2008.

SILENCE AS A RESOURCE

68   *"To study the self"*: Hee-jin Kim, *Eihei Dogen: Mystical Realist* (Boston: Wisdom Publications, 2004), p. 125. In general see chapter 9 of Dogen's "Genjokoan."

68   *"If my poems and paintings"*: Alford, "Don't Stop Thinking About . . . Yesterday," p. 34.

68   *"What difference"*: Foucault (citing Samuel Beckett), p. 222.

69   *collective ignorance*: For Thoreau on ignorance, see Lewis Hyde, *The Essays of Henry D. Thoreau* (New York: North Point Press, 2002), pp. xvi–xxiii.

69   *VisiCalc*: Zittrain, p. 2.

69   *cell biologists in San Diego*: Andrew Pollack, "Drug Makers Prepare to Argue Against a Patent," *The New York Times*, 19 April 2005.

69   *survey of scientists*: Sulston and Ferry, p. 268.

70   *"Out of unhandselled savage nature"*: Emerson, vol. 1, *Nature, Addresses and Lectures*, pp. 99–100; www.vcu.edu/engweb/transcendentalism/authors/ emerson/essays/amscholar.html, accessed 23 October 2009.

70   *"Silence is audible"*: Henry D. Thoreau, *A Week on the Concord and Merrimack Rivers* (Princeton, N.J.: Princeton University Press, 2004), p. 391.

71   *"The very same olive-wood rafters"*: Illich, p. 52.

71   *"On the same boat"*: Ibid., p. 53.

71   *buses are equipped*: Winnie Hu, "Radio on Bus Fosters Quiet, but Not Peace," *The New York Times*, 17 April 2008.

71   *the only sugared drink*: Mary B. W. Tabor, "Schools Profit from Offering Pupils for Market Research," *The New York Times*, 5 April 1999.

72   Classical Graffiti: Randy Cassingham, "Silence Is Golden—for Some," www .peg.com/forums/comm/200209/msg00250.html, accessed 23 October 2009.

73   *"It informed me"*: Ben Greenman, "Silence Is Beholden," *The New Yorker*, 30 September 2002.

73   *"This is intellectual property"*: Ibid.

73   *"making this gesture"*: Cassingham, op. cit.

73   *"copyright infringement"*: Ibid.

74 *"The issue was entirely"*: The e-mail exchange with Riddle is posted online at http://johncage.org/blog/hyde_riddle_exchange.html, accessed 23 October 2009.

74 *"I used them to free myself"*: Richard Kostelanetz, *Conversing with Cage* (New York: Limelight Editions, 1991), p. 229.

74 *"the imprint"*: Carolyn McColley, "Limitations on Moral Rights in French Droit d'Auteur," *Copyright Law Symposium*, no. 41 (New York: American Society of Composers, Authors and Publishers, 1997), p. 424.

74 *"an artist who draws from life"*: Bleistein v. Donaldson Lithographing Co. (1903), 188 U.S., p. 250.

74 *"Personality"*: John Cage, *Silence* (Middletown, Conn.: Wesleyan University Press, 1961), p. 90.

76 *"every Free-Man"*: The Great Charter of the Forest §13, as found in Linebaugh, p. 299.

76 *entitled to glean*: Neeson, pp. 284 and 313.

4: FRAMING A COMMONWEALTH

78 *Wisdom and knowledge*: Constitution of the Commonwealth of Massachusetts (Boston: Wright & Potter, 1918), p. 30.

"LEACHES HAVE SUCKED THE COMMON-WEALTH"

79 *"What Des-Cartes did"*: Merton, p. 31.

79 *"If there be any thing"*: Camden, col. 999.

80 *"The general rule of law"*: International News Service v. Associated Press, 248 U.S. 215 (1918), p. 250.

81 *"Luther, I answer"*: Cited in Hesse, p. 34.

81 *"exclusive Right to the Property of published books"*: Mark Rose, *Authors and Owners*, p. 35.

81 *"every jot as unjust"*: Ibid.

81 *"A Book is the Author's Property"*: Ibid., p. 39.

82 *"His Brain, which was his Estate"*: Ibid., p. 40.

82 *"The ancient Patriarchs of Poetry"*: Ibid., p. xiii.

82 *"it was on the model"*: Ibid., p. 7.

82 *"The mind of a man of Genius"*: Edward Young, *Conjectures on Original Composition* (London: A. Millar, 1759), p. 9.

83 *"who will be apt to think"*: Mark Rose, "Nine-Tenths of the Law," p. 82.

83 *"When an author prints and publishes"*: Ibid., p. 79n (citing Yates's dissent in *Millar v. Taylor* [K.B. 1769], *The English Reports*, vol. 98, p. 234).

83   res publicae: For a good discussion of the categories of Roman property law, see Carol Rose, "Romans, Roads, and Romantic Creators."

84   *"We conceive [that] this property"*: Mark Rose, *Authors and Owners*, p. 44.

84   *"Newton, Milton, Locke"*: Camden, col. 1000.

85   *"upon herself to grant patents"*: Macaulay, *Works*, vol. 1, p. 66.

85   *"could be bought only"*: Ibid.

85   *the queen's printer*: Hesse, p. 30.

85   *"Copyright is monopoly"*: Macauley, "A Speech," pp. 232–33.

85   *"injurious to learning"*: Locke, "Memorandum," p. 208.

86   *"It is very absurd"*: Ibid., pp. 208–209.

86   *authors yet living*: Ibid.; see also Mark Rose, *Authors and Owners*, pp. 32–33; Starr, pp. 118–19.

86   *"in an angry and determined mood"*: Macaulay, *Works*, vol. 1, p. 66.

87   *"were merely privileges"*: Yates, p. 186.

87   Wheaton v. Peters: Travis, p. 816.

87   *the problem continued*: Drahos, pp. 29–30.

87   *"a Nest of Wasps"*: www.british-history.ac.uk/report.aspx?compid=74922, accessed 24 October 2009.

88   *"let Mother Church"*: Locke, "Memorandum," p. 207.

89   *Wesleyan Methodists*: Macaulay, "A Speech," pp. 241–42.

89   *printers in London*: Locke, "Memorandum," p. 207, and Camden, col. 963.

89   *"restrictions against monopolies"*: Smith, vol. 1, p. 512.

89   *"the incitements to ingenuity"*: Ibid., p. 545.

90   *"With regard to Monopolies"*: Ibid., p. 566.

90   *"perpetual monopolies of every sort"*: Madison, "Monopolies," p. 552.

90   *"If nature has made any one thing"*: Jefferson, *The Complete Jefferson*, p. 1015.

91   *"the braking and beating [of] hemp"*: Jefferson, *The Jefferson Cyclopedia*, p. 432.

91   *"Certainly an inventor ought"*: Ibid., p. 679; Jefferson, *The Writings of Thomas Jefferson*, vol. 11, p. 201.

"EASY AND CHEAP AND SAFE"

92   *elected the surveyor of highways*: Page Smith, *John Adams*, 2 vols. (New York: Doubleday, 1962), vol. 1, pp. 57–59.

94   *Adams's thesis*: Adams, "A Dissertation," pp. 448–56. I present Adams's position on its own terms; it should be noted, however, that Adams himself mythologizes his Puritan ancestors. As Michael Warner has shown, Adams treats his own emerging republicanism as if it were "the latent mean-

ing of Puritan history." Contrary to Adams's reading of the past, Puritan print culture was not "routinely opposed to authority," nor identified with "emancipatory reflection," nor linked to "a protonationalist consciousness." See Warner, pp. 2 and 31.

94   *"continued Protestants through the reign of Queen Mary"*: Franklin, *Auto-biography*, pp. 4–5.

95   *the overarching themes*: Adams, "A Dissertation," pp. 455–57.

96   *"There shall be . . . paid unto his majesty"*: §7 of the Stamp Act; see www .lexrex.com/enlightened/laws/stampact.htm, accessed 25 October 2009.

96   *smaller duty on fees*: Ibid., §54.

96   *"the Duties upon Admissions"*: Morgan, p. 57.

97   *destroy the German-language newspapers*: Starr, p. 65.

97   *a 50 percent sales tax*: Ibid., p. 38.

97   *"The stamp tax made it impossible"*: Ibid., p. 39.

97   *"foolish curiosity"*: Ibid.

98   *"And you, Messieurs printers"*: Adams, "A Dissertation," p. 457.

98   *"Printed by Authority"*: Starr, pp. 34–35.

98   *Printers in the American Colonies*: Ibid., pp. 53–55.

99   Cato's Letters: Ibid., p. 62.

99   *it bore Gridley's name*: Adams, "A Dissertation," p. 447.

THE FRAMERS' ESTATE

100   *allodial land*: On the distinction between allodial and feudal land, see Alexander, pp. 51–55.

100   *"his own and the commonwealth's"*: Pocock, p. 386.

101   *freeholders are distinct*: Alexander, pp. 53–54.

102   *Jefferson mythologized it*: Jefferson, "A Summary View," pp. 132–33.

102   "The earth belongs in usufruct": James Morton Smith, vol. 1, p. 632 (Jefferson letter of 6 September 1789).

103   *"This principle that the earth belongs to the living"*: Ibid., p. 635.

103   *"eighteen years, eight months"*: Ibid., p. 633.

104   *"It seems very manifest"*: Adams, "A Dissertation," p. 464.

104   *"hold . . . their lands allodially"*: Ibid., p. 455.

104n   *three kinds of land*: Alexander, pp. 41 and 55.

107   *"compensation for a benefit"*: Madison, "Monopolies," p. 551.

107   *democracy is democracy*: I recommend Neil Netanel's 1996 essay "Copyright and a Democratic Civil Society" for a more contemporary analysis of how a well-designed copyright regime strengthens democratic ends. Assuming that democracy requires "robust public debate, the spread of knowl-

edge, and the questioning of cultural hierarchy," Netanel defines copyright as "a state measure that uses market institutions to enhance the democratic character of civil society." It does this in part by supporting "a sector of creative and communicative activity that is relatively free from reliance on state subsidy, elite patronage, and cultural hierarchy." Copyright gives authors and publishers "room for risk taking and independence from government and private patronage." See Netanel, pp. 288, 296, and 335–36.

108 *"imported from Holland Tully's Works"*: Locke, "Memorandum," p. 208.

108 *"by this act scholars are subjected"*: Ibid., p. 204.

109 *"As artists, we find"*: www.negativland.com/news/?page_id=23, accessed 26 October 2009.

110 *how this Latin phrase is used today*: *Black's Law Dictionary*, edited by Bryan A. Garner (St. Paul, Minn.: West, 2009), s.v. *publici juris*.

110 *twenty thousand commercials each year*: Bollier, *Silent Theft*, p. 154.

110 *investing in loudspeakers*: Starr, p. 9.

5: BENJAMIN FRANKLIN, FOUNDING PIRATE

"THE INVENTIONS OF OTHERS"

112 *a typical display*: Cohen, *Benjamin Franklin's Science*, p. 44.

112 *"enjoying . . . Leisure to read"*: Cohen, *Science and the Founding Fathers*, p. 149.

113 *"Insist on yourself"*: Emerson, vol. 2: *Essays: First Series*, p. 83.

113 *each man made contributions*: Franklin, *Benjamin Franklin's Experiments*, pp. 60–66.

113 *room at the Pennsylvania State House*: Chaplin, p. 106.

113 *series of foundational contributions*: Cohen, *Science and the Founding Fathers*, pp. 141–43.

114 *"We made what we called an* electrical-battery": Franklin, *Benjamin Franklin's Experiments*, p. 192.

114 *terms that first found their modern usage*: Van Doren, p. 173.

114 *"I have been much amused"*: Cited by Cohen in Franklin, *Benjamin Franklin's Experiments*, p. 106.

114 *"electrical fluid agrees with lightning"*: Franklin, *Benjamin Franklin's Experiments*, p. 112.

115 *The experiment he went on to suggest*: Ibid., p. 122.

115 *Sparks leaped from an iron rod*: Van Doren, p. 163.

115 *he substituted a kite*: Cohen, *Benjamin Franklin's Science*, p. 68; see also Joseph Priestley's account in Van Doren, p. 165.

115 *"The experiment depended on the 'power of points'"*: Cohen in Franklin, *Benjamin Franklin's Experiments*, p. 113.

116 *lightning rods were erected*: Cohen, *Benjamin Franklin's Science*, pp. 68, 82, and 229.

116 *results of the kite experiment*: *The Pennsylvania Gazette*, 19 October 1752. Also printed in Joseph Priestley, *The History and Present State of Electricity, with Original Experiments* (London: J. Dodsley, 1767), pp. 179–81.

116 *"securing . . . Buildings from Mischief"*: Franklin, *Benjamin Franklin's Experiments*, p. 129 (citing *Poor Richard Improved*, 1753).

117 *offered a patent*: Franklin, *Autobiography*, p. 98.

117 *Much of the language . . . was easily at hand*: Cohen, *Benjamin Franklin's Science*, p. 52; Chaplin, pp. 111–13.

117 *"balance of power"*: Cohen, *Science and the Founding Fathers*, p. 210.

117 *"aether (like our air) may contain particles"*: Cohen, *Benjamin Franklin's Science*, p. 19; Cohen, *Science and the Founding Fathers*, p. 141.

118 *proto-scientific journals*: Cohen, *Benjamin Franklin's Science*, pp. 61, 64, and 227.

118 *"Hence have arisen some new terms"*: Cohen, *Benjamin Franklin's Science*, p. 65.

118 *the existence of contrary electricities*: Ibid.

118 *"a striking illustration of the doctrine"*: Ibid., p. 65.

119 *"the labor of his body"*: Locke, *Second Treatise*, p. 19 (§27).

120 *"If I own a can of tomato juice"*: Nozick, p. 174, commenting on Locke's labor theory.

120 *The innovation of the Franklin stove*: See Samuel Y. Edgerton, Jr., "Supplement: The Franklin Stove," in Cohen, *Benjamin Franklin's Science*, pp. 199–211; Chaplin, p. 87.

120 *"That as we enjoy great Advantages"*: Franklin, *Autobiography*, p. 98 (italics deleted).

"UNLOCKING SECRETS"

121 *"as printing is this man's trade"*: Cited in Chaplin pp. 361–62.

121 *"the trade secret died"*: Ibid., p. 362.

122 *Apprentices initiated into these mysteries*: Ibid., p. 12.

122 *"guild structure was weak or absent"*: Ibid.

122 *"missing link"*: William Eamon, *Science and the Secrets of Nature: Books of Secrets in Medieval and Early Modern Culture* (Princeton, N.J.: Princeton University Press, 1994), p. 9.

123 *publications had turned craft-specific*: Chaplin, p. 20.

123 *"unlock[ing] . . . Secrets"*: Ibid.

123   *"To offer a thing to the Publick"*: Ibid., p. 54.

123   *"such Hints . . . as may contribute"*: *The Pennsylvania Gazette*, 2 October 1729.

123   *anti-emigration laws*: Ben-Atar, pp. 12 and 52–53.

124   *"a special Law might easily be obtain'd"*: Franklin, *The Papers of Benjamin Franklin* (Franklin letter of 4 January 1782).

124   *"If Books can be had much cheaper"*: Ibid. (Franklin letter of 21 April 1785.)

125   *"Gentlemen, A Ship having been fitted out from England"*: Ibid. (Franklin letter of 10 March 1779.)

126   *"Franklin never became an intellectual property nationalist"*: Ben-Atar, p. 75.

126   *new method for casting printer's type*: Ibid., pp. 75–76.

126   *"produce something for the common Benefit of Mankind"*: Cohen, *Science and the Founding Fathers*, p. 149.

127   *"humanity, regardless of national boundaries"*: Ben-Atar, p. 77.

"IMPROVEMENT FLASHED UPON IMPROVEMENT"

127   *"copper plate and letter printing"*: Franklin, *The Papers of Benjamin Franklin* (Franklin letter of 27 November 1755).

127   *"many useful Particulars remain uncommunicated"*: Ibid. (Broadside of 14 May 1743.)

128   *"the Knowledge of small Matters"*: Ibid. (Franklin letter of 27 November 1755.)

128   *surmised that the Gulf Stream gave rise to the difference*: Ibid. (Franklin letter of 29 October 1768.)

128   *Mariners had known about the Gulf Stream*: Chaplin, p. 175.

128   *Captain Cook tried to chart the shores*: Ibid., p. 197.

129   *Nantucket whalers*: Ibid.

129   *"that the Whales are found"*: Franklin, *The Papers of Benjamin Franklin* (Franklin letter of 29 October 1768).

130   *"Maritime Observations"*: Chaplin, p. 323.

131   *"the art of printing"*: Franklin, *The Papers of Benjamin Franklin* (Franklin letter of 2 October 1783).

131   *"the powerful and opulent"*: Owen Biddle, *An Oration, Delivered the Second of March, 1781, at the Request of the American Philosophical Society for Promoting Useful Knowledge* (Philadelphia: Francis Bailey, 1781), p. 25.

131   *"improvement flashed upon improvement"*: Ibid.

132   *"Our Birth is nothing but our Death begun"*: Edward Young, *The Complaint: or, Night-Thoughts on Life, Death, & Immortality* (London: A. Millar and R. Dodsley, 1750), p. 128.

132 *"why is Property to be represented"*: Franklin, *The Papers of Benjamin Franklin* ("Queries and Remarks on a Paper entitled 'Hints for the Members of Convention No II in the *Federal Gazette* of Tuesday Nov 3d 1789 . . .'").

133 *In explaining this position*: Ibid. (Franklin letter dated 2 June 1750.)

133 *a right to tax their members*: Ibid. ("Revisions of the Pennsylvania Declaration of Rights," 29 July 1776); and see Morgan, pp. 307–308.

6: LIBERTY TO COMMUNICATE

TRUTH HAS NO THINKER

135 *"These Thoughts, my dear Friend"*: Cohen, *Benjamin Franklin's Science*, p. 38.

136 *"I have never entered into any Controversy"*: Franklin, *Benjamin Franklin's Experiments*, pp. 137–38 (Franklin letter of 4 October 1777).

137 *"The lie requires a thinker"*: Bion, p. 102.

137 *"work that corroborates the discovery of others"*: Ibid., p. 105.

137 *"The lie and its thinker are inseparable"*: Ibid., p. 102.

138 *"it is wrong to say"*: Rimbaud, pp. 303–305.

138 *Turks in Constantinople*: The example comes from one of the "Paradoxes" in *Poor Richard Improved*, 1757; see Franklin, *The Papers of Benjamin Franklin*.

138 *"Rules of Reasoning in Philosophy"*: Isaac Newton, *The Principia: Mathematical Principles of Natural Philosophy*, translated by I. Bernard Cohen and Anne Whitman (Berkeley: University of California Press, 1999), p. 795.

139 *how Franklin persuaded the delegates*: "Speech in the Convention on the Constitution," delivered 17 September 1787; see Franklin, *The Papers of Benjamin Franklin*.

"I'M NOBODY!"

140 *letter to the* Journal of Paris: "Proposal re Daylight Saving," 26 April 1784; see Franklin, *The Papers of Benjamin Franklin*.

143 *"What has he done that he is so modest"*: Merton, pp. 163n and 296.

143 *"philosophical levity"*: Herman Melville, *Israel Potter* (New York: G. P. Putnam, 1855), p. 81.

143 *"You will see it perhaps often"*: Franklin, *Autobiography*, p. 76.

144n *"There is none so proud"*: Ibid., p. 76n.

144 *"I scarce ever heard"*: Ibid., p. 2.

146 *"The Tatler tells"*: Franklin letter to Jared Eliot dated 12 April 1753; see Franklin, *The Papers of Benjamin Franklin*.

SPECULATIVE STATESMEN AND THE COMMON HIVE

147 *Boston's first-ever newspaper*: Starr, p. 57; for the *New-England Courant*, see Van Doren, pp. 18ff.

147 *"I took some of the Papers"*: Franklin, *Autobiography*, p. 11.

148 *"I have observed," he writes*: Joseph Addison, *The Spectator*, edited by George A. Aitken (London: John C. Nimmo, 1898), vol. 1, pp. 1–7.

149 *"Since it is observed"*: "Silence Dogood, No. 1," from the *New-England Courant*, 2 April 1722; see Franklin, *The Papers of Benjamin Franklin*.

150 *"Cato's Letters"*: For background on these, see Bailyn, p. 43.

150 *"not themes or subjects fit for vulgar persons"*: Starr, p. 24.

151 *"Opportunity of Judging"*: Cited in Warner, p. 37.

151 *the public realm then consisted of show*: Habermas, pp. 7–10.

151 *"a refeudalization of the public sphere"*: Ibid., p. 195.

152 *"I . . . put my self as much as I could out of sight"*: Franklin, *Autobiography*, p. 64.

152 *"In the Introduction to these Proposals"*: Ibid., pp. 98–99.

153 *"any private Views or Ends"*: Cited in Warner, p. 38.

153 *In the following sheets*: Thomas Paine, *Collected Writings* (New York: Library of America, 1995), pp. 5ff.

154 *"The Bee gathers honey from all sorts of Flowers"*: Cited in Warner, p. 39.

I AM OTHER BIRDS

155 *in England he had been a customs officer*: For Paine's early life, see the first chapter of A. J. Ayer, *Thomas Paine* (New York: Atheneum, 1988).

155 Frederick Douglass' Paper: see Lewis Hyde, *Trickster Makes This World* (New York: Farrar, Straus and Giroux, 1998), pp. 240–47.

156 *"The present little Sacrifice of your Vanity"*: Franklin, *Autobiography*, p. 64.

157 *the house sparrow*: See for example Anders Pape Møller, "Social Control of Deception Among Status Signalling House Sparrows," *Behavioral Ecology and Sociobiology*, vol. 20, no. 5 (May 1987), pp. 307–11.

157 *"a Number of Friends"*: Franklin, *Autobiography*, p. 64.

157 *"Every man must seriously set himself"*: *Warren-Adams Letters*, 2 vols. (Boston: The Massachusetts Historical Society, 1917–25), vol. 1, p. 223.

158 *"purity of heart"*: Ibid., p. 222.

158 *"the principles of society may be virtuous"*: John Taylor, *An Inquiry into the Principles and Policy of the Government of the United States* (Union, N.J.: The Lawbook Exchange, 1998; originally published Fredericksburg, Va.: Green and Cady, 1814), p. 460.

158 *"The interest of vice"*: Ibid., p. 461.

158   *"an avaricious society"*: Ibid.; see also Wood, pp. 588–92.

160   *"not freedom from, but freedom to"*: Isaiah Berlin, *Liberty*, edited by Henry Hardy (New York: Oxford University Press, 2002), p. 178.

7: THE COMMON SELF

162   *"The mind / Is so hospitable"*: John Ashbery, *Houseboat Days* (New York: Viking, 1977), p. 38.

162   *"The polis was for the Greeks"*: Arendt, p. 51.

"DIGNITY"

163   *British critics of the Declaration*: Carl L. Becker, *The Declaration of Independence* (New York: Vintage, 1958), pp. 227–29.

163   *"The whole basis of natural freedom"*: Webster, "Examination," p. 59 (italics deleted).

164   *"the very soul of a republic"*: Ibid., p. 59.

164   *"dangerous to liberty and republican government"*: Ibid., p. 60.

164   *"irrevocable laws . . . destroying and barring entailments"*: Ibid., p. 59.

165   *"auxiliary supports"*: Ibid., p. 60.

167   *"utter nonsense"*: Derrick Z. Jackson, "Rumsfeld's 'Fungible' Facts," *The Boston Globe*, 21 April 2004.

167   *"In the kingdom of ends everything has either a price or a dignity"*: Immanuel Kant, *Groundwork of the Metaphysics of Morals*, translated by Mary Gregor (New York: Cambridge, 1998), p. 42.

ALLOTMENT VERSUS THE COMIC GOOD

169   *"there is no enterprise to make your home any better"*: Washburn, p. 17.

169   *"wear civilized clothes"*: Cited in the PBS documentary *The West* (September 1996); www.pbs.org/weta/thewest/resources/archives/eight/dawes.htm, accessed 16 October 2009.

169   *lifted from the enclosure movement in England*: See, for example, Patrick Edward Dove, *The Theory of Human Progression, and Natural Probability of a Reign of Justice* (Boston: Sanborn, Carter and Bazin, 1856), p. 409.

170   *"education and civilization" of the Indians*: Dawes Act, p. 390 (§5).

171   *the Supreme Court had ruled*: Washburn, p. 23.

171   *"every Indian . . . who has voluntarily taken up"*: Dawes Act, p. 390 (§6).

171   *"Indian police"*: Ibid., §5.

171   *"plucked the Indian like a bird"*: Washburn, p. 7.

171 *"Had I known then, as I now know"*: Ibid., p. 67.

171 *"the main purpose of this bill is not to help the Indian"*: Ibid., pp. 37–39.

172 *"is formed solely upon a theory"*: Ibid., p. 35.

172 *"for centuries" the system of holding property in common*: Ibid., p. 38.

172 *"Barbarism has no rights"*: Ibid., p. 16.

172 *"a Christianizing power"*: Ibid., p. 57.

172 *Indians eventually lost 86 million acres*: "Dawes General Allotment Act," *Encyclopaedia Britannica* (online), 7 November 2009; www.britannica.com/ EBchecked/topic/152952/Dawes-General-Allotment-Act, accessed 6 November 2009.

173 *contempt of court*: Timothy Egan, "Indians Win Major Round in Fight over Trust Accounts," *The New York Times*, 23 February 1999. A lawsuit over the mismanaged revenue was finally settled in December 2009; see Charlie Savage, "U.S. Agrees to $3 Billion Deal in Indian Suit," *The New York Times*, 9 December 2009.

173 Arnold v. Mundy: Supreme Court of New Jersey, 6 N.J.L. 1 (1821); http://fas -history.rutgers.edu/clemens/NJLaw/arnold1821.html, accessed 6 November 2009; see also *Illinois Central Railroad v. Illinois*, 146 U.S. 387 (1892).

173 *"divest . . . all the citizens of their common right"*: Cited by Carol Rose, *Property and Persuasion*, p. 120.

173 *applies to the seashores*: See for example *Thornton v. Hay*, 254 Ore. 584, 462 P.2d 671 (1969).

174 *"the common property of all the people"*: Constitution of the Commonwealth of Pennsylvania, article I, section 27; www.legis.state.pa.us/WU01/ VC/visitor_info/creating/constitution.htm, accessed 6 November 2009.

174 *"traditional public forums"*: Hague v. Committee for Industrial Organization, 307 U.S. 496 (1939).

174 *"in the classical sense of a story with a happy outcome"*: Carol Rose, *Property and Persuasion*, p. 111.

174 *"inherently public property"*: Cited in Loux, p. 145.

175 *a system called Gopher*: Lessig, *The Future of Ideas*, p. 43.

175 *from "time out of memory," to dance*: *The English Reports,* vol. 83, p. 357 (the case being *Abbot v. Weekly* [1665]).

175 *a right to play cricket on otherwise private ground*: Carol Rose, *Property and Persuasion*, p. 141.

175 *"who shall resort thither"*: Loux, p. 131.

175 *"the inhabitants of a parish to erect a Maypole"*: *The Law Times*, vol. 33, n.s. (January 29, 1876), p. 697 (the case being *Hall v. Nottinghan*).

175   *the right to hold an annual horse race*: *The English Reports*, vol. 158, p. 1077 (the case being *Mounsey v. Ismay* [1863]).

175   *"in great jollity"*: Carol Rose, *Property and Persuasion*, p. 141.

175   *"Jocular Customs"*: Ibid.

176   *"indefinite and unlimited numbers of persons"*: Ibid., p. 146.

"NOURISHED BY COUNTLESS INDIVIDUALS"

177   *"Where is the master who could have instructed Franklin"*: Emerson, vol. 2: *Essays: First Series*, p. 83.

177   *"Everything that I have seen, heard, and observed"*: Martha Woodmansee and Peter Jaszi, "The Law of Texts: Copyright and the Academy," *College English*, vol. 57, no. 7 (November 1995), p. 769.

178   *"I nearly got myself into a scrape"*: Frances Trollope, *Domestic Manners of the Americans* (New York: Dodd, Mead and Co., 1927), pp. 349–50.

179n   *"Persons—single actors—are not thought in South Asia to be 'individual'"*: Marilyn Strathern, *The Gender of the Gift* (Berkeley: University of California Press, 1988), p. 348.

179n   *"Far from being regarded as unique entities"*: Ibid., p. 13.

180   *"the nonchalance of boys"*: Emerson, vol. 2: *Essays: First Series*, p. 48.

180   *"is always a child"*: Emerson, vol. 1: *Nature, Addresses and Lectures*, p. 9.

181   *A sturdy lad from New Hampshire or Vermont*: Emerson, vol. 2: *Essays: First Series*, p. 76 (italics deleted).

182   *"I shun father and mother and wife and brother"*: Ibid., p. 51.

182   *"It is a true rule that particular estates"*: John Winthrop, "A Model of Christian Charity," *The Norton Anthology of American Literature*, 2 vols. (New York: Norton, 1979), vol. 1, pp. 23–24.

182   *"'Tis the Business of the Legislature"*: Shain, pp. 26–27.

182   *"Brethren, we were born not merely for ourselves"*: Ibid., p. 39.

182   *"A people is traveling fast to destruction"*: Ibid., p. 44.

183   *Not only does democracy make every man forget*: Alexis de Tocqueville, *Democracy in America*, 2 vols., edited by Phillips Bradley (New York: A. A. Knopf, 1987), vol. 2, pp. 98–99.

183   *"Individualism . . . saps the virtues of public life"*: Ibid., vol. 2, p. 98.

183   *As Hannah Arendt has shown*: Arendt, chapters 1 and 2.

183   *the word "idiot"*: Ibid., p. 35.

184   *sets liberty and privacy in opposition*: Ibid., pp. 26–27 and 35.

185   *1826 letter to his cousin*: Webster, "Origin of the Copy-Right Laws," pp. 175–76.

185   *denied the "natural justice" claim*: Ibid., p. 176.

185 *built it on the foundations of existing books*: Ibid., p. 173.

185 *drew on more than two dozen existing works*: Joseph W. Reed, "Noah Webster's Debt to Samuel Johnson," *American Speech*, vol. 37, no. 2 (May 1962), p. 100.

186 *Webster lifted fully a third of his definitions*: Ibid., pp. 97–98.

186 *Make laws, irrevocable laws in every state*: Paraphrasing and altering Webster, "Examination," pp. 59–60.

8: THE COMMON SELF NOW

187 *Near the end of March, 1845, I borrowed an axe*: Henry D. Thoreau, *Walden and Resistance to Civil Government* (New York: W. W. Norton, 1992), p. 27.

187 *I don't believe in the individual Writer so much as in Writing*: Quoted in Veronica Marie Gregg, *Jean Rhys's Historical Imagination* (Chapel Hill: University of North Carolina Press, 1995), p. 49.

"LIKE A TERMITE MOUND"

189 *"I am one of those who feel that the earth is a common good"*: Sulston and Ferry, pp. 266–67.

190 *"[The] . . . monopoly . . . ought to be temporary"*: Madison, "Monopolies," p. 551.

190n *he "watermarked" it to contain a code*: Andrew Pollack, "Synthetic Genome: Signed, Sealed, Decoded," *The New York Times*, 29 January 2008.

190 *DNA is not a simple substance*: Sulston and Ferry, pp. 3, 11–12, and 243.

191 *The resources needed to sequence but one bit of the genome*: Ibid., p. 201.

191 *"no public sequencing lab could even look at the data"*: Ibid., p. 234 (and see also pp. 204 and 206).

191 *like a termite mound*: Ibid., p. 228.

192 *Some of what once seemed barren*: Ibid., p. 40.

192 *"This is sometimes called 'ignorance-driven'"*: Ibid., p. 44.

193 *"But who made the inventive step?"*: Ibid., p. 268.

193 *"many of the most important potential applications"*: Sulston, *C. elegans*, p. 379.

193 *Science Commons*: See http://sciencecommons.org, accessed 6 November 2009.

194 *"What Money Can't Buy"*: Sandel, "What Money Can't Buy."

194 *"an assumption that informs much market-oriented thinking"*: Ibid., p. 104.

196   *"was immediately obvious . . . that Celera had made no attempt"*: Sulston and Ferry, pp. 239–40.

196   *their own piecemeal set*: Ibid., pp. 48, 155, 160, and 192.

"I AM THOUGHT"

197   *"Over the next few weeks I listened to it"*: Dylan, pp. 283–85.

197   *"That day I listened all afternoon to Guthrie"*: Ibid., pp. 244–45.

198   *"I could rattle off all these songs"*: Ibid., p. 240.

198   *"he wasn't much interested in playing; he wanted to listen"*: Eric von Schmidt and Jim Rooney, *Baby, Let Me Follow You Down: The Illustrated Story of the Cambridge Folk Years*, 2nd ed. (Amherst: University of Massachusetts Press, 1994), p. 75.

198   *"Do you know what Dylan was when he came to the Village?"*: www.bob dylanroots.com/inter02.html#sponge, accessed 23 February 2006.

198   *"I didn't have many songs"*: Dylan, p. 227.

199   *"You could write twenty or more songs off that one melody"*: Ibid., p. 228.

199   *"not a melodist"*: Interview with Robert Hilburn, *Los Angeles Times*, 4 April 2004, reprinted in *Bob Dylan: The Essential Interviews*, edited by Jonathan Cott (New York: Wenner Books, 2006), p. 437.

199   *"Almost every song . . . had a clear predecessor"*: Harvey, p. xi.

199   *"What happens is, I'll take a song I know"*: Interview with Hilburn, op. cit., p. 437.

200   *variants of it can be found*: Harvey, pp. 84–86, 111–13.

200   *"a show-stopping ballad"*: Dylan, p. 273.

200   *"I found myself taking the song apart"*: Ibid., p. 275.

200   *"If I hadn't . . . heard the ballad 'Pirate Jenny'"*: Ibid., p. 288.

200   *"When I read those words the bells went off"*: Ibid.

201   *"Right now I'm debauching myself as much as possible"*: Rimbaud, pp. 303–305.

201   *"idiotic generations"*: Ibid., p. 307.

201   *"strange, unfathomable, repulsive, delicious"*: Ibid., p. 309.

202   *"Immature poets imitate"*: T. S. Eliot, *The Sacred Wood and Major Early Essays* (Mineola, N.Y.: Dover Publications, 1998), p. 72.

202   *"All artists borrow"*: Attributed to Picasso, and variously phrased ("Good artists copy; great artists steal"; "Mediocre artists borrow; great artists steal"); see Ralph Keyes, *The Quote Verifier* (New York: St. Martin's, 2006), p. 96.

202   *from an essay by Jonathan Lethem*: "The Ecstasy of Influence: A Plagiarism," *Harper's*, February 2007, pp. 59–71; www.harpers.org/archive/2007/02/0081387, accessed 6 November 2009.

INTELLECTUAL PROPERTIES MANAGEMENT, INC.

205 *"rise to the level of a legally cognizable appropriation"*: Bridgeport Music, Inc. v. Dimension Films, 383 F.3d 390 (6th Cir. 2004); http://fsnews.findlaw.com/cases/6th/04a0297p.html, accessed 2 July 2009.

205 *"is never accidental"*: Ibid.

205 *"were conscious of the fact that they"*: Bright Tunes Music v. Harrisongs Music, 420 F. Supp. 177 (S.D.N.Y. 1976); http://cip.law.ucla.edu/cases/case_brightharrisongs.html, accessed 2 July 2009.

205 *"I conclude," the judge wrote*: Ibid.

206 *Harrison ordered to surrender the majority of royalties*: http://en.wikipedia.org/wiki/My_Sweet_Lord, accessed 6 November 2009.

207 *Dexter King established*: Information on corporations related to the King Estate can be found on the website of the Georgia secretary of state, http://sos.georgia.gov/Corporations, accessed 20 June 2009.

208 *"T-shirts, posters, pens, key chains"*: A copy of the December 1993 opposition to the registration of the mark "We Have a Dream" can be found on the website of the U.S. Department of Commerce Patent and Trademark Office, www.uspto.gov/web/offices/com/sol/foia/tab/2aissues/1999/96881.pdf, accessed 6 November 2009.

208 *tried to erect a monument to Dr. King*: "Cashing In on the Legacy of Martin Luther King Jr.," *The Journal of Blacks in Higher Education*, no. 36 (Summer 2002), p. 52.

208 *threatened to sue vendors selling T-shirts*: Robbie Brown, "King Estate Considering Suit over Unlicensed Obama Items," *The New York Times*, 15 November 2008.

208 *As for the archives, the estate has received*: Steven A. Holmes, "U.S. to Spend $20 Million to Acquire King's Papers," *The New York Times*, 30 October 1999; Errin Haines, "King Estate Seeks Halt to Auction," Associated Press, 8 April 2007.

208 *the estate has exploited the copyright it holds for the "Dream" speech*: See Paul Farhi, "King's 'Dream' Becomes Commercial," *The Washington Post*, 28 March 2001; Darryl Fears, "Critics Say King's Family Is Dishonoring His Legacy," *The Washington Post*, 8 April 2002; Bollier, *Brand Name Bullies*, pp. 172–74.

208n *All proceeds from this*: Michael Eric Dyson, *I May Not Get There with You: The True Martin Luther King, Jr.* (New York: Free Press, 2000), p. 262.

208 *"I called the commercial agency"*: Farhi, op. cit.

209 *juxtapose Dr. King's image with Kermit the Frog*: Fears, op. cit.; Bollier, *Brand Name Bullies*, p. 175.

209   *Alcatel used the "Dream" speech in a thirty-second commercial*: http://
youtube.com/watch?v=4pSWMgfA0wQ, accessed 17 March 2008.

210   *"I don't see how it's any different"*: Fears, op. cit.

210   *"rabbit in the bushes" sermon*: Hansen, p. 96.

211   *"are best heard in this light"*: Ibid.

211   *All the major themes of the speech have roots*: See Sundquist, p. 70, and
Hansen, pp. 154–55. For a discussion of the broader question of Dr. King's
appropriations, especially in regard to his Ph.D. thesis from Boston University, see *The Journal of American History*, vol. 78, no. 1 (June 1991), a
special issue titled "Becoming Martin Luther King, Jr.—Plagiarism and
Originality: A Round Table."

211   *Dr. King once told his graduate adviser*: Sundquist, p. 23.

212   *"I have dreamed a dream"*: Daniel 2:3.

212   *presents himself as one who has come before us, like Daniel*: Sundquist,
pp. 136–37.

212   *"counsel with the Lord"*: Hansen, p. 68.

9: ENDURING COMMONS

214   *One Law for the Lion & Ox*: William Blake, *The Marriage of Heaven and
Hell*, edited by Sir Geoffrey Keynes (Oxford: Oxford University Press,
1994), p. xxvii.

215   *a statutory tort is a statutory tort*: Patry, p. 121.

215n *"The primary goal of copyright is not to reward authors"*: Ibid., p. 128, citing *Feist Publications v. Rural Telephone Service Co.*, 499 U.S. 340 (1991).

215   *"We have often recognized the monopoly privileges"*: Ibid., p. 129, citing
Fogerty v. Fantasy, Inc., 510 U.S. 517 (1994).

COPYDUTY

216   *They moved in tracks of shining white*: Samuel Taylor Coleridge, *The Rime
of the Ancient Mariner* (New York: Newson & Company, 1906), p. 17 (lines
275–85).

217   *"encumbered self"*: Sandel, *Democracy's Discontent*, p. 12.

217   *"Where freedom of conscience is at stake"*: Ibid., p. 66.

218   *"liberty depends on self-government"*: Ibid., p. 117 (and see p. 274).

218   *an often-told story*: Lessig, *The Future of Ideas*, pp. 52–53.

219   *"general public license"*: Ibid., p. 59.

220   *The word "common" is said by some to derive from*: Raymond Williams,
Key Words (New York: Oxford University Press, 1976), p. 61; *Barnhart*

Concise Dictionary of Etymology, edited by Robert K. Barnhart (New York: HarperCollins, 1995), p. 143.

221 *"It is in the nature of tyranny"*: For the original version of this text, see Blaise Pascal, *The Pensées*, translated by J. M. Cohen (Harmondsworth, England: Penguin Books, 1961), p. 96; see also Walzer, p. 18.

222 *"whether this surplus value is convertible"*: Walzer, p. 315.

223 *"in the United States today"*: Ibid., p. 316.

223 *A 2006 letter*: The "Copyright Compliance Notice" sent 23 August 2006, "to all students at USC," signed by Michael Pearce, deputy chief information officer, University of Southern California. For a copy of the letter annotated by Cory Doctorow, see http://craphound.com/usccopyrightcompliance .html, accessed 17 October 2009.

224 *no "deterrent technology" yet exists*: Letter from Jerrold M. Grochow, dated 31 October 2007, to the members of the Massachusetts Delegation to Congress regarding the Higher Education Act reauthorization bill, H.R. 3746. Posted as a pdf at www.educause.edu, accessed 4 August 2008.

225 *"What is 'proper' or appropriate"*: Carol Rose, *Property and Persuasion*, p. 58.

FREEDOM OF LISTENING

226 *"expressly for the Use of any Preacher"*: Franklin, *Autobiography*, p. 88 (and see p. 99).

227 *initial building of the Philadelphia Academy*: Ibid., pp. 98–100.

227 *One line of political thought*: Chantal Mouffe, *The Democratic Paradox* (London: Verso, 2000).

228 *Adam Phillips has explained*: Adam Phillips, "Superiorities," *Equals* (London: Faber and Faber, 2002), pp. 3–31.

228 *Van Winkle goes hunting in the mountains*: Washington Irving, *The Sketch-Book of Geoffrey Crayon, Gent*, edited by Susan Manning (New York: Oxford University Press, 1996), pp. 42–43; see also Starr, p. 84.

229 *Hannah Arendt's reading of the Greek distinction*: Arendt, p. 35.

230 *"image of all of us holding hands"*: Carol Martin and Anna Deavere Smith, "Anna Deavere Smith: The Word Becomes You. An Interview," *TDR* [*The Drama Review*], vol. 37, no. 4. (Winter 1993), p. 54.

230 *"Crown Heights is no melting pot"*: Ibid., p. 46.

230 *"Put on your headphones"*: Ibid., p. 56.

230 *"Many of the characters have chiseled away"*: Ibid., p. 57.

231n *The phrase referred originally*: Webster, "Examination," p. 38; Bailyn, pp. 216–29.

232 *"traditional public forums"*: Hague v. Committee for Industrial Organization, 307 U.S. 496 (1939).

233 *"Men in high stations . . . increase their ambition"*: Cited in Wood, p. 22.

233 *"whetted, not cloyed, by possession"*: Ibid., p. 21, quoting James Burgh.

233 *"all men and women are either free or slaves"*: Skinner, pp. 9–10.

233 *"To enjoy liberty . . . it is not sufficient to be free from coercion"*: Ibid., p. 11.

234 *"the most miserable feature of this condition"*: Ibid., p. 20.

234 *"the highest law is the well-being of the people"*: Ibid., p. 12.

234 *"perpetual monopolies of every sort are forbidden"*: Madison, "Monopolies," p. 552.

235 *"well established"* that copyright *"must serve public, not private, ends"*: Eldred v. Ashcroft, 537 U.S. 186 (2003), Justice Stephen Breyer, dissenting, p. 6 (brackets in original).

APHASIA

235 *lyricist Lorenz Hart*: Eldred v. Ashcroft, 537 U.S. 186 (2003), brief for College Art Association, et al. as Amici Curiae, 20 May 2002, p. 9n.

236 *niece of James McNeill Whistler refused*: Zechariah Chafee, "Reflections on the Law of Copyright: II," *Columbia Law Review*, vol. 45 (1945), p. 726; Paul Goldstein, "Copyright and the First Amendment," *Columbia Law Review*, vol. 70, no. 6 (June 1970), p. 1003n. Both authors comment on *Phillip v. Pennell*, 2 Ch. 577 (1907).

236 *Church of Scientology*: www.wired.com/wired/archive/3.12/alt.scientology.war_pr.html; http://altlaw.org/v1/cases/557492, accessed 24 July 2009.

236 *John Lennon's heirs*: www.law.stanford.edu/news/pr/88, accessed 24 July 2009.

236 *the widow of E. E. Cummings refused*: A Poetry Reading Against the Vietnam War, edited by Robert Bly and David Ray (Madison, Minn.: Sixties Press, 1966).

236 *"the Pro-Choice view" of abortion*: http://altlaw.org/v1/cases/557492, accessed 24 July 2009; the case was *Maxtone-Graham v. Burtchaell*, 803 F.2d 1253 (2d Cir. 1986).

236 *Picasso estate refused*: Anthony Haden-Guest, "Picasso Pic Has Heirs Seeing Red!," *The New Yorker*, 21 and 28 August 1995, pp. 53–54.

236 *a book on children's art and modern artists*: Eldred v. Ashcroft, 537 U.S. 186 (2003), brief for College Art Association, et al. as Amici Curiae, 20 May 2002, p. 9.

236   *The estate of the poet Countee Cullen refused*: See the interview with Robert Pinsky at www.duke.edu/web/thearchive/fall07interview.html, accessed 25 July 2009.

236   *conservative talk show host Michael Savage*: http://latimesblogs.latimes .com/webscout/2008/10/brave-new-films.html, accessed 24 July 2009.

237   *a history of Depression-era American photography*: *Eldred v. Ashcroft*, 537 U.S. 186 (2003), brief for College Art Association, et al. as Amici Curiae, 20 May 2002, pp. 13–14.

237   *NBC refused to license a video clip*: Patricia Aufderheide and Peter Jaszi, *Untold Stories: Creative Consequences of the Rights Clearance Culture for Documentary Filmmakers* (Washington, D.C.: Center for Social Media, 2004); www.centerforsocialmedia.org/resources/fair_use, accessed 24 July 2009.

237   *Greenwald's 2004 Outfoxed: Rupert Murdoch's War on Journalism*: Robert S. Boynton, "How to Make a Guerrilla Documentary," *The New York Times Magazine*, 11 July 2004.

237   *Samuel Beckett's estate refuses*: For examples, see the following *New York Times* articles: Mel Gussow, "A Reading Upsets Beckett's Estate," 24 September 1994; Alan Riding, "Moral Rights or the Outraged Heir: Real-Life Drama at House of Molière," 29 May 2007; and Jason Zinoman, "Guided by Beckett From the Grave," 2 January 2008.

237   *Robert Frost's publisher refuses*: Letters dated 6 August 2002 and 22 April 2003 from Henry Holt and Company to the playwright Peter Langman, on file with the author.

237   *Soviet refugee artist Mihail Chemiakin*: Cox, p. 1; e-mail exchange with Sarah de Kay Chemiakine, 5–6 August 2009, on file with the author.

237   *Disney managed to impede the importation of How to Read Donald Duck*: John Shelton Lawrence, "Donald Duck v. Chilean Socialism: A Fair Use Exchange," *Fair Use and Free Inquiry: Copyright Law and the New Media* (Norwood, N.J.: Ablex Publishing, 1989), pp. 53 and 68–69.

237   *Harvard University refused*: Hal Abelson et al., *Blown to Bits: Your Life, Liberty, and Happiness after the Digital Explosion* (Upper Saddle River, N.J.: Addison-Wesley, 2008), p. 125.

238   *John McCain commercials be removed from YouTube*: Saul Hansell, "McCain in Fight over YouTube," *The New York Times*, 20 October 2008; Lawrence Lessig, "Copyright and Politics Don't Mix," *The New York Times*, 20 October 2008.

238   *the Yes Men*: Wendy Seltzer, "The Chill in Practice," an excerpt from "Free

Speech Unmoored in Copyright's Safe Harbor: Abuses of the DMCA and the First Amendment," p. 3, unpublished essay, on file with author.

238 *Diebold, Inc., the maker of electronic voting machines*: Ibid., pp. 7–8.

238n *"For a demonstration I suggest you fake it"*: Cited in ibid., p. 7.

239n *"the right of privacy may not be asserted"*: Melville B. Nimmer, "Does Copyright Abridge the First Amendment Guaranties of Free Speech and the Press?," *UCLA Law Review*, vol. 17 (1970), p. 1193n.

240 *"everyone outside the* polis*"*: Arendt, pp. 26–27.

240 *"Those who won our independence believed"*: Whitney v. California, 274 U.S. (1927), p. 375.

241 *"An aphasiac is not without thought"*: Sheila Hale, *The Man Who Lost His Language* (London: Allen Lane, 2002), pp. 89 and 94.

241 *amounted to $240,000*: http://news.stanford.edu/news/2009/september28/ shloss-joyce-settlement-092809.html, accessed 6 November 2009.

242 *amounted to $125,000*: www.eff.org/press/archives/2004/10/15, accessed 6 November 2009.

GOVERNING THE COMMONS

242 *How might the public domain be converted*: James Boyle has been address- ing this question for many years; see for example, chapter 10 of *The Public Domain*.

243 People's Songs: "We Will Overcome" was first published in *People's Songs*, vol. 1, no. 5 (June 1946) as song number 281. The introductory note says the song "was learned by Zilphia Horton of the Highlander Folk School . . . , from members of the CIO Food and Tobacco Workers Union."

243 *"In the early '60s our publishers said to us"*: Pete Seeger, *Where Have All the Flowers Gone: A Singer's Stories, Songs, Seeds, Robberies*, edited by Peter Blood (Bethlehem, Pa.: Sing Out, 1993), p. 34.

244 *"in a social system where everything has to be owned"*: Ibid., p. 76.

244 *"signed a 'Songwriter's contract'"*: Ibid., p. 34.

244 *"royalties derived from this composition are being contributed"*: Ibid.

245 *Creative Commons offers a set of licenses*: http://creativecommons.org, accessed 16 October 2009.

246 *"parasitic patenting"*: Cited in Donna M. Gitter, "Resolving the Open Source Paradox in Biotechnology," *Houston Law Review*, vol. 43 (2006– 2007), p. 1484.

247 *"etiquette of sharing"*: Sulston and Ferry, p. 144.

247 *At first they considered a claim-and-release license*: Ibid., p. 272 (and see p. 213).

247   *"Bermuda Principles"*: Of the Bermuda meeting, Sulston has written: "As I
stood at the white board, scribbling away, erasing and rewriting, we eventually came up with a statement. The Wellcome Trust . . . still has a photo
of that handwritten statement with its three bullet points:

• Automatic release of sequence assemblies larger than 1 kb (preferably
within 24 hours).
• Immediate publication of finished annotated sequences.
• Aim to make the entire sequence freely available in the public domain
for both research and development in order to maximise benefits to
society."

See http://mondediplo.com/2002/12/15genome, accessed 6 November 2009.

248   *would have contravened the Bermuda Principles*: Sulston and Ferry,
p. 182.

248   *"I knew I had written the best brief I possibly could"*: Peter Ben Friedman,
"What is a Judicial Author?"; http://ssrn.com/abstract=1538633, accessed
19 March 2010.

249   *"it is the* user's *purpose that matters"*: www.gnu.org/philosophy/free-sw
.html, accessed 16 October 2009.

249   *"Free software does not mean non-commercial"*: Ibid.

250   *"enough, and as good"* has been *"left in common"*: Locke, *The Second
Treatise*, p. 19 (§27).

BIBLIOGRAPHY

Adams, John. "A Dissertation on the Canon and Feudal Law." *The Works of John Adams.* 10 vols. Boston: Charles C. Little and James Brown, 1850–1856. Vol. 3, pp. 446–64.

Alexander, Gregory S. *Commodity and Propriety: Competing Visions of Property in American Legal Thought 1776–1970.* Chicago: University of Chicago Press, 1997.

Alford, William P. "Don't Stop Thinking About . . . Yesterday: Why There Was No Indigenous Counterpart to Intellectual Property Law in Imperial China." *Journal of Chinese Law,* vol. 7, no. 1 (Spring 1993), pp. 3–34.

———. *To Steal a Book Is an Elegant Offense: Intellectual Property Law in Chinese Civilization.* Stanford, Calif.: Stanford University Press, 1995.

Arendt, Hannah. *The Human Condition.* New York: Doubleday Anchor, 1959.

Bailyn, Bernard. *The Ideological Origins of the American Revolution.* Cambridge, Mass.: Harvard University Press, 1992.

Barlow, John Perry. "The Economy of Ideas." *Wired,* vol. 2, no. 3 (March 1994); www.wired.com/wired/archive/2.03/economy.ideas_pr.html, accessed 4 July 2003.

Barnes, Peter. *Capitalism 3.0: A Guide to Reclaiming the Commons.* San Francisco: Berrett-Koehler, 2006.

———. *Who Owns the Sky? Our Common Assets and the Future of Capitalism.* Washington, D.C.: Island Press, 2001.

Ben-Atar, Doron S. *Trade Secrets: Intellectual Piracy and the Origins of American Industrial Power.* New Haven: Yale University Press, 2004.

Benkler, Yochai. "Free as the Air to Common Use: First Amendment Constraints on Enclosure of the Public Domain." *New York University Law Review,* vol. 74, no. 2 (May 1999), pp. 354–446.

———. "Overcoming Agoraphobia: Building the Commons of the Digitally Networked Environment." *Harvard Journal of Law and Technology,* vol. 11, no. 287 (Winter 1997–1998), pp. 287–400.

———. *The Wealth of Networks: How Social Production Transforms Markets and Freedom.* New Haven, Conn: Yale University Press, 2006.

Best, Stephen Michael. *The Fugitive's Properties: Law and the Poetics of Possession.* Chicago: University of Chicago Press, 2004.

Bion, Wilfred R. *Attention and Interpretation.* New York: J. Aronson, 1983.

Blackstone, William. *Commentaries on the Laws of England.* Edited by Wayne Morrison. 4 vols. London: Cavendish Publishing, 2001.

Bollier, David. *Brand Name Bullies.* Hoboken, N.J.: John Wiley, 2005.

———. *Silent Theft: The Private Plunder of Our Common Wealth.* New York: Routledge, 2002.

Bollier, David, and Laurie Racine, eds. *Ready to Share: Fashion and the Ownership of Creativity.* Los Angeles: The Norman Lear Center, Annenberg School for Communication, 2006.

Boyle, James, ed. *Collected Papers, Duke Conference on the Public Domain.* Durham, N.C.: Center for the Study of the Public Domain, 2003.

———. *The Public Domain: Enclosing the Commons of the Mind.* New Haven, Conn.: Yale University Press, 2008.

———. *Shamans, Software, and Spleens: Law and the Construction of the Information Society.* Cambridge, Mass.: Harvard University Press, 1996.

Bracha, Oren. "Owning Ideas: A History of Anglo-American Intellectual Property." S.J.D. thesis, Harvard Law School, 2005.

Buck, Susan J., et al. *The Global Commons: An Introduction.* Washington, D.C.: Island Press, 1998.

Bushaway, Bob. *By Rite: Custom, Ceremony and Community in England* 1700–1880. London: Junction Books, 1982.

Byrne, David. "David Byrne's Survival Strategies for Emerging Artists—and Megastars." *Wired,* vol. 16, no. 1 (December 18, 2007); www.wired.com/print/entertainment/music/magazine/10.01, accessed 11 December 2008.

Camden, Earl (Charles Pratt). [1774 speech on literary property.] *The Parliamentary History of England,* vol. 17 (1771–1774). London: T. C. Hansard, 1813, cols. 992–1001.

Chafee, Zechariah. "Reflections on the Law of Copyright: II." *Columbia Law Review,* vol. 45 (1945), pp. 719–38.

Chaplin, Joyce E. *The First Scientific American: Benjamin Franklin and the Pursuit of Genius.* New York: Basic Books, 2006.

Coalition Provisional Authority. [L. Paul Bremer's "100 Orders."] www.cpa-iraq.org/regulations/#Orders, accessed 16 October 2009.

Cohen, I. Bernard. *Benjamin Franklin's Science.* Cambridge, Mass.: Harvard University Press, 1990.

——. *Science and the Founding Fathers: Science in the Political Thought of Jefferson, Franklin, Adams and Madison.* New York: W.W. Norton, 1995.

Considerations on the Nature and Origin of Literary Property. Edinburgh: Donaldson, 1767. Reprint: *Freedom of the Press and the Literary Property Debate: Six Tracts 1755–1770.* Edited by Stephen Parks. New York: Garland, 1974.

Coombe, Rosemary J. *The Cultural Life of Intellectual Properties: Authorship, Appropriation, and the Law.* Durham, N.C.: Duke University Press, 1998.

Cox, Susan Jane Buck. "No Tragedy in the Commons." *Environmental Ethics* [Albuquerque, N.M.], vol. 7, no. 1 (Spring 1985), pp. 49–61.

Crawford, Rachel. *Poetry, Enclosure, and the Vernacular Landscape, 1700–1830.* Cambridge: Cambridge University Press, 2002.

Dawes Act. An Act to Provide for the Allotment of Lands in Severalty to Indians on the Various Reservations ("General Allotment Act" or "Dawes Act"), U.S. Statutes at Large, vol. 24, pp. 388–91, NADP Document A1887; www2 .csusm.edu/nadp/a1887.htm, accessed 6 November 2009.

Deazley, Ronan. *On the Origin of the Right to Copy: Charting the Movement of Copyright Law in Eighteenth-Century Britain (1695–1775).* Oxford, U.K.: Hart, 2004.

——. *Rethinking Copyright: History, Theory, Language.* Cheltenham, U.K.: Edward Elgar, 2006.

Drahos, Peter. *A Philosophy of Intellectual Property.* Aldershot, U.K.: Ashgate, 2002.

Drahos, Peter, and John Braithwaite. *Information Feudalism.* New York: The New Press, 2002.

Dylan, Bob. *Chronicles.* New York: Simon and Schuster, 2004.

Emerson, Ralph Waldo. *The Complete Works of Ralph Waldo Emerson.* 12 vols. Boston: Houghton Mifflin, 1903.

Encyclopaedia Britannica. 11th ed. London: The Encyclopaedia Britannica Company, 1911.

English Reports, The. 176 vols. London: Stevens, 1900–1911. Reprint: Abingdon, U.K.: Professional Books Ltd., 1980.

Enquiry into the Nature and Origin of Literary Property, An. London: Flexney, 1762. Reprint: *Horace Walpole's Political Tracts 1747–1748 with Two by William Warburton on Literary Property 1747 and 1762.* Edited by Stephen Parks. New York: Garland, 1974.

Fauchart, Emmanuelle, and Eric von Hippel. "Norms-Based Intellectual Property Systems: The Case of French Chefs." *Organization Science*, vol. 19, no. 2

(March–April 2008), pp. 187–201; http://unjobs.org/authors/emmanuelle -fauchart, accessed 16 October 2009.

Fisher, William W. III. *Promises to Keep: Technology, Law, and the Future of Entertainment*. Stanford, Calif.: Stanford University Press, 2004.

———. "Theories of Intellectual Property." *New Essays in the Legal and Political Theory of Property*. Edited by Stephen R. Munzer. New York: Cambridge University Press, 2001, pp. 168–200; www.law.harvard.edu/faculty/tfisher/ iptheory.html, accessed 5 November 2009.

Foucault, Michel. "What Is an Author?" *Aesthetics, Method, and Epistemology*. Edited by James D. Faubion. New York: The New Press, 1998, pp. 205–22.

Franklin, Benjamin. *Benjamin Franklin's Autobiography*. Edited by J. A. Leo Lemay and P. M. Zall. New York: W. W. Norton, 1986.

———. *Benjamin Franklin's Experiments: A New Edition of Franklin's Experiments and Observations on Electricity*. Edited by I. Bernard Cohen. Cambridge, Mass.: Harvard University Press, 1941.

———. *The Papers of Benjamin Franklin*. Online digital edition produced by the Packard Humanities Institute. Sponsored by the American Philosophical Society and Yale University; www.franklinpapers.org/franklin, accessed 16 October 2009.

Gates, Kelly. "Will Work for Copyrights: The Cultural Policy of Anti-Piracy Campaigns." *Social Semiotics*, vol. 16, no. 1 (April 2006), pp. 57–73.

Gillespie, Tarleton. "Characterizing Copyright in the Classroom: The Cultural Work of Anti-Piracy Campaigns." *Communication, Culture, and Critique*, vol. 2, no. 3 (September 2009), pp. 274–318.

Goldstein, Paul. "Copyright and the First Amendment." *Columbia Law Review*, vol. 70, no. 6 (June 1970), pp. 983–1057.

Gordon, Wendy J. "A Property Right in Self-Expression: Equality and Individualism in the Natural Law of Intellectual Property," *Yale Law Journal*, vol. 102, no. 7 (May 1993), pp. 1533–1609.

Gordon, Wendy J., and Richard Watt, eds. *The Economics of Copyright*. Cheltenham, U.K.: E. Elgar, 2003.

Habermas, Jürgen. *The Structural Transformation of the Public Sphere*. Translated by Thomas Burger. Cambridge, Mass.: MIT Press, 1991.

Hansen, Drew D. *The Dream: Martin Luther King, Jr., and the Speech That Inspired a Nation*. New York: Ecco, 2003.

Hardin, Garrett. "Extension of The Tragedy of the Commons." www.garrett hardinsociety.org/articles/art_extension_tragedy_commons.html, accessed 23 April 2004.

———. "The Tragedy of the Commons," *Science*, vol. 162 (1968), pp. 1243–48.

Harvey, Todd. *The Formative Dylan.* Lanham, Md.: Scarecrow Press, 2001.

Heller, Michael. "The Tragedy of the Anti-Commons." *Harvard Law Review,* vol. 111, no. 3 (January 1998), pp. 621–88.

Hess, Charlotte, and Elinor Ostrom, eds. *Understanding Knowledge as a Commons: From Theory to Practice.* Cambridge, Mass.: MIT Press, 2006.

Hesse, Carla. "The Rise of Intellectual Property, 700 B.C.–A.D. 2000." *Daedalus,* vol. 131, no. 2 (Spring 2002), pp. 26–45.

Honohan, Iseult. *Civic Republicanism.* New York: Routledge, 2002.

Illich, Ivan. "Silence Is a Commons." *Mirror of the Past.* London: Marion Boyars, 1992, pp. 47–54.

Ivey, Bill. *Arts, Inc.: How Greed and Neglect Have Destroyed Our Cultural Rights.* Berkeley: University of California Press, 2008.

Jaszi, Peter. "On the Author Effect: Contemporary Copyright and Collective Creativity." *Cardozo Arts and Entertainment Law Journal,* vol. 10 (1991–1992), pp. 293–320.

———. "Toward a Theory of Copyright: The Metamorphoses of 'Authorship.'" *Duke Law Journal,* vol. 1991, no. 2 (April 1991), pp. 455–502.

Jefferson, Thomas. *The Complete Jefferson.* Edited by Saul K. Padover. New York: Buell, Sloan, and Pearce, 1943.

———. *The Jefferson Cyclopedia.* Edited by John P. Foley. New York: Funk and Wagnalls, 1900.

———. "A Summary View of the Rights of British America." *The Papers of Thomas Jefferson.* Edited by Julian P. Boyd. 21 vols. Princeton, N.J.: Princeton University Press, 1950, vol. 1, pp. 121–37.

———. *The Writings of Thomas Jefferson.* 18 vols. Edited by Andrew A. Lipscomb. Washington, D.C.: Thomas Jefferson Memorial Association, 1903.

Langland, William. *Piers the Ploughman.* Translated by J. F. Goodridge. Harmondsworth, U.K.: Penguin Books, 1959.

Lessig, Lawrence. *Free Culture: How Big Media Uses Technology and the Law to Lock Down Culture and Control Creativity.* New York: Penguin Press, 2004.

———. *The Future of Ideas: The Fate of the Commons in a Connected World.* New York: Random House, 2001.

Lethem, Jonathan. "The Ecstasy of Influence: A Plagiarism." *Harper's* (February 2007), pp. 59–71.

Letter from an Author to a Member of Parliament Concerning Literary Property, A. London: Knapton, 1747. (Attributed to William Warburton.) Reprint: *Horace Walpole's Political Tracts 1747–1748 with Two by William Warburton on Literary Property 1747 and 1762.* Edited by Stephen Parks. New York: Garland, 1974.

Linebaugh, Peter. *The Magna Carta Manifesto: Liberties and Commons for All.* Berkeley: University of California Press, 2008.

Litman, Jessica. *Digital Copyright.* Amherst, N.Y.: Prometheus Books, 2000.

———. "The Public Domain." *Emory Law Journal,* vol. 39, no. 4 (Fall 1990), pp. 965–1023.

Locke, John. "Memorandum." *The Life and Letters of John Locke, with Extracts from His Journals and Common-Place Books.* Edited by Peter King. London: G. Bell, 1884, pp. 202–209. Reprint: New York: Burt Frankling, 1972.

———. *Second Treatise of Government.* Edited by C. B. Macpherson. Indianapolis: Hackett Publishing, 1980.

Loux, Andrea. "The Great Rabbit Massacre—A 'Comedy of the Commons'— Customary Community and Rights of Access to the Links of St. Andrews." *Liverpool Law Review,* vol. 22 (2001), pp. 123–55.

Macaulay, Thomas Babington. "A Speech Delivered in the House of Commons on the 5th of February, 1841." *Miscellaneous Works of Lord Macaulay.* New York: Harper, 1880, pp. 228–43.

———. *The Works of Lord Macaulay.* 12 vols. London: Longmans, Green, and Co., 1898.

Madison, James. "Monopolies. Perpetuities. Corporations. Ecclesiastical Endowments." *The William and Mary Quarterly,* third series, vol. 3, no. 4 (October 1946), pp. 551–62.

———. "Property." *The Papers of James Madison.* 17 vols. Edited by William T. Hutchinson and William M. E. Rachal. Chicago: University of Chicago Press, 1983, vol. 14, pp. 266–68.

Marshall, Eliot. "Bermuda Rules: Community Spirit, with Teeth." *Science,* vol. 291, no. 5507 (16 February 2001), p. 1192; www.sciencemag.org/cgi/content/full/291/5507/1192, accessed 2 August 2009.

Merton, Robert K. *On the Shoulders of Giants: A Shandean Postscript.* San Diego: Harcourt Brace Jovanovich, 1985.

Mitchell, Henry C. *The Intellectual Commons: Toward an Ecology of Intellectual Property.* Lanham, Md.: Lexington Books, 2005.

Morgan, Edmund S. *Benjamin Franklin.* New Haven, Conn.: Yale University Press, 2002.

Morgan, Edmund S., and Helen M. Morgan. *The Stamp Act Crisis.* Chapel Hill: University of North Carolina Press, 1953.

Motion Picture Association of America/Junior Achievement. "What's the Diff? A Guide to Digital Citizenship for Volunteers and Teachers." www.respectcopyrights.org/CG_FINAL.pdf, accessed 16 October 2009.

Motion Picture Association of America/Los Angeles Area Boy Scouts. "Respect

Copyrights: Curriculum for the Los Angeles Area Boy Scouts." www.mpaa .org/press_releases/RespectCopyrightsCurriculum.pdf, accessed 2 October 2009.

Neeson, J. M. Commoner. *Common Right, Enclosure, and Social Change in England, 1700–1820.* Cambridge: Cambridge University Press, 1993.

Negativland. www.negativland.com, accessed 8 November 2009 (regarding "fair use," see www.negativland.com/news/?page_id=23, accessed 8 November 2009).

Netanel, Neil. "Copyright and a Democratic Civil Society." *Yale Law Journal,* vol. 106, no. 2 (November 1996), pp. 283–387.

Nimmer, Melville B. "Does Copyright Abridge the First Amendment Guaranties of Free Speech and the Press?" *UCLA Law Review,* vol. 17, no. 6 (June 1970), pp. 1180–1204.

Nozick, Robert. *Anarchy, State and Utopia.* New York: Harper and Row, 1974.

Ostrom, Elinor. *Governing the Commons.* New York: Cambridge University Press, 1991.

Ostrom, Elinor, Roy Gardner, and James Walker. *Rules, Games, and Common-Pool Resources.* Ann Arbor: University of Michigan Press, 1994.

Patry, William F. *Moral Panics and the Copyright Wars.* New York: Oxford University Press, 2009.

Pocock, J.G.A. *The Machiavellian Moment: Florentine Political Thought and the Atlantic Republican Tradition.* Princeton, N.J.: Princeton University Press, 1975.

Radin, Margaret Jane. *Contested Commodities.* Cambridge, Mass.: Harvard University Press, 1996.

———. "Market-Inalienability." *Harvard Law Review,* vol. 100 (1987), pp. 1849–1937.

Raustiala, Kal, and Christopher Sprigman. "The Piracy Paradox: Innovation and Intellectual Property in Fashion Design." *Virginia Law Review,* vol. 92, no. 8 (December 2006), pp. 1687–1777.

Reed, Joseph W. "Noah Webster's Debt to Samuel Johnson." *American Speech,* vol. 37, no. 2 (May 1962), pp. 95–105.

Rimbaud, Arthur. *Complete Works, Selected Letters.* Translated by Wallace Fowlie. Chicago: University of Chicago Press, 1966.

Rose, Carol M. *Property and Persuasion: Essays on the History, Theory, and Rhetoric of Ownership.* Boulder, Colo.: Westview Press, 1994.

———. "Romans, Roads, and Romantic Creators: Traditions of Public Property in the Information Age." *Law and Contemporary Problems,* vol. 66 (Winter/ Spring 2003), pp. 89–110.

Rose, Mark. *Authors and Owners: The Invention of Copyright*. Cambridge, Mass.: Harvard University Press, 1993.

———. "Nine-Tenths of the Law: The English Copyright Debates and the Rhetoric of the Public Domain." *Collected Papers, Duke Conference on the Public Domain*. Edited by James Boyle (Durham, N.C.: Center for the Study of the Public Domain, 2003), pp. 75–87.

Sandel, Michael J. *Democracy's Discontent*. Cambridge, Mass.: Belknap Press of Harvard University Press, 1996.

———. "What Money Can't Buy: The Moral Limits of Markets." The Tanner Lectures on Human Values, delivered at Brasenose College, Oxford, May 11 and 12, 1998; www.tannerlectures.utah.edu/lectures/atoz.html#s, accessed 1 July 2009.

Shain, Barry Alan. *The Myth of American Individualism*. Princeton, N.J.: Princeton University Press, 1994.

Skinner, Quentin. "Classical Liberty and the Comings of the English Civil War." *Republicanism: A Shared European Heritage*. Edited by Martin van Gelderen and Quentin Skinner. 2 vols. Cambridge: Cambridge University Press, 2002, vol. 2, pp. 9–28.

Smith, James Morton, ed. *The Republic of Letters: The Correspondence Between Thomas Jefferson and James Madison 1776–1826*. 3 vols. New York: W. W. Norton, 1995.

Smith, Page. *John Adams*. New York: Doubleday, 1962.

"Stamp Act, The." www.lexrex.com/enlightened/laws/stampact.htm, accessed 16 October 2009.

Starr, Paul. *The Creation of the Media: Political Origins of Modern Communications*. New York: Basic Books, 2004.

Statute of Anne (An Act for the Encouragement of Learning, by Vesting the Copies of Printed Books in the Authors or Purchasers of such Copies, During the Times therein mentioned, 1710, 8 Anne, c.19). www.copyrighthistory.org/cgi-bin/kleioc/0010/exec/ausgabe/%22uk_1710%22, accessed 21 October 2009.

Sulston, John. "Autobiography." http://nobelprize.org/nobel_prizes/medicine/laureates/2002/sulston-autobio.html, accessed 10 November 2009.

———. "*C. elegans*: The Cell Lineage and Beyond." Nobel lecture, December 8, 2002. http://nobelprize.org/nobel_prizes/medicine/laureates/2002/sulston-lecture.html, accessed 10 November 2009.

Sulston, John, and Georgina Ferry. *The Common Thread: A Story of Science, Politics, Ethics, and the Human Genome*. Washington, D.C.: Joseph Henry Press, 2002.

Sundquist, Eric J. *King's Dream*. New Haven, Conn.: Yale University Press, 2009.

Thompson, E. P. *Customs in Common: Studies in Traditional Popular Culture*. New York: The New Press, 1993.

Travis, Hannibal. "Pirates of the Information Infrastructure: Blackstonian Copyright and the First Amendment." *Berkeley Technology Law Journal*, vol. 15 (2000), pp. 777–864; http://ssrn.com/abstract_id=758885, accessed 24 October 2009.

Vaidhyanathan, Siva. *Copyrights and Copywrongs*. New York: New York University Press, 2001.

Van Doren, Carl. *Benjamin Franklin*. New York: The Viking Press, 1956.

Vindication of the Exclusive Right of Authors to Their Own Works, A. London: Griffiths, 1762. Reprint: *Horace Walpole's Political Tracts 1747–1748 with Two by William Warburton on Literary Property 1747 and 1762*. Edited by Stephen Parks. New York: Garland, 1974.

von Schmidt, Eric, and Jim Rooney. *Baby, Let Me Follow You Down: The Illustrated Story of the Cambridge Folk Years*. 2nd edition. Amherst: University of Massachusetts Press, 1994.

Walterscheid, Edward C. *The Nature of the Intellectual Property Clause: A Study in Historical Perspective*. Buffalo, N.Y.: Hein and Co., 2000.

———. *To Promote the Progress of Useful Arts: American Patent Law and Administration, 1798–1836*. Littleton, Colo.: F. B. Rothman, 1998.

Walzer, Michael. *Spheres of Justice: A Defense of Pluralism and Equality*. New York: Basic Books, 1983.

Warner, Michael. *The Letters of the Republic: Publication and the Public Sphere in Eighteenth-Century America*. Cambridge, Mass.: Harvard University Press, 1990.

Washburn, Wilcomb E. *The Assault on Indian Tribalism: The General Allotment Law (Dawes Act) of 1887*. Philadelphia: J. B. Lippincott Company, 1975. Reprint: Malabar, Fla.: Robert E. Krieger, 1986.

Webster, Noah. "Examination of the Leading Principles of the Federal Constitution, 1787." *Pamphlets on the Constitution of the United States*. Edited by Paul Leicester Ford. Brooklyn: 1888, pp. 29–65.

———. "Origin of the Copy-Right Laws in the United States." *A Collection of Papers on Political, Literary and Moral Subjects*. New York: Webster and Clark, 1843, pp. 173–78.

Wood, Gordon S. *The Creation of the American Republic: 1776–1787*. Chapel Hill: University of North Carolina Press, 1998.

Woodmansee, Martha, and Peter Jaszi, eds. *The Construction of Authorship*. Durham, N.C.: Duke University Press, 1994.

———. "The Genius and the Copyright: Economic and Legal Conditions of the

Emergence of the 'Author.' " *Eighteenth-Century Studies*, vol. 17, no. 4 (Summer 1984), pp. 435–48.

———. "On the Author Effect: Recovering Collectivity." *Cardozo Arts and Entertainment Law Journal*, vol. 10 (1991–1992), pp. 279–292.

Yates, Joseph. "Speech for the Defendant in Tonson v. Collins." *The English Reports*, vol. 96. Edinburgh: William Green, 1909, pp. 185–88.

Zittrain, Jonathan. *The Future of the Internet and How to Stop It*. New Haven: Yale University Press, 2008.

ACKNOWLEDGMENTS

I began thinking seriously about this book around 1998 when Archibald Gillies, then president of the Andy Warhol Foundation, kindly offered to publish a pamphlet based on a talk he had heard me give, one that included reflections on the pamphlet's eventual title, "Created Commons." Another five years passed, however, before I actually started to write, encouraged first by Jonathan Galassi at Farrar, Straus and Giroux and then by a grant from the Lannan Foundation that allowed me to take a year's leave from my teaching duties at Kenyon College.

I returned to Kenyon with several chapters in hand and, since then, almost every part of the book has benefited from feedback offered by the members of the Kenyon Faculty Seminar. Particularly helpful have been comments by Erika Boeckeler, Jeff Bowman, Jim Carson, Jennifer Clarvoe, Deborah Laycock, Jesse Matz, Pat Urban, and Yang Xiao. At Kenyon I always appreciate the support as well of Peter Rutkoff and David Lynn. Carolin Hahnemann kindly sorted out some mysteries having to do with Latin nomenclature. Tess Hardcastle helped me put the notes and bibliography in order. I owe a large debt as well to Richard L. Thomas, whose unstinting generosity allowed Kenyon to create the chair in creative writing that I currently hold.

In 2003, Eric Saltzman invited me to become a Fellow at the Berkman Center for Internet and Society at the Harvard Law School. That association proved remarkably fruitful; almost everything I know about copyright law I learned during my subsequent years at Berkman. In addition to Eric, I am especially grateful for the support, instruction, feedback, and advice given over the years by David Ardia, John Clippinger, Terry Fisher, Colin Maclay, Phil Malone, Charles Nesson, Dotan Oliar, John Palfrey, Carolina Rossini, Wendy Seltzer, David Weinberger,

Jonathan Zittrain, and Ethan Zuckerman. At Berkman I also had invaluable research assistance from Max Choi and Adam Holland.

For the gift of a quiet and spacious office in which to write I'm most grateful to Maryann Thompson and the staff at Maryann Thompson Architects in Cambridge, Massachusetts. Many's the time I found my solitary labors slipstreaming the group energy of an M.T.A. charrette.

Over the years I have been able to enjoy several periods of concentrated work time, first at the Mesa Refuge in Point Reyes, California, and later at the Lannan Residency Program in Marfa, Texas, and at the MacDowell Colony in New Hampshire. In addition to the initial Lannan Literary Fellowship, financial support for this book has come from the Center for the Public Domain, LEF New England, the Guggenheim Foundation, the American Council of Learned Societies, and the National Endowment for the Humanities.

I have always found that the best research is the fruit of conversation and correspondence, my own aphorism being: "I have no thoughts but in the presence of other thoughts." I cannot possibly name all the friends and strangers whose creative work provided the seed ground for my own, but beyond those already mentioned, the list must surely include Jonathan Abrahamson, Pat Aufderheide, Linda Bamber, Peter Barnes, David Bollier, Oren Bracha, Jo Chapman, Jesse Coleman, Ronan Deazley, Jaune Evans, Tony Falzone, Peter Friedman, Tarleton Gillespie, Wendy Gordon, Douglas Humble, Bill Ivey, Peter Jaszi, Henry Jenkins, Martha Jessup, Rob Kunzig, Lyda Kuth, Peter Linebaugh, Louisa McCall, Kembrew McLeod, Vijaya Nagarajan, Laurie Racine, Jonathan Rowe, Wendy Salinger, Barry Sanders, Scott Russell Sanders, Mona Simpson, Taylor Stoehr, Lee Swenson, Edward Walterscheid, John Wilbanks, and Martha Woodmansee.

Final and fullest gratitude, as always, goes to Patsy Vigderman.

INDEX

Page numbers in *italics* refer to illustrations.

Venice, printers in, 55
Venter, J. Craig, 190*n*, 191
Versailles, 151
villeins (serfs), 31
Virgil, 82
Virginia, 102, 158, 199
virtue, 92–93, 163, 165, 226; *see also*
 civic virtue
VisiCalc, 69
vitamins, 61
Volta, Alessandro, 60
von Schmidt, Eric, 198
voting rights, 25, 40–41, 92, 168, 171,
 194, 195, 207

Walzer, Michael, 221–23, 225
Warner, Michael, 289*n*–90*n*
Warren, Mercy, 157–58
Warren, Robert Penn, 262
Warren, Rosanna, 261–62, 271, 272–74
Washington Post, 208, 236
Waste Land, The (Eliot), 202
water, 13, 19, 162–63, 168, 244
Waters, Muddy, 202
waterways, 164, 173–75, 196,
 217–18, 251
wealth, 10, 107, 133, 167, 176, 215
Webster, Daniel, 185
Webster, Noah, 30, 163–66, 168, 170,
 184–87, 253
Weill, Kurt, 200
"We Shall Overcome," 243–44, 306*n*

Wesley, John, 89
Wesleyan Methodists, 89
West, Benjamin, 180, *181*
"What Money Can't Buy"
 (Sandel), 194
wheat, 17, 37, 165
Wheaton v. Peters, 87
Whigs, 99, 150
Whistler, James McNeill, 236
Whitefield, George, 226–27
widows, 28, 76
Wikipedia, 14
William the Conqueror, 102
Winthrop, John, 182
Wired, 63
Wöhler, Friedrich, 194
wool, wool market, 39, 42
Wordsworth, William, 40
Works and Days (Hesiod), 20
World Trade Organization (WTO),
 16–17
World Tree, 19
World Wide Web, 13, 62, 65, 174–77,
 247, 249
W. W. Norton, 261

Yates, Joseph, 83
Yes Men, 238, 239, 241
Young, Edward, 83, 132
YouTube, 3, 238

Zittrain, Jonathan, 65